YAMAHA

TED MACAULEY

*In recognition of
my valued friend Mike Hailwood's efforts
to further the legend.*

ISBN 0 85429 419 8

A FOULIS Motorcycling Book

This revised and updated 1983 edition first published
in 1979

Published & distributed in North America by:
Haynes Publications Inc.
861 Lawrence Drive,
Newbury Park,
California 91320, USA

Produced by:
Cadogan Books Ltd.
15 Pont Street,
London SW1X 9EH,
England

Printed in England

Contents

Torakusu Yamaha and the Birth of a Legend

The man who gave his name to one of the most successful marques in the history of motor cycling was born in 1851, the third son of Wakayama clansman Konosuke Yamaha. At the age of 20, Torakusu Yamaha took the first steps towards fulfilling a passionate vocation to be an engineer. Leaving home for Nagasaki, he embarked upon a 10-year apprenticeship under the guidance of an English clockmaker. This was to provide the groundwork for the young man's meticulous appreciation of precision work. Innately gifted in all things mechanical, he soon developed a high degree of expertise that he was to maintain throughout his life.

At 30 Torakusu took up an apprenticeship in a medical equipment shop at Osaka. Here again he proved to be a quick learner, eager to put his ideas into practice. In 1883 he was sent to carry out a repair job for the Hamamatsu Hospital. Falling in love with the tremendous scenic beauty of the Hamamatsu area, he decided that this was the place for him to live. He was confident that he could make a reasonable living with his background of work on clocks and his growing knowledge of complicated machinery.

His reputation grew and in 1887 he was called to his most important job yet—an urgent repair to an organ owned by the Hamamatsu Elementary School. The year before, ambitious education planners had ruled that singing lessons should make up a regular part of the elementary school curriculum. The school had bought an American-built organ and installed it in a classroom. It was something of a novelty to the entertainment-starved citizens and its melodious tones drew vast crowds into the school grounds. Worried that these crowds might interrupt the children's classes, the authorities designated the 16th of each month as a sort of open day when anyone could attend the school to listen to the music. It became one of the most popular dates in the calendar for the Hamamatsuans. Their numbers grew—but their joy was short-lived, for the organ broke down after only two and a half months.

It seemed to be a total disaster because the school knew of nobody who could repair it. Then news of the breakdown reached Tomisaku Fukushima, the president of Hamamatsu hospital and the man who had summoned Torakusu Yamaha from the repair shop in Osaka. Torakusu was happy to accept the challenge presented by the ailing organ, even though it was outside his range of experience. He recruited the help of a metal worker, Kisaburo Kawai, and together they were able to fix the damage, to the delight of the school, its pupils and the scores of people who turned up on every 16th day of the month.

Excited by the complexities of the organ, Torakusu then decided to make a harmonium—from scratch. It took him two and a half months. Though he was happy with his handiwork, he wanted to have it examined by the music certification office in Tokio, now the Tokio University of Art. But that was more than 200 miles away, and there was no readily available means of transport. So he walked. With his partner, Kisaburo Kawai, he carried the weighty instrument along the dusty track called the Tokaido, the route to Tokio. Only their incredible determination could have seen them through such a gruelling journey, and with pride and hope burning in their hearts they arrived at the certification office.

But there was only disappointment for them in Tokio. The harmonium failed to pass the examination set by the experts in the office, because of imperfect tuning. After such an effort, Torakusu could not hide his bitter disappointment. But he so impressed the head of the office, Shuji Izawa, that he was invited to stay on and listen to the university lectures, so that his zeal and ability could benefit from some advanced teaching on the art of tuning. For a month he attended lectures and absorbed information. Refreshed, he then returned to Hamamatsu to start all over again. This time he was armed with greater knowledge, a more appreciative feel for the instrument he was trying to build, and therefore a far better chance of achieving his goal.

His second harmonium was completed in March 1888, when he was 37. Once more he travelled to Tokio and, heart in mouth, listened while it was rigorously tested by the experts in the certification office. This time there was only high praise. The president, Mr Izawa, extolled Yamaha's achievement and rated the harmonium equal to any foreign-produced instruments in the country.

His incredible determination to succeed had seen him through a traumatic period. The expert standard of his work guaranteed that his effort was not wasted. Soon afterwards, when his workmanship had earned even wider acclaim than that given it by the officials in the certification office, orders began to roll in. The Shizuoka Prefecture wanted five full size organs. The authorities at the Hamamatsu Normal School ordered two more. And the name Yamaha had begun its journey around the world and across the years . . .

He established a partnership with Kisaburo Kawai, the man who had accompanied him on the memorable first trek to Tokio. They rented a rundown Fudaiji temple in Sugawaracho, Hamamatsu, for a few yen a month and set about meeting the orders from this make-do workshop. Working until the early hours of the morning, they were soon rewarded by success. A year after the second harmonium had been built, the company had a capital of 30,000 yen with 250 brand new organs manufactured and sold. A year later the capital had risen to 50,000 yen and Yamaha Organ Manufacturing was in full swing.

Yamaha and Kawai had been joined in the company by the president of Hamamatsu hospital, Tomisaku Fukushima, the man who had given

Yamaha his first job. In the third year of its existence, just after one of their organs had been awarded the medal for merit at the Third Industrial Exhibition in Tokio, internal strife caused the break-up of the company. Yamaha went his own way and set up the privately managed "Yamaha Musical Instrument Manufacturing". He kept on filling his order books, exporting 80 organs to England in 1892, but ran into difficulties in 1895 after the Sino-Japanese war. Because of the boom that followed the war and the growing popularity of musical instruments of a western type, the company found it impossible to keep pace wth the increasing numbers of orders. Two years later, after struggling to meet ever increasing demands, Yamaha joined forces with other businessmen to found Nippon Gakki. Supported by a 100,000 yen capital base, he set about turning the business into the internationally known company it is today.

From 1900 pianos were produced—the Imperial household even had a Yamaha piano in its drawing room. Five years later at the 1905 World Exposition held in St. Louis, in the United States, Yamaha's organs and pianos were awarded top honours. It was, he felt, the final proof that his workmanship had reached an international standard and that he could compete on equal terms with any other company in the world. Business boomed and expansion was called for. In 1913 Torakusu Yamaha welcomed the prestigious Chiyomaru Amano, Governor of the Hamana District, into the company as vice-president. And three years later a new factory was built in Nakazawacho, Hamamatsu City, the site of the present-day headquarters of Nippon Gakki.

But that year, 1916, Torakusu Yamaha died at the age of 64. He left behind an empire firmly established upon a foundation of his hard work and his unique ability to make sweet sounds for a world wide market.

Chiyomaru Amano became the company's second president and soon the capital was raised to more than three million yen. A branch factory was established in Kushiro to take advantage of the extensive wood supplies in Hokkaido. A harmonica factory, with 600 women workers, was set up there as business improved even further in the boom associated with World War I. But after the war, the serious decline of the German mark resulted in a large quantity of German-made pianos and harmonicas being imported by Japanese companies. This and the burning down of the Tokio branch in the great Kanto earthquake of 1923, dealt the company a severe financial blow; and inevitably there were management problems, too. In 1926 a strike for improved labour conditions and the laying off of 350 employees wracked the company. For more than 100 days all work at the factories was suspended. Despite petitions from his directors, President Amano refused to reform, and the company went into a sharp decline—until Amano was replaced by a man who shared Torakusu Yamaha's great love of his brainchild.

The new president was Kaichi Kawakami, then 43 years old. A brilliant and greatly respected engineer, he had been one of the few to major in technical engineering at the exclusive Tokio University. He was recommended to the ailing company by Sumitomo Metal Industries, a huge business in his homeland, for whom he was then working as technical director.

He happily accepted the massive responsibility thrust on to his shoulders: he certainly did not want to see people being pushed out of work and he immediately stressed his readiness to shoulder whatever responsibilities were necessary, to revitalize the company, put right the crippling deficit, restore good relations with the disenchanted workforce and end the long drawn-out dispute. His words then were an apt demonstration of his determination to carry on the good works established by the company's lamented founder, Torakusu Yamaha: "The underlying motive that led me to accept this position is that the work of Nippon Gakki is not just that of a business interested only in profits. I have prepared myself to make sacrifices to realize the need for adjustment and to rationalize the company and I pledge to devote all my energies toward this end."

Yamaha was Japan's solitary Western music plant. The business they brought to the Shizuoka Prefecture, the area around the factory, was vital to the economy and to the further employment of hundreds of locally based workers. To them, Kawakami said: "I make a solemn oath to all employees that I want to make this company a good one. I call upon you to co-operate in a united effort to make it a company *par excellence* so that in the future we will earn admiration and trust the world over for the products of Nippon Gakki."

They were the brand of fighting words needed to haul the company back onto its feet. It was probably the worst period in the history of the firm but Kaichi Kawakami pulled it back from the brink of disaster.

In 1950, after a long illness, Kaichi Kawakami retired from the presidency of Nippon Gakki. During his long reign as president, he had groomed his son, Gen-Ichi, to take over his position. In latter years, his ill health had meant that Gen-Ichi was already assuming this role in almost every aspect but the title. Like his father an extremely able man, and with the benefit of long experience in the highest echelons of the company, Gen-Ichi Kawakami was a natural successor. And it was Gen-Ichi, the fourth president of Nippon Gakki, who decided to diversify the company's interests and venture into the tough commercial field of motor cycle manufacture. For this purpose, a separate company was created, while Gen-Ichi assumed dual presidency of both the parent company and its progeny—Yamaha Motor.

Enter the Red Dragonfly

In the mid-50s the Japanese motor cycle industry was in a state of chaos. There were around 100 manufacturers, all fighting tooth and nail, designing and launching endless models. None of them could hold a substantial market lead over the others. Even Honda, a big home name, had a desperate struggle with Meguro, Tohatsu, Showa, Miyata and dozens of other companies whose names have long since passed from the memory into history. Europe, a long way off, had no idea of what was coming. The vast markets that existed there, rich new grounds ripe for exploitation by any manufacturer with the ability to build machines quickly and cheaply, were foremost in the minds of the Japanese.

It was this highly competitive and rapidly expanding field of manufacture that Gen-Ichi Kawakami decided to enter in 1955. In the midst of such expansion, it would have been madness for a newly formed company such as Yamaha Motor to battle for a share of the market with no sure basis for success. And in fact the first Yamaha motor cycle to be produced, the YA1, was the near offspring of the thoroughbred German marque, the DKW, and in particular of the RT 125. It was a natural instinct for mechanical perfection that had steered Yamaha's designers towards DKW. Taking its name from the initials of 'Das Kleine Wunder'—'The Little Wonder'—this company had been founded by a Danish engineering genius called Jorgen Skafte Rasmussen. It had started producing two-stroke petrol engines in 1919 and between the wars was leading the field in the bid to produce a simple and inexpensive two stroke—at a time when most manufacturers preferred the four-stroke engine. The RT 125 was first marketed in 1949 and became such a roaring success that it very quickly earned the title of 'the world's most frequently copied motor cycle'. Yamaha were by no means the only company to produce replicas of the DKW—its pedigree and Rasmussen's genius had guaranteed both that it would be a success and that it would be copied. For that very reason, there was more to praise than criticise in Yamaha's decision to use the RT 125 as the basis for their very first motor cycle.

The success of this policy was proved immediately. With its maroon framework and cream tank sides, hand polished by workers from the Nippon Gakki piano division, the YA1 was first produced at the rate of 300 a month—and sold rapidly. In three years, no less than 11,088 units had been produced at Hamamatsu.

The way through to the buying public was publicity, a new factor in Japan as far as motor cycles were concerned. The sport was in its infancy in the country and there was hardly a race track worth calling by that name. But with ever increasing numbers of machines on the road, the speed-conscious began to turn their attention to competitive interests—

motor cycle racing became almost a necessity for both manufacturers and buyers.

That is how the Asama Volcano Road Race came into being—soon to become the Mecca of motor cycle racing in Japan. A track was built at the foot of Mount Asama, 120 miles to the north of Tokio. Daredevil riders risked life and limb, hurtling prototype racers into the darker reaches of technology on a surface of volcanic ash. For 20 terrifying kilometres (120 miles) on the shifting, blinding ash of Asama, the first shots in the battle for commercial supremacy were fired.

The first Asama Volcano Road Race was held in 1955, a few months after Yamaha introduced their first model—the 125-cc YA1, nicknamed Akatombo, "the Red Dragonfly". With telescopic front forks and an oil damper system, it was the first motor cycle to carry the symbol of the triple tuning fork. The newest of all the factories bidding for a place in the sales battle, Yamaha naturally entered several YA1 specials in the race—and then proceeded to stagger the opposition by winning it outright. Few people at Asama had realized the strength of their challenge—until it was too late. The YA1 quickly became a prized possession. To the hundreds of young motor cycle enthusiasts, who were being tempted on all sides, it had proved itself as a true race winner. None of the other manufacturers could top that.

The team manager, Zenzaburo Watase, one of the great names in Yamaha racing history, was the company's first racing chief. He planned the victory in meticulous detail. The stakes, remember, were high: the rewards immense. As he pointed out, "We went to the race just for a win."

The first Yamaha, the 125 cc YA1. Built 1954, marketed 1955, it won the Mount Fuji Race on its first competitive outing.

He moved his team into living quarters as close to the course as possible. "We could command a view of the whole track even when we were in our quarters," he said," and this enabled us to collect all the speed data of rival machines while they were out practising on the course. We made long checks on the course ourselves. Our preparation had to be perfect—and I tried to make sure that it was. Accompanied by a team member who had majored in civil engineering, I walked round every metre of the 20 kilometre circuit, checking most carefully every bend and turn in the road. We passed on all our findings to the team's mechanics so that they could set up the machines in the best possible condition. I also took every rider aside and instructed each one on how best to negotiate Asama's particularly gruelling course.

"We took an early morning session of training. I ordered the Yamaha team to be at the course at 5.30 am—the others did not appear until 8.00 am or 9.00 am. I wanted absolute secrecy; it was vitally important to our tactics that everything about our machines, our riders and our preparation should be kept secret even during official practice. I believe this hit the mark. The other teams knew very little about us before the actual race, while we had collected as much pre-race information as possible—and we knew nearly everything about them.

"Then there was the question of teamwork. We were new to racing and, naturally, every rider wanted to win. But I was team manager and it was up to me to nominate just one of them as the 'ace', depending on their racing technique and their performance in training. It was not easy to convince them of the need for teamwork—that was something to which they were less accustomed. I had a job to persuade them that my way was right.

"As it turned out, everything in the race went precisely as we had planned. Yamaha won a great victory in the big national race and it was the finest imaginable public relationship exercise for the company at a critical time. Additionally, the race and the victory gave us precious technical data for the development of the production models that were to follow the YA1."

The second Yamaha model to be produced, the YC1, was also a replica of a DKW design, this time the RT 175. The lessons learned from the YA1 had seen the Yamaha designers through their apprenticeship, and with the YC1, finished in a reddish-grey colour, they had mastered the art. They became restless to incorporate their own ideas into their next design—the YD1 250cc machine. The planners had been instructed by the management to follow another German design, the highly successful Adler MB 250, but at a meeting with President Kawakami they insisted that they would prefer to follow their own inspiration. He gave them complete sanction.

Given full rein, the designers made full sized and detailed drawings and from these the engineers, dispensing with all the intermediate stages, built the prototypes for the beautiful YD1 machine. The only Adler influence lay in the construction of the crankcase, Thus, having copied only two models, the quick-to-learn designers at Yamaha, the students of motor cycle design, had already become the teachers.

Zenzaburo Watase took the team back for the second Mount Asama Road Race in 1957. The conditions of entry had by now been tightened up. Each team was allowed to enter two machines. Any further machines entered had to be built to different specifications, as follows: in stroke by more than 5 per cent, in valve format, valve drive system, transmission, number of cylinders, exhaust volume by 5 per cent, and lastly in fuel supply equipment.

Yamaha entered two teams—A and B. Team A consisted of a YA 125-cc and a YD 250-cc with a bore and stroke of 54 x 54 mm, Team B of a YA 125-cc and a YD 250-cc with a bore and stroke of 56 x 50 mm.

The YA machines were genuine racing bikes modelled on their famous forerunner, a direct development from the successful YA1. To comply with race regulations, they differed in bore and stroke, but were otherwise identical. The forward inclined single-cylinder, two-stroke engine had a large fin area. The crank case and transmission system were constructed singly, and the Mikuni carburettor had a separate float chamber and wire-net air cleaner. The compression ratio was said to be 9.5. Starting was by means of a magneto on the right-hand side of the crank shaft. On the left side was the primary transmission gear, with a tachometer on the outside. The clutch was wet multi-plate and the transmission figures were as follows: 1st—2.121; 2nd—1.510; 3rd—1.227; and 4th—1.000. The 90-kg machines were 1,925 mm long, 660 mm wide, 970 mm high, with a ground clearance of 145 mm. The tyres, front and back, were 2.75 x 18 block pattern. Both machines were fitted with dolphin cowlings, a rather long fuel tank, short handlebars, and drawn-back footrests forcing the rider into a forward inclination in a bid to search out some extra streamlining. Significantly, neither machine was to suffer the durability problems that seemed to hit many of their competitors during the race.

The YD machines were similar to the two-stroke, twin-cylinder 250-cc model marketed by Yamaha the previous year. In contrast, the engines were less compact than on the production model, and both the YD-A and YD-B had larger fuel tanks, holding 20 litres. There were two fuel cocks, each combined with a strainer, connected to two carburettors. Each carburettor was a Mikuni racing type with a separate float chamber and a wire-net air cleaner. The engine was fired up by means of a magneto on the right side of the crankshaft. The bore and stroke of the YD-A was 54 x 54 mm square (the same as that on the YD production model). The YD-B was 56 x 50 mm oversquare. Both machines were reputed to have a maximum output of 20 hp at 7,500 rpm. The clutch of the YD production model had been coaxial, with the crankshaft mounted at the left end, but on the two racers it was mounted on the primary-reduced transmission drive shaft. Gear figures were: 1st—2.213; 2nd—1.510; 3rd—1.220; and 4th—1.000. The racing trim of cowling, fuel tank and seat was the same as on the YA-A and YA-B. Weighing 100 kg, the machines were 1,925 mm long, 660 mm wide, and 970 mm high, with a road clearance of 125 mm.

One of the Yamahas entered in the second Asama Volcano Road Race.

Yamaha's results in the second Mount Asama Road Race could not have been more impressive. They were overwhelmingly triumphant in both the 125-cc and 250-cc classes. In the 125-cc event, a YA-A ridden by Oishi came home first, followed into second place by Miyashiro on a YA-B. Masuko won the 250-cc class on a YD-A, with team mates Sunako and Shimora gaining second and third places on YD-Bs. The machines also won the Good Design Mark awarded by the Japanese Ministry of International Trade and Industry—the first time a motor cycle had been given this accolade.

In 1957, Kawakami gave a speech to his employees in which he explained the motives behind such a seemingly incongruous development from the manufacture of musical instruments to motor cycles. The reasons are intriguing in themselves, but Kawakami's speech also gives a fascinating insight into that particular mix of commercial aggression and paternalistic concern for employees that has always characterized the Yamaha organization:

"The musical instrument industry is considered to be somewhat restricted in materials and scope, and can be expected to face difficulties in the future. We at Nippon Gakki cannot remain passive, assuming the responsibility for a large number of people just on the basis of present-day good business. Unless management, as part of its responsibility, conducts research to determine possible future business activities, at a time when adequate financial reserves are at hand, it will not be able to take any necessary drastic action when some day there prove to be more workers than work. Nippon Gakki must look forward to tomorrow's business activity whilst today's business is still expanding.

Masuko on his way to victory in the second Asama Volcano Road Race.

"It so happens that machine tools constructed during the period when we were manufacturing wooden aeroplane propellers, were removed to another town, Futamata, for safety and placed in a bark-roofed shack. After ten years in storage the tools were becoming rusty. Somehow this equipment had to be transported back to town and utilized. However, to construct a building to house so much equipment, and to allocate sufficient funds to restore it, presents a problem for a business enterprise. Once the funds are invested, some tangible benefit must be realized. The question is simply: what can be made with company-owned machine tools such as these?"

Kawakami then went on to list the possible areas of diversification open to the company: "One idea put forward was to make parts for sewing machines, motor cycles, three-wheeled vehicles, scooters or cars. But, as is well known, sewing machines are being over-produced, which makes our entry into that field quite out of the question. What about scooters? The sales networks are established and production is essentially monopolized by two producers, Silver Pigeon and Rabbit. Moreover, it became clear after investigation that both these companies are very large with well-equipped facilities capable of high-volume production. Again, although three-wheeled vehicles can be made most easily by our company's machinery and equipment, it turned out that Mazda and Daihatsu have full command of the market, with large-scale production facilities built around a well-grounded research programme.

"All of this led us to the conclusion that our energies would be better directed towards some other type of undertaking. As to the idea of our becoming a sub-contractor for automotive parts, we cannot place the name of Yamaha on such parts, no matter how good the quality. Up to now we have always produced complete, finished products under our own brand name. As a sub-contractor, we would be at the mercy of the parent firm: should they decide that they did not need to use us any more, we would be placed in the untenable position of having to liquidate facilities and dismiss employees. However, if finished products are sold by our own organization, we can manage to pull through hard times. Thus, in the final analysis, it is necessary for us to produce the finished articles.

"The outcome of the above thought process is that we consider the possibility of motor cycle production to be our best opportunity for success, even though the best point of entry might have already passed us by. As a result of information gained from Mr. Takai, the chief of our research section, who has undertaken a study tour of the major motor cycle manufacturing facilities in Japan, we were able to take the view that we could survive in the motor cycle field, despite out late entry and the existing manufacturers.

"Since we lacked experience in this type of business, we had to study the type of products we would have to make. In our efforts to minimize setbacks and shorten the time from entry to profitability, we observed factories in Germany. After examining various types of motor cycles, we made our first 125-cc model (the YA1). We were able to start out confident that, after thorough investigation and research, we would never be overtaken by our competitors. Thus, you can now understand that we cannot view such a move as being born of some superficial idea or as some kind of sideline or corporate hobby."

Kawakami then went on to outline the startling progress achieved by the new company during its first two years of production:

"All concerned have put their best efforts into our enterprise, and the business results have been as good as was anticipated in the early planning stages. In the area of sales policy we have taken a stance quite the opposite to that of the rest of the motor cycle industry. As a result, we can demonstrate that Yamaha is number one in the field of motor cycle production in Japan in only two years' time.

"We could sell 3,000 to 3,500 motor cycles now if we had followed the pattern set by other manufacturers, producing to the limits of our capacity and marketing the goods immediately. But generally speaking, this method of selling is not the most effective. At present we are directing our sales in order to achieve steady progress and minimize selling expenses, so that we can maintain a constant flow of operating funds."

He concluded: "I have explained to you the reasons why I boldly chose motor cycles as a new undertaking, at a time when motor cycles were not selling well and when general business conditions were slacking off. Thinking back, I can say that we began this enterprise with the firm conviction that to do so would be best for the future of our company— particularly if sufficient plans could be formulated after I had toured Europe and asked the technology chief to prepare his study.

"However, I must say that at the time the reaction of some people was to question very strongly the advisability of our entering the field of motor cycle production at all."

There must have been widespread embarrassment amongst those doubters as the Yamaha success story began to unfold.

The company built its first factory at Hamakita and with a 200-strong workforce began turning out 200 motor cycles a month. From these humble beginnings production facilities and representation spread dramatically, to cover almost every part of the globe. By 1975 there were 8,165 people working for Yamaha. Trade had been stepped up to include snowmobiles, outboard motors, engines for four-wheel vehicles, power boats, sailing boats, fishing boats, multi-purpose engines, generators, go-karts, fun bikes, swimming pools, and the development and administration of a network of leisure parks.

The growth rate was phenomenal. Production of motor cycles had reached well over one million a year with exports totalling more than 773,000. Outboard motors, answering the needs of a new, fast-growing water-borne pastime, were manufactured at a rate of 90,000 a year; boats, including fishing smacks and pleasure craft of all sizes, rolled from the factories at Arai, Nakaze, Amakusa, Gamagori and Ofunado, at a volume exceeding 150,000 a year. Snowmobiles, for winter sport and rescue work, were reaching annual production figures of 50,000. Turnover for the company was upwards of £245,000,000 a year, while its capital had risen to £560,250,000.

Aside from the headquarters at Iwata, the tentacles of the Yamaha empire stretched six ways across Japan with branch offices in Sendai, Tokio, Nagoya, Osaka, Shikoku and Kyushu. There were 47 business offices, 7 service centres and more than 20 sales companies. Yamaha International was set up in Los Angeles on the Californian coastline of America, a growing market zone; in Europe, as the Common Market gathered momentum, Yamaha Motor NV was established in Amstelveen, Holland; then there was Yamaha Motor, Brazil; Yamaha Motor, Canada—and more than 300 agencies world-wide.

Gen-Ichi Kawakami retired as president of Yamaha in 1974 but retained his presidency of Nippon Gakki for a further three years, to be succeeded by Hiroshi Kawashima. (It is interesting that Mr Kawashima's brother was a member of the Honda hierarchy, Yamaha's greatest rivals). While Mr Kawakami remained the chairman of Yamaha, overseeing the company's business, the all-powerful office in the factory, that of president, was taken over by Hisao Koike. Under his leadership Yamaha made another change of direction, moving into what was an entirely new area for them—the four-stroke branch of motor cycle development. Within only two years, Yamaha were once more challenging Honda, the market pacemakers.

In only two decades, the first president of Yamaha Motor had seen his dream develop into a massive multi-million concern. And through it all, the link—symbolized by the triple tuning fork emblazoned on every Yamaha motor cycle ever produced—went back to that Wakayama clansman's home and the name Torakusu Yamaha.

Contesting the Classics

Yamaha's victory at the two Asama Road Race meetings had exceeded even their own initial expectations. Now a wider world beckoned. Heartened by their domestic success, Yamaha struck out from the shores of Japan to seek rewards and experience thousands of miles away. Their first stop lay across the Pacific at Catalina Island, the holiday playground for the wealthy, off the coast of Los Angeles. It was 1958.

The race meeting at Catalina was not that important. In fact, as an event guaranteed to bring world-wide recognition to its winner, it was a non-starter. But in the 1950s, motor cycle racing in the United States was very much in its infancy, with little public interest or response. It failed quite miserably to generate the same excitement or attendances that were a feature of the sport in Britain and Europe.

What Catalina did have to offer was a chance for Yamaha to broaden their experience, to look around and see what others were doing, how they were organized, how they went about the business of racing. It also presented a good opportunity to spread the company's reputation, through its improving brand, over a much bigger area than that bounded by the shoreline of Japan.

It was the first time a Yamaha had been taken out of the country to be matched against a line-up of foreign bikes and riders, in totally unfamiliar circumstances. By later standards of back-up and even team numbers, their bid to take the laurels at Catalina was a pathetic affair, but Yamaha were happy to be learning all the time.

The course was dreadful. Six miles of gravelled track, rough and bumpy like a moto-cross test. The man selected to be the first to carry the Yamaha banner into action on foreign ground was the team rider, Itoh. He had done well enough in the first Asama Volcano race and his outstanding potential had been recognized by team manager Zenzaburo Watase.

The machine was a 249 cc YD, fundamentally the same as the tried and trusty YD-B that had performed so well in the second Asama race the previous year. It was a two-stroke, forward-inclined two-cylinder engine with a bore and stroke of 56 x 50 mm. It had two Mikuni racing carburettors, a wet multi-plate clutch and could, depending on the course, be fitted with either four or five speeds. Because of the state of the course at Catalina the muffler was positioned high and a perforated and plated heat insulating cover was fixed over it. The frame was the same as on the YD-B, but the tank had thinner knee grips and was a little smaller. The front fork was telescopic with the spring exposed, and with a friction steering damper. The rear was swing-arm with hydraulic dampers front and rear.

Two works Yamahas trying out the bumpy gravelled track at Catalina, 1958—Yamaha's first race away from Japan.

It was a tough race for Itoh. He had not even seen the course before and could hardly remember his way round after the first lap. He was brought down by another faller and had to get back to the pits for a plug change. This put him in last position, way behind the rest of the field, but he fought back and finished sixth. Yamaha were delighted.

Back in Japan, top-level board meetings thrashed out a budget for Grand Prix racing. The racing and research department worked flat out to design and build a competitive set of racing machines to match the best in the world. 1961 was designated the target for an onslaught on the world championships that were staged across Europe, Scandinavia and, more particularly, in the Isle of Man at the TT—the most testing of all race courses in the world.

The Japanese motor cycle industry as a whole was poised on the threshold of its most important and memorable era. In line with Yamaha, the development experts at Suzuki were working furiously to get Grand Prix machinery into the front line. And in 1959, Honda launched the spearhead of the Japanese attack. After a great deal of careful planning, they ventured boldly to the Isle of Man with a factory team for the 125 cc TT.

Across the Irish Sea, off Britain's west coast, the Isle of Man was in a turmoil of excitement at the strange sight of a Japanese racing team in action. Neat and tidy in Honda overalls, with endless supplies of money, tools and spares, the Honda mechanics busied themselves around closely guarded lines of machinery with a precise efficiency that had hardly ever been seen before. That they never touched an engine unless they were wearing white gloves and that not a soul could understand a word of what

Yamaha's Catalina entrant: Itoh and his 249 cc YD.

they were saying only added to their mystique; all that and the fact that they seemed to work right round the clock without a break.

Hardly anyone realized that right behind the Honda vanguard was a second wave of Japanese motor cycle workmanship. Both Yamaha and Suzuki were preparing to follow with equal determination—perhaps those at Honda had guessed as much, but they could not be certain. Rumours swept around the tracks like wildfire. A few riders, blessed with enough skill to make them the best in the world, dreamed of the huge amounts of money that might be heading their way if the Japanese challenge remained on a firm footing. In truth, they were standing at the end of the rainbow. The 1960s were to provide the real pot of gold.

Yamaha moved swiftly. Hiroshi Naito, later to be appointed to the board as head of motor cycle technology, was put in charge of research and development; another expert, Noriyuki Hata, was invited to join the company. Naito told me: "We wanted to get our machines abroad as quickly as we could. Grand Prix success was necessary to bolster sales. Efforts were concentrated on a two-stroke 250 cc racing model—the RD48—based on the abundant technical data we had collected through our successful experience in national racing. The RD48 was later further developed into the RD56."

The second weapon in the Yamaha armoury was the 125 cc YX18. That was Hata's baby. He explained: "I got my job with Yamaha in 1959 and my first task was to develop a 125 cc racer. Ever since I have been concentrating on this line of work."

Hata was appointed General Manager of the company's Research and Development Division as the department grew. He later recalled the early problems that hit the prototype racers in his care. "Our first problem was how to test the new machine. Yamaha had no test course so we had to conduct the first series of proving runs on the normal expressways. But the results, anyway, were more than miserable. The new bikes were hit by piston seizure even after a small distance had been covered. Our machines had too many faults—poor materials, imperfect casting, defective chrome-plating and so on. But the design, I felt, held something noteworthy. We just had to work harder to get the machine right.

"The maximum output of the Asama-winning machines was only 12-13 hp. But the new racers we were developing were up to 18 hp mainly through the adoption of the rotary disc valve mechanism. In those days only the East German MZs were a match for the four-stroke machines in the 125 cc class. Therefore, we followed a similar pattern. We did, however, feature several refinements exclusive to Yamaha: rear exhausts and forced lubrication. But we realized we needed more time to make our machines competitive."

In a bid to sort out the problems, in 1960 Naito flew to Europe on a fact-finding mission. By then Suzuki had joined Honda in the Grand Prix contest for the world championship and both companies were fielding full-strength teams. Naito followed their progress at several European Grands Prix. It took him two months—but he came back with a head full of ideas and a notebook packed with information. He was able to give Yamaha a positive lead on what they should do.

Looking back on his mission to Europe, he recalled: "It was a wonderful experience for me, and an eye-opener, too. The new machines that were raced by Honda and Suzuki did well enough, but the longer established machinery that MV and MZ used was fantastic. Carlo Ubbiali, the great Italian champion, and Gary Hocking, from Rhodesia, were in the MV-Agusta team. Their lightweights were absolutely unrivalled. The two-stroke machines from MZ were also incredibly fast, but at the same time they lacked the durability that was just as vital as speed. The battles between MV and MZ went on at every Grand Prix and provided by far the greatest highlight of the racing. Most of the time the MZ was beaten by the MV but, nevertheless, I never lost confidence in two-stroke machines or their potential. I was convinced that we could build two-strokers that were much more raceworthy . . . provided we could find an answer to the problem of durability."

Yamaha firmly upheld the principle of the two-stroke engine. Their conviction was based mainly on the simple truth that there are fewer moving parts than in four-stroke engines, and that the power impulses are delivered at twice the rate. The recurring problem with two-strokes has always been the vexing issue of the petrol-oil mixture. Yamaha's answer was the auto-lube system. This constantly metered the amount of oil fed to the engine, in accordance with rev speed and throttle opening. It was the first pressure-lubrication device to be fitted on a production model after it had been used in racing machinery. The system was thorough; the build-up of carbon deposits and spark plug fouling was reduced drastically and exhaust fumes cut right down.

After concentrating tremendous effort on producing their racing machines, in line with rapidly increasing sales at home and abroad, in 1961 Yamaha announced that they were ready and willing to take on the rest of the world. For the first time Yamaha works bikes were to contest the classics. Cablegrams were sent off for entries in the Grand Prix rounds in France, Holland and Belgium, and for the Isle of Man TT—the race that would give them universal publicity and fame if only they could pull it off.

From the 14-strong racing department—10 engineers and 4 mechanics, a team of 8 was chosen for Europe. Naito was nominated team manager, and the chief engineer was Hasegawa. The money manager was a 29-year-old called Miyake. He carried with him all the cash for the running of the team abroad—around £30,000 ($60,000) and picked up the tabs for the riders—Itoh, who later became a cab driver in America; Noguchi, one of the biggest motor cycle dealers in Japan by the 1970s; Sunako, Masuko and Oishi.

The team had no European base. It was simply a three-truck caravan rolling across Britain, France, Holland and Belgium, loaded with machines, spares, tools, mechanics' clothing and personal belongings. Additional needs were requested by telex or phone and collected at American Express offices around Europe. It was a tough existence for everybody but there were few complaints, not even from the mechanics who were paid £40 ($80) a month and worked upwards of 15 hours a day for it. In their opinion, seeing some of the world at Yamaha's expense was far more pleasant than being on the production lines at the home-base factory.

According to Naito, their objective was to contest the races in order to amass as much tehnical data as possible and convert it to good use in the further development of Grand Prix bikes. "The results" he pointed out, "were not always satisfactory. Problems hit our machines and it was difficult for us to locate them in order to cure them, because neither our riders nor our mechanics had worked under similar conditions before.

"Aside from various irritating faults and shortcomings, we had to admit that our machines were much less powerful than the MVs and the Hondas. We had problems with the fairings, the carb settings and the ignition. In those days the carb was built in such a way that the float chamber and the mixing body were separate. The gas became bubbly and couldn't be absorbed into the cylinder. It had very poor response under rapid acceleration and deceleration. But that was only one of the many difficulties we had to cope with."

The two machines were the 125 cc RA41 and the 250 cc RD48. They were nothing like any other racing bikes that had emerged from the factory. Thoroughbred racers were what Yamaha needed and, though there was a base of experience upon which to draw, the designers realized that the earlier models were not the answer. Custom-built equipment became the priority.

Yamaha's first European racers: (above) the 250 cc RD48, developed by Naito for 1961; (below) the 125 cc RA41 developed by Hata from the YX18.

The RD48 had a two-stroke air-cooled twin-cylinder power unit which was pretty much the same as its predecessors. What had been altered was the suction method. Rotary valve suction, which allowed freer suction timing compared with the conventional piston valve, was installed. It was short stroke, the bore and stroke being 56 x 50 mm. It had a Mitsubishi racing magneto and two Mikuni racing carburettors. Maximum power output at 10,000 rpm was 35 hp. As with the 125 cc machines, the RD48 had porous plating cylinders, dry sump transmission and forced lubrication to the crank shaft bearing and connecting rod big end.

The frame was double cradle, molybdenum chromium steel. The front fork was telescopic with exposed spring, and there was a rear swinging arm . The front brake had a leading-trailing double panel and the rear another leading-trailing type. Both the 125 cc RA41 and the 250 cc RD48 had an air scoop. The RD48 weighed in at 100 kg, mainly because of the wide use of aluminium, and it had a top speed in the region of 130 mph, certainly a match for its rivals. It was rated at 246.33 cc.

The RA41 was a two-stroke, air-cooled, single cylinder. It was fitted with right and left rotary valves, Yamaha's unique suction system. This ensured higher intake efficiency for the two-stroke engine, opening or closing the intake port independently of the piston's reciprocating motion. The watchphrase among technicians at Yamaha was given to me by a former team member: "Fill in as much gas as possible and make it explode." The RA41 had a large cylinder fin, larger even than the fin area on the 250 cc. The cylinder wall was porous plated as a counter measure against the treachery of seizures.

With a six speed transmission, Yamaha avoided the wet sump: they felt it could bring about a power loss and a temperature rise in the oil. Instead it was designed so that oil was slightly put to each gear end and splashed from above—the dry sump. There was a deep fin in the oil pan. Maximum output at 10,000 rpm was 20 hp.

It had an expansion chamber that was both thin and short—the Yamaha engineers insisted that a 125 cc machine need not use two cylinders. The double cradle frame was made of molybdenum chromium steel and there was a telescopic front fork, spring exposed. The rear swing arm type had a damper located quite close to the swing arm centre—a design that the company had seen used on the Suzuki moto cross model. Its main characteristic was that the cushion stroke could be made longer, but the spring was fairly finely pitched for pliable setting. The brakes were leading-trailing type with 260 mm diameter double panels mounted on the front and a one-sided leading-trailing type on the rear. Both had big air scoops. For the Isle of Man TT, the RA41 was fitted with a special cowling, or fairing, that completely enclosed the handlebars.

At the French Grand Prix this largely experimental outfit opened Yamaha's world challenge. Noguchi, who had started racing with Yamaha by competing in the Fuji climbing race, following the rather peculiar Japanese prediliction for racing up volcanoes, showed up as a strong contender. He managed to steer his RA41 into a respectable eighth place. His team mate Itoh, notably the most promising of the Japanese riders, also earned an eighth place in the 250 cc class, with Noguchi two places behind him.

The TT, staged over $37\frac{3}{4}$ gruelling, hilly and twisty miles, gave the team its first look at the most severe test devised for any racing motor cycle. They had struggled hard to get the machines right for the race that was undoubtedly the most important of the short series they had chosen to contest. In the event Itoh was eleventh and Oishi twelfth in the 125 cc class. Under the circumstances, these two placings were excellent. But they were plainly not nearly good enough for the team itself, who were full of self-criticism and regret. However, they were a good deal happier with the results of the hotly contested 250 cc lightweight TT. Showing great bravery, Itoh picked up sixth place and thus entry on the leader board.

1961 was the beginning of the Japanese domination of the lightweight classes of the Isle of Man TT. At the head of the board, in a 1-2-3 formation in both the 125 cc and the 250 cc events, were Yamaha's great rivals—Honda. Mike Hailwood scored a fantastic double with a win in the 188-mile 250 cc race in 1 hr. 55 min. 03.6 sec., and a second victory in the 113-mile 125 cc race in 1 hr. 16 min. 58.6 sec. Tom Phillis, from Australia, was second in the 250 cc race, ahead of Jim Redman, the London-born Rhodesian. In the 125 cc class Luigi Taveri, from Switzerland, came second and Phillis—a big man, really, for the ultra-lightweights—was third. Yamaha might have been forgiven for feeling totally crestfallen, but when they left for Holland and Belgium, they were determined to do well, even in the face of such mastery from Honda. Their experience had been painful and, at times, embarrassing. But they learned from their own mistakes and from the successes of their rivals.

Holland and the Dutch TT gave Sunako a ninth place and Itoh an eleventh in the 125 cc class; Itoh, coming to grips with the erratic 250 cc bike, made it into sixth place, ahead of Noguchi who was eighth. Itoh picked up his best result with a fifth place at Spa in Belgium—and the team set off for home. They were chastened, but not despondent. And, anyway, Itoh was ninth in the world rankings, which was considered not bad for a beginner.

The engineering staff had already managed to fashion some improvement out of the machines, but they realized quite quickly that they still needed some extra pep and reliability. Both the 125 cc and the 250 cc had been troubled by plugs oiling, shocking vibration, carburation, and a shortfall on power and durability. The engineers were pressed into an exhaustive programme in preparation for the 1962 season. In the event, Yamaha's attack on the world championships of 1962 stuttered to a halt in the throes of the recession which followed the settlement of the Korean issue. Their target now became 1963. They built another 125 cc, the RA55, and developed the RD48 into the rather more sophisticated RD56. At last, Yamaha were turning the corner, and other

Itoh aboard the RA41 at the 1961 Isle of Man TT.

manufacturers began to fear the threat they offered.

For the Japanese, the highlight of 1962 was the domestic Grand Prix held at the new circuit, Suzuka, in November. It was the first all-Japan championship, a tremendous showpiece for the home market, and, at last, a chance for Yamaha to match their new machines against the best of the rest of the world's bikes. They fielded five Japanese riders—Itoh, who was fast becoming famous as a serious contender in the championships— if only the bike would match his ambitions for it; Sunaka, Masuko, Oishi and a new man, Hasegawa.

The race generated a great deal of excitement, both in Japan and abroad. Jim Redman, Irishman Tommy Rob and Luigi Taveri were there on Hondas; Englishman Frank Perris—later team manager of the ill-fated Norton line-up, had teamed up with a tough New Zealand competitor, Hugh Anderson, under Suzuki colours. The race had the look and the entry list of a full-status Grand Prix. It presented riders and manufacturers with a chance to test each other to the full in the battle for domination in the lightweight classes. Big things were expected of the new 125 cc and 250 cc Yamahas.

Any chance of victory in the 125 cc class faded for Yamaha when Hasegawa, at one stage running sixth, had to pull out with engine trouble on the tenth lap. The old bogey of reliability had hit the team again. But there was still the 250 cc class . . .

Redman, on the Honda RC163, was quickest in practice with a time of 2 min.36.0 sec. Itoh, to the great delight of his back-up team, was second fastest with a time of 2 min.36.7 sec. In the race, Redman stretched out a lead, chased by Robb, another Honda RC163 rider, and Itoh, who got into third place on lap two. On the sixth lap, Itoh passed Robb and held

With these two models, both raced at Suzuka 1962, Yamaha posed their first real threat to their competitors: (above) the 125 cc RA55, later developed into the RA75; (below) the 250 cc RD56.

his place until the fourteenth lap when the little Irishman forced him back into third spot. Itoh would not quit and stole back into second place two laps later, only to lose the advantage again on the twentieth lap. This time Robb made sure of his second place and came home one second

The engineering staff had already managed to fashion some improvement out of the machines, but they realized quite quickly that they still needed some extra pep and reliability. Both the 125 cc and the 250 cc had been troubled by plugs oiling, shocking vibration, carburation, and a shortfall on power and durability. The engineers were pressed into an exhaustive programme in preparation for the 1962 season. In the event, Yamaha's attack on the world championships of 1962 stuttered to a halt in the throes of the recession which followed the settlement of the Korean issue. Their target now became 1963. They built another 125 cc, the RA55, and developed the RD48 into the rather more sophisticated RD56. At last, Yamaha were turning the corner, and other manufacturers began to fear the threat they offered.

For the Japanese, the highlight of 1962 was the domestic Grand Prix held at the new circuit, Suzuka, in November. It was the first all-Japan championship, a tremendous showpiece for the home market, and, at last, a chance for Yamaha to match their new machines against the best of the rest of the world's bikes. They fielded five Japanese riders—Itoh, who was fast becoming famous as a serious contender in the championships— if only the bike would match his ambitions for it; Sunaka, Masuko, Oishi and a new man, Hasegawa.

The race generated a great deal of excitement, both in Japan and abroad. Jim Redman, Irishman Tommy Rob and Luigi Taveri were there on Hondas; Englishman Frank Perris—later team manager of the ill-fated Norton line-up, had teamed up with a tough New Zealand competitor, Hugh Anderson, under Suzuki colours. The race had the look and the entry list of a full-status Grand Prix. It presented riders and manufacturers with a chance to test each other to the full in the battle for domination in the lightweight classes. Big things were expected of the new 125 cc and 250 cc Yamahas.

Any chance of victory in the 125 cc class faded for Yamaha when Hasegawa, at one stage running sixth, had to pull out with engine trouble on the tenth lap. The old bogey of reliability had hit the team again. But there was still the 250 cc class . . .

Redman, on the Honda RC163, was quickest in practice with a time of 2 min.36.0 sec. Itoh, to the great delight of his back-up team, was second fastest with a time of 2 min.36.7 sec. In the race, Redman stretched out a lead, chased by Robb, another Honda RC163 rider, and Itoh, who got into third place on lap two. On the sixth lap, Itoh passed Robb and held his place until the fourteenth lap when the little Irishman forced him back into third spot. Itoh would not quit and stole back into second place two laps later, only to lose the advantage again on the twentieth lap. This time Robb made sure of his second place and came home one second ahead of his Japanese tormentor.

The sensational RD56, which was to give Yamaha their first Grand Prix win in 1963.

A confidential report, circulated among high management officials from the racing department at Yamaha at the time, claimed firmly that their riders had gained great confidence in the new machines. It stressed: "With a little more development the RD56 will not fail in winning the championship."

In 1963 Naito once again took a team to Europe. They had a brand new RA75 and the sensationally fast RD56, even further developed after its run-out against the Hondas and Suzukis in Japan only a few months before. Hata was the chief engineer, controlling two other engineers and five mechanics. There was the usual money manager, that unique institution among Japanese teams abroad, and five riders, all Japanese: the by now regular line-up of Itoh, Sunako, Masuko, Oishi and Hasegawa. The programme, still modest by anybody's standards, was to compete for the prizes at the Isle of Man, Holland and Belgium, and at home at Suzuka, the Japanese Grand Prix.

Before the party set off for the Isle of Man, Itoh was flown to America by Naito, to take part in a short series of international meetings Grand Prix warm-up and to test the capability of the RD56, soon to show itself as the fastest 250 cc machine in the world. He clinched two wins, one in a straight 250 cc event and the second in an open class race. The threat from Yamaha was looming larger.

The RA75, the 125 cc model, did not make an appearance until the Japanese Grand Prix later on in 1963, despite its expected arrival at the TT, the first of the Grand Prix races on Yamaha's schedule. Yamaha still maintained that 125 cc single-cylinder machines were ideal for the job. Twins were not part of their planning. The two stroke, forward inclined engine was basically the same as the conventional RA41 and RA55—but the carburettor lay-out had been halved. There was only one, installed on the right-hand side of the crank case. The machine had enjoyed a power lift and its output at 12,000 rpm had been raised to 25 hp. Like the RA55, it had a forced lubrication system by means of an oil pump. The frame, double cradle, was the same sort that had been used on the RA41, while the swing arm and telescopic suspension remained unchanged.

The main challenge for honours was to come, of course, from the 250 cc machine, the RD56 revamped from its first showing at Suzuka in 1961. With no test track, the company had had to try out the ultra-fast RD56 in its initial stages of development on a 9-foot-wide path alongside the river Tenryu—not a happy thought for a test rider who had a machine capable, though not proved, of taking him along the bank at 135 mph! That speed was thought to be the flat-out figure, but a report from the research and development department at the time pointed out laconically: "This could not be confirmed with a tester."

The two-stroke forward-inclined engine, a parallel twin, had rotary valves and was of a generally conventional layout. But in the search for high power, the cooling fin was made a little larger and the rotary valves were fitted at the right and left crankshaft ends. It was over-square with a bore and stroke of 56 x 50.7 mm. The overall displacement was 249.7 cc and it had a maximum output of 45 hp at 11,000 rpm. Compression was 7.8. Ignition was by means of a gear-driven Mitsubishi racing magneto.

The carburettor was a Mikuni M34 racing type—but with a separate float chamber. As has been explained, Yamaha had had a lot of trouble in the opening stages of the Grand Prix era with bubbling petrol. These problems continued, as team chief Naito related: "We were very worried at the Belgian Grand Prix. It was as if somebody had set an ambush for us. Not a new rival, but certainly a troublesome enemy. We discovered a big fault with the RD56 itself, while it was running at high speed through a long downward straight section during practice at Francorchamps.

"Engine response became extremely poor and wilted at full throttle when speed exceeded 130 mph. Why? We could not find an easy solution and our riders failed more than once to cover the prescribed number of practice laps. It was a big puzzle. Something, we reasoned, must have gone wrong with the mixing or float chamber.

"We concentrated our efforts on tracking down the trouble, all through the night. We took a gamble and decided to attach one more float chamber to the carburettor so that the mixing body was sandwiched by

The sensational RD56, which was to give Yamaha their first Grand Prix win in 1963.

both chambers. We had no idea whether it would be an effective solution to the problem. But we made a bet as it were—and it paid off."

In fact it paid off handsomely, for Itoh and his friend Giichi Sunako, seasoned campaigners in the Yamaha cause, finished first and second in the 250 cc class at Belgium, to give Yamaha its first Grand Prix win.

"The average speed was well in excess of 190 kmh (118 mph) on this ultra-fast circuit," recalled Naito. He added proudly: "One by one the two of them, Itoh and Sunako, rode past the chequered flag as I looked on. It was one of the most unforgettable moments of my life. All our work and effort, our faith in what we were doing and our confidence in the RD56, had come to fruition."

The date was 7 July 1963, a red-letter day in the history of Yamaha. But those of us who were there to see it had to cast our minds back barely one month, to the Isle of Man and the TT, to appreciate the tremendous escalation in Yamaha's threat to the dominance of Honda. It is worth retracing the saga of that TT in detail, for it was this race, more than any other, that made the racing world sit up and take notice of what Yamaha had to offer.

Once again, the arrival of Yamaha on the island triggered off an almost ritual surveillance from press and television men, who were curious and impatient to discover what, if any, improvements had been made by Yamaha technicians in their bid to unseat Honda and Suzuki.

Interest was heightened by the withdrawal of the Italian MV works team—though Mike Hailwood competed in the Senior 500 cc class as a *private* entry—particularly since it had monopolized four solo classes in the 1960 TT. Count Agusta, the company chief, was wise enough to

Part of Yamaha's Grand Prix team for 1963, with an RD56 at the Isle of Man. Left to right, back row: *Kosugi, Kaneyoshi Suzuki, Seki, Hata;* front row: *Naito, riders Itoh and Sunako.*

foresee that his lightweight machinery was no match for the two-stroke Japanese bikes, and that Honda, Suzuki and Yamaha, the precocious newcomers, would soon be bitterly contesting a three-cornered fight. The East German MZ had also been withdrawn. Plainly, the lightweight events of the 1963 TT were to be a sort-out between the threesome from the Land of the Rising Sun.

So far as the 125 cc class went, it was a non-contest. Suzuki were 1-2-3 with Hugh Anderson, Frank Perris and Ernst Degner, the East German defector, crossing the finishing line in that order. The 50 cc race was another Suzuki benefit: Mitsuo Itoh gave Japan her first ever TT victor with Anderson shadowing him to the chequered flag.

That left the 250 cc race as Yamaha's only hope. Fumio Itoh—no relation to the 50 cc ace—had Hasegawa to support him and they were joined by an Englishman, Tony Godfrey, surprisingly signed just for the TT. They were up against the mighty Jim Redman, captain of Honda, who had Tommy Robb, the likeable Belfast-born TT expert, and Luigi Taveri to help him. In practice, as expected, Redman was quickest, Robb second, Itoh third and Godfrey, despite his unfamiliarity with the complex machine, fourth.

Race day was hot and sticky. The tar melted and made the roads treacherous. Flies spattered screens and visors and half-blinded the riders. Footholds for the sharply accelerating motor cycles on the bubbling, shifting rivulets of tar were hazardous. But at 1.30 pm prompt Robb's

Honda led off. In the staggered start there was a ten-second time lag;
Takahashi, balloted to go next, screamed away, followed by Redman and
Luigi Taveri. The main Honda men had gone, anxious to open up as big
a gap as possible between them and the Yamahas that were waiting their
turn to be flagged away. Behind the pack of Hondas, with everything to
play for, went Itoh and Godfrey.

They were quickly into their stride. And by the end of the first lap they
had the whole island aghast. Itoh, with Godfrey right behind him, had
overtaken Redman into first place; the Honda star was trailing in the
wake of the flying Yamahas. Their speeds measured at a trackside radar
trap were: Godfrey, a breathtaking 225.6 kmh (140.2 mph), and Itoh
222.6 kmh (138.3 mph), with Redman's Honda slower by 15 kmh.

Without the same sort of power that the Yamahas had found, Redman
had to work really hard to make up for his lost ground. It was a matter of
sheer determination and skill. He was well-equipped with both. He got
ahead of Itoh while Godfrey, who had been running consistently well in
second place, had to stop for two minutes to make adjustments. When he
rejoined the race Itoh had fought back and was one second ahead of
Redman. Takahashi and Taveri had to pull out, soon followed by
Godfrey, who fell disastrously as he was chasing the leading pair.

The race was won and lost in the pits at the half-way, three-lap stage.
Redman refuelled inside 30 seconds. Itoh lost 19 seconds in the long haul
over the mountain, before the sloping road back to the grandstand area.
He lost a further 55 seconds in the refuelling, too much to make up
against a man of Redman's talent for TT racing. He did, however, hold
onto his second place. Redman came in 27.2 seconds in front. Bill Smith,
from Chester in the north of England, was third on another Honda—but
he was more than five minutes adrift of Itoh's Yamaha. Hasegawa was
fourth—a fair reward for the game of patience he had played in
supporting his team mate from behind the leaders.

Thus, even before that famous 1-2 Yamaha triumph in Belgium, when
the company gained its first Grand Prix success, Itoh's second place at the
TT, the most testing of all road races, was being hailed as the big
breakthrough. Naito recalled: "After the 1963 Isle of Man TT, when Itoh
finished second to Jim Redman's Honda, we had a great boost of
confidence in our machines." And to the world at large, it showed that
Yamaha were on to something—and that something big in Grand Prix
glory was in the offing.

I can recall Jim Redman telling me later—with as much enthusiasm as
he was ever able to show with that lazy drawl of his: "Boy, those Yamahas
were going like hell. I had to pull out all the stops to get some advantage
back." Redman had enough vision then to realize that his reign as the
kingpin of 250 cc racing was being seriously threatened. "We'll have to
get some more speed from somewhere", he said. "The bike I had was
nowhere near as quick. If Yamaha had been fielding a rider with a good
knowledge of the TT, I think I might have lost it. But I'm sure they'll
soon put tht right. They're obviously in the business seriously. And,

Itoh racing the RD56 in the Isle of Man TT. His second place in 1963 was Yamaha's biggest breakthrough, heralding their famous 1-2 triumph in Belgium.

knowing the Japanese, they'll move heaven and earth to build on what they've got . . and that means getting some real good men."

He was absolutely right. They did. And it triggered off not only the most glorious era in Yamaha racing history, but the most exciting period I hae ever seen in Grand Prix racing. The mid-sixties is, I think, firmly established in everybody's minds as the battle of the giants of racing. Yamaha-vrsus-Honda-versus-Suzuki. The big bangers, the 500s, were pushed back in order of appearance and the 250s were given top billing, promoted to the lastrace of the day. Nobody moved until that race had been won.

The riders embroiled in this three-way struggle lived on their nerves, and on whatever skill they had that separated them so starkly from the rest. Their names read like racing's roll of honour: Mike Hailwood, Jim Redman, Phil Read, Bill Ivy, Mike Duff, Luigi Taveri, Ralph Bryans, Tommy Robb, Frank Perris, Kel Carruthers, Stuart Graham, Barry Smith, Ernst Degner. They gave Grand Prix racing a closeness it had never had before—nor since. And a speeds hitherto undreamt of among the lightweights.

Phil Read
and the 1964 250-cc
Championship

Phil Read did not wait to be asked to become a member of the Yamaha
line-up. He invited himself.

Never a man to play down his own talent, Read approached Itoh, the
established Japanese rider in the team, at the 1963 Isle of Man TT. At 24
the rather abrasive young Englishman demonstrated a fierce will to win,
allied to a burgeoning skill that was to give him a reputation as a rider
who could be relied upon to be in the thick of the final action at the
chequered flag. He was just the sort of man Yamaha needed—and they
were quick to recognize his potential, even if he himself had been the one
to underline it.

His character was investigated; his skill rating, based on his results,
spoke for itself. Whether he could marry that talent to Yamaha's need for
it was another matter. There was only one way to find out; he had to be
invited to Japan. He was offered a test ride and then a machine for the
Japanese Grand Prix at Suzuka.

Whatever differences cropped up later between Read and Yamaha, and
there were many that left the factory displeased with the rider, he most
certainly was instrumental in putting them on the map in a racing sense.
He, really, was the turning point. He was the x-factor that had been
missing from their plans. The Japanese riders were good—especially
Itoh, but they did not have Read's resolve nor the final edge of genius that
lifted him out of the ordinary and into the extra-ordinary as a competitor.
He hardly ever inspired affection or friendship, his ready recognition of
his own brilliance made sure of that, but he enjoyed the grudging respect
of those who raced against him.

The truth of the matter was that Yamaha and the RD56 in particular—
a machine that was getting closer and closer to the desired standard,
needed a man of Read's calibre and special qualifications. Yamaha were
lucky. Read was absolutely right for the factory at a time when many
other first-class riders had slotted in perfectly with their factory's
requirements. He was a hard, tough rider who gave away nothing,
expected as much, and was prepared to be as daring as the next man.
Honda had such a rider in Jim Redman.

Read performed expertly enough in the 1963 Japanese Grand Prix at
Suzuka, on his first race outing aboard the RD56, to earn the respect of
Redman, the eventual winner, and the admiration of Itoh. The Japanese
star finished second, which gave him enough points for a third place in

Phil Read: the man who really put Yamaha on the map in Grand Prix racing. First signed in late 1963.

the world 250 cc championships. Read's machine was plagued with engine troubles. But he had headed Redman and Itoh in what had been an uncompromisingly fierce race, and had done enough to excite the assembly of Yamaha officials. Right after the race they drew up a contract for him to race for them in 1964. They were to pay him around £10,000 ($20,000)—and when you remember that AJS, Matchless and Norton used to contract riders for £1,000 a season, it is easy to understand his anxiety to be signed as an official works team man. Yamaha bought greatness—but trouble, too.

Mike Duff, a handsome and friendly Canadian, joined Read in the team. Itoh, with three years of hard labour on Yamaha's behalf behind him, was scheduled for duty only at the Isle of Man TT. The new team manager was Hasegawa, with chief engineer Nagayasu leading three

Frank Perris, Suzuki team captain. He was approached by Yamaha in 1961 but by then had already signed up with Suzuki.

engineers and five mechanics. Read's personal mechanic was called Seki and Duff's Suzuki.

With the publicity and backing of their racing successes, Yamaha had accelerated their sales efforts. The market began to expand on a world-wide scale. The huge amounts of money earned from sales at home and abroad were channelled straight back into the racing programme; cash was no object, success was vital. The targets were the titles held by Honda and the cost of getting them just did not matter. Redman's all-conquering four-stroke four-cylinder 250 cc Honda, slower than both the Yamaha and the Suzuki but more durable, was about to receive its direst threat. Read, almost on a par with the more experienced Redman as a rider, was after him; with Duff in support. The company entered their two-stroke twins for all the world championship rounds.

The RD56 had benefited from a massive cash flow into the research and development section—but it was losing ground to the Suzuki on the issue of water-cooling. It still had an air-cooled engine when Suzuki were improving their water-cooling system. All the big companies were working flat out in a bid to achieve stability in temperatures, and thus avoid the terrifying problem of seizures. This was particularly frightening for the Suzuki riders—the super-fast 250 cc model was called "Whispering Death" in that whimsical way riders have, because of its habit of nipping up without giving the man aboard it time to react. Frank Perris, the team captain and another £10,000 ($20,000) a year capture from British racing, once had five seizures in practice and two in an actual race, and was thrown off each time.

"I know that all of us, the men on Yamahas, Suzukis and even Hondas, though they were not nearly so bad, had this fear," he recalled later. "So much so that we developed a quick draw left-hand action on the clutch. You just had to get it in as quickly as possible or you were down on the road before you knew what had hit you. That's why water cooling was so vital. With air cooling the temperature was up and down like a yo-yo and it was frighteningly erratic. We and Yamaha had another problem that was peculiar to both factories. Neither had electronic ignition and the thing used to advance and retard itself, causing seizures on each cylinder. The worst threat of all for us at Suzuki was a seizure of a disc valve. When that happened the seizure was instantaneous and you were off the bike in a heap and hurting before you could react."

Suzuki, with a racing budget of more than £250,000 ($500,000) a year, headed Yamaha in the experiments on water-cooling, but they could not get over the dreadful problems they suffered with the handling of their machines. The bike twitched in the middle as if it was hinged whenever it was aimed into a corner. "Straight lines were a piece of cake," said Perris, "but as soon as you showed it a corner all hell was let loose. You just had to hang on and hope for the best."

Redman's Honda was good mannered, though a little slower than the diabolically behaved Suzuki. The Yamaha had speed and handled reasonably well. "At least," said Perris, "I don't recall hearing Read complain too often about it. But then we had little to do with him. He was a bit of a loner, not really part of the group of us who went round the world racing. So we never talked about bikes at all. Redman and I, as team captains, had long chats and were great friends. Read was a man apart. But that, I suppose, was good for Yamaha. He was certainly the sort of rider they needed—he only thought about winning. He was always trying, right to the last. And he wasn't too worried about jabbing his elbows and his legs out in the corners.

"I suppose there was still a lot that was gentlemanly about racing then, but Phil altered all that. He brought a professionalism to the sport that was not there before: I don't mean in his dealings in money, I mean in his riding technique. He was pushy, a sort of Cassius Clay. There was great rivalry between us all, and great friendship. But Phil was never part of it. He just got on with his job. His job wasn't making friends, it was winning races.

"We all had so much money then, such big contracts were paid out, that we lived the high life. In fact other riders who were not works contracted used to call us "Nob Hill". We all lived in the best hotels, had the finest food and spent our time jetting to and from Japan or other exotic places.

"Yamaha were the last of the big three—Suzuki and Honda were the others—to come into Grand Prix racing. And there were not so many really top class riders left to sign."

As early as 1961, over dinner in the Argentine after the Grand Prix there, Perris was aproached by Yamaha and invited to abandon his Norton racing and join the company. He had, however, committed himself to Suzuki and went on to race for them when the fully developed factory team went into competition. "When Read joined Yamaha for the Japanese Grand Prix at Suzuka, late on in 1963, he did so well the first time out that he looked all over a natural for them," said Perris. "He had all sorts of problems, but he got third place and the Yamaha people were really chuffed. It was a very good race and Read was right up front in the thick of things. It looked to me then as if Yamaha were going to be very difficult to beat in the following season.''

He was right. The RD56s prepared for Read and Duff had undergone an involved process of revitalization. The total displacement was 249.8 cc with a bore and stroke of 50.7 mm, unchanged from the previous model. But power, the eternal plea from riders, was increased dramatically from 40 hp to 54-plus hp at 11,000 rpm—and the bike was an absolute flyer. Stability and durability, said the race department, were improved and, indeed, there were few mechanical troubles throughout 1964 and 1965.

The compression ratio was 7.8—the combustion chamber was semi-spherical for better efficiency on the two-stroke engine. The cleaning ports were an orthodox shape, but cleaning port number three was made especially large. The floating rotary valve was lubricated by an oil pump, as was the crankshaft bearing. The carburettor was a Mikuni adapted to prevent petrol from bubbling and frothing and causing cut-outs, an old bogey with Yamaha. The parallel twin crankshafts were independent of each other, each respectively transmitting power through gears to the idler shaft. The bearing was a needle type.

Power transferred through the idler shaft energized the Mitsubishi inner rotary racing magneto set above the transmission at the rear of the crank. Rotation was reduced to half turns and the magneto end points, two of them, formed two crests. At the drive shaft end was a multi-plate dry clutch. The bike had seven gears and in order to minimize the length of the engine the drive shaft was located in an upper position and slanted. The oil tank, fitted under the transmission, had a complex separator built into it. Oil was fed to the speed adjuster and corner ring. The frame was a Kuromori double cradle, fundamentally unchanged from the RD56s forerunners.

Another RD56, bored out to 252 cc, was prepared for Read to race in the Junior TT in the Isle of Man. With the 1 mm widening of the bore, it was so incredibly quick that Yamaha's engineers felt it would present enough of a problem to Jim Redman's RC172 Honda. The mechanics were instructed to do nothing other than alter the bore. This challenger for the 350 cc class was only a sideline to the main issue. Yamaha were interested in capturing the world 250 cc title from Honda and Redman, and anything outside that priority received only secondary attention.

It most certainly held all of Read's concentration. It appealed to his great sense of determination and his natural enjoyment of personal glory. Even his love of money took a backward step; he rarely, if ever, joined forces with Redman and Perris when they were negotiating appearance-money terms for their respective teams, Honda and Suzuki. Redman, a notoriously tough and immovable man when it came to haggling with race organizers, did not feel the need to have Read by his side when he was trying to force purses to open a little wider. Nor, for that matter, did Perris. Read, it seemed, was quite happy to go it alone and to stand by his own considerable and distinguished talents when it came to

Itoh, the great Japanese rider who pioneered many of Yamaha's early bids. With an RD56 at Singapore 1964, just before his last race.

performances on the track. It all added spice to what turned into a season of spectacular racing in the lightweight division, a sort of high-noon situation between the two fastest men in the west—Redman and Read.

The first race of the 1964 campaign was the United States Grand Prix at Daytona. Honda did not send a team but Yamaha entered Read and Itoh on the RD56s. Itoh went out on the first lap and Read lasted only nine more before he was forced out with engine trouble. Alan Shepherd won on an MZ and Yamaha's earlier confidence had received a severe jolt. It was not helped when Itoh went off to contest the Singapore Grand Prix. He fell and injured his head. After his release from hospital he disappeared and was later believed to be a taxi driver in America.

Then the world championship contest started up in Europe. In Spain, Tarquino Provini abroad a four-cylinder Benelli picked up the major haul of points; Redman, the reigning world champion, was second and Phil Read third. In France, after a tremendous race, Redman had to quit with ignition troubles and Read triumphed with Luigi Taveri, Redman's supporting rider, 20 miles behind in second place.

By the time the teams reached the Isle of Man for the TT, the championship was wide open and the pace was getting hotter. The promise of a gruelling tussle between Redman and Read had been fulfilled and massive crowds flocked to watch them. Each man was feeling the pressure of the huge publicity build-up that heralded their appearance on the island's desperately tricky and arduous $37\frac{3}{4}$ mile course. In that respect the Isle of Man is claustrophobic—there is no escaping the atmosphere. Few people in TT week are on the island for anything but the racing; riders, by the very nature of this unique atmosphere, are embraced totally. For the big stars, freedom of movement without recognition is an impossibility. But they have to live with it.

Tommy Robb, the Belfast man sacked by Honda, joined Read and Duff in the Yamaha line-up—determined to show his former bosses that they had made a costly error in letting him go. The Yamahas were widely tipped to clean up and, indeed, many people considered that Redman was wasting his time in even bothering to enter. He, of course, had other ideas. With the backing of £100,000-worth of machines and engines in the Honda garage below a beachside hotel in Douglas, he had fair reason to be confident.

Only minutes after the start, almost before the crowd had settled into their places, Mike Duff was out with engine trouble. Read made it back to the pits at the grandstand, second to Redman, and had to pull in for a plug change. The mechanics worked quickly but he had still lost more than one minute. Redman was steady, relentless, and, in his own words, unhurried. Whatever speed anybody else wanted to go was alright by him; he knew what pace he was safe at and he would not step beyond that limit. Read was outside even his wider margins of safety, carving a path through the backmarkers to break Redman's stranglehold on the race.

Redman was forced to refuel at the end of the third lap, and even as he looked back over his shoulder, along the Glencrutchery road in front of the grandstand, Read swept through, his heart soaring. But his joy, and the unbridled happiness of the men in the Yamaha pits, was short-lived. For only a mile or so farther on, at Quarter Bridge, the spirit of the Yamaha suddenly flagged. And a grim-faced Read, staring hard at the dead engine, looking for some clue as to its sudden demise, pulled in.

He was still there when Redman angled the lustier Honda round the curve of Quarter Bridge and opened the taps to accelerate away towards Braddan. Redman was not sure that the Yamaha had been killed off—but he did not want to take any risks. He had seen what it could do in Read's hands and he had learned his lesson. But he need not have feared—Read was out.

Even then Redman was lucky. A dribble of oil from a seal almost put the skids under his victory. Behind him lay 200 gruelling miles. In front, only 14 miles off, stood the official with the chequered flag. In between them lay an avenue of applause. But as Redman lined up to round Ramsey Hairpin, the Honda suddenly slewed crazily sideways and started to keel over. He shifted his weight and balance and heaved the skidding machine back into an upright position. It still ran wide but somehow he turned it round onto the correct line and headed back towards the finish at Douglas.

Phil Read racing the RD56 at the Isle of Man. Mechanical failure forced him out of both the 1964 and the 1965 250 cc races, although he went on to win both world championships.

He explained: "There was oil bleeding out of a seal and it got onto the back tyre. It almost put me down but I managed to get it back upright. It was a close call. It was a relief to see Phil by the roadside at Quarter. I doubt that I would have caught him again. He was in the groove and the Yamaha was really flying."

Alan Shepherd was second on an MZ. Behind him came Alberto Pagani, riding a Paton. Tommy Robb, the only Yamaha finisher, took it steady to clinch seventh place.

At Francorchamps Spa, Belgium, the two seemingly nerveless adversaries, Read and Redman, fought another round in their fierce duel for the 250 cc championship. Their bright and breezy veneer tended to overshadow the apprehensions they felt about the dangers of racing at the speeds they were forced to go. This time, those apprehensions were spiced by the knowledge that Francorchamps is Europe's fastest track.

Indeed, Redman had one of the most frightening moments of his career at the Belgian Grand Prix. He recalled later: "I'd got off to a flyer of a start down that cresta run of a road in front of the pits. I moved on as quickly as I could, knowing full well that Phil would be after me like a shot out of a gun. I could only sit there, going as fast as I could, waiting for him to arrive and wondering what to do when he passed. In fact, I must have been going good because I got much farther along the course before he caught me—but then he went by me like the wind. As soon as I felt the draught I tucked in on his tail, but slightly to the side of his slip-steam. I knew all about the two-strokes and their terrible habit of seizing in full flight, and I wasn't going to be caught out. I'd seen it happen too often not to worry about the effects it could have—not only on the man on the machine but on the guy right up his exhausts. Just ahead of me Phil was riding in the usual two-stroke man's style, his left hand hooked gently over the clutch ready to squeeze it in at the slightest feel of a seizure.

"I saw a puff of smoke—hardly discernible, but it was there—come out of his exhaust. I knew what had happened and instantly I knew his bike would seize. I started to swing out of his slip-stream just as we entered the Masta-S bend, a full 140 mph swoop. As I swerved, Phil sat up and pulled the clutch in and though the Yamaha swerved and snaked off its line he stayed aboard.

"I was left with no place to go. I threw the bike sideways, out of Phil's way, but I went off the circuit at about 130 miles an hour. In a split second I was on the grass verge, the bike bucking all over the place. A telegraph pole loomed up and I missed it by fractions, then I missed the wall of a house by about a foot. Don't ask me how but I managed to get the bike back under control and onto the track. Then, still swallowing hard and trying to forget the nightmare of it all, I set off after Mike Duff and Alan Shepherd. My stomach was in a knot and though I managed to get past Alan Shepherd I couldn't catch Mike Duff, who won in record time.

"It was some sort of instinct that told me Phil's bike had seized when I saw that tell-tale puff of smoke. I'd never noticed that happen before. If I had waited for Phil to sit up, indicating that he had seized, I would have

*Ulsterman Tommy Robb,
who joined Read and Duff in
the Yamaha team for the 1964
Isle of Man TT. His RD56 was
the only Yamaha to finish.*

rammed him at about 140 mph. Everybody else was so close at that stage—Mike Duff, Alan Shepherd and Bertie Schneider—we'd all have been down in a heap.

"Strange, really, how you get over a fright like that. I still managed to get round at an average of more than 116 mph, even though my heart wasn't really in it."

Phil Read's failure to finish meant that Redman's lead in the world 250 cc championships had increased to 10 points; Redman had 28, Read 18. And the advantage was distinctly Redman's, for the two of them were to race in the next round at Solitude, West Germany, a track familiar to Redman but completely new to Read.

Read remembered: "The races between us were getting harder all the time—but we dare not ease up or lose concentration. Redman was desperate to retain his title. I wanted it off him. It was as simple as that."

At Solitude Read played a clever waiting game; he allowed Redman to show him the way round, being careful not to let the Honda get clear. Redman tried everything he knew to throw Read off the scent—he started fast, went for a decisive lead and rode superbly. But he could not shake off the equally determined Englishman. It is a twisty circuit, difficult to learn, and Redman used all the knowledge he had built up over his experiences there. He even tried to lure Read into the lead, in the hope that the Yamaha might break when trying to get away—but Read was having none of that. For ten of the eleven laps Read was a carbon copy of Redman. Then, on the back straight of the eleventh lap, he darted out of Redman's slip-stream, left the Honda for dead by at least 100 yards, and surged over the line for a memorable victory. On his final lap Read logged 99.37 mph, a record on a track he had never even seen before.

Afterwards Read revealed that he could have passed Redman's Honda any time he wanted on the straights. He preferred to learn the circuit as Redman's shadow and save all his effort for a last-ditch burst. His tactics paid off handsomely—he had taken his championship tally to 26 points. Redman had reached 34, but he knew he was going to be hard-pressed to stay in the lead.

When the 250 cc battle moved to East Germany, 300,000 people covered the hillsides of the Sachsenring circuit. There were 30,000 in the grandstand that curved from the final, upward turn and stretched beyond the start-and-finish line 300 yards or so away. As if Read and Redman did not have enough problems in contending with each other, Mike Hailwood had eagerly accepted an offer from MZ to race their 250 cc machine. Alan Shepherd, the rider from Lancashire, England, who had done really exceptional things for the MZ factory, had crashed in practice and was out of the race. Hailwood did not have to be asked twice—and the partisan crowd was behind him to a man.

Both the Yamaha and the Honda teams were worried, conscious that Hailwood could upset all the predictions for the race by winning. The somewhat fragile MZ had the knack of going superbly on home ground, and with Hailwood aboard a record-breaking performance seemed assured. Hailwood felt that the 250 cc was the class where the true racing was being staged. Before the race, he told me that he was determined to split the Honda and the Yamaha. If he upheld any alliance other than to MZ, it was to Redman on the Honda—they were old friends. He knew that even if he could not win, by making it into second place he would at least push Read back a little in his rush towards the title.

The atmosphere was quite incredible—a massive crowd prepared to cheer themselves hoarse, stirred with excitement and anticipation. The riders were edgy, the mechanics even more so. From the start Read demonstrated his steely determination not to be trapped by the two friends. He got off to a punishing start ahead of Redman's Honda and Hailwood's MZ, and swooped round the long right-hander after the start as though the devil were after him. The phenomenal acceleration of the RD56 carried Read swiftly out of the reach of Redman's Honda, but Hailwood's MZ was another matter. Half-way through the first lap, Hailwood caught Read and passed him, with Redman viewing it all from far back. Redman managed to close the gap to about 10 yards but he simply could not get by to chase Hailwod—Read kept him firmly back in third place.

Hailwood, enjoying every milli-second of his new responsibility, battered his two-year-old lap record out of sight, rounding the hilly $5\frac{1}{2}$ mile circuit at 102.06 mph. With 40 yards on the Yamaha and the Honda, he tried desperately to open up an even wider margin as he swept through the cobbled streets of Hohenstein-Ernstthal. But he let loose too much power too soon and the brave little MZ slithered sideways and threw him off. Read, right behind, violently heaved the Yamaha off its racing line as Hailwood's unconscious figure rolled in front of him. Redman had to take avoiding action as well and the two of them headed up the hill into the town, looking over their shoulders at the comatose form of Hailwood. When they came round again he was already on his way to hospital— with a lacerated scalp, injured shoulder muscles, bruises and a splitting headache, but otherwise okay.

Redman took advantage of Read's diversion round Hailwood to snatch the lead and the pair of them, still tied together by their equal talents, lapped everybody else on the circuit. With three laps to go Read eased back into the number one position, and no matter how hard he strived Redman could not shake him loose.

I looked left towards the final turn as the two of them, straining every sinew and reaching deep into the reserves of their strength, leaned their machines as tightly as possible into the finishing straight. Read was ahead by a yard. His black and white helmet was thrust low behind the screen. Redman's silver helmet glinted as he shoved his chin down onto the tank and turned his fist backwards, in a ferocious effort to feed enough winning power through the twist grip to carry him past Read's Yamaha. Behind them, in a marvellous backcloth of waving handkerchiefs and programmes, the people in the grandstand leapt to their feet with a thunderous roar of encouragement, straining their eyes towards the

Phil Read racing the RD56 at the Isle of Man. Mechanical failure forced him out of both the 1964 and the 1965 250 cc races, although he went on to win both world championships.

official with the chequered flag.

Redman tried to guide his Honda out of Read's slip-stream, but even then the Yamaha still had too much power aboard to relinquish the advantage so close to the line. There was no stopping Read in that mood. Redman's lead was reduced to only six points: the world championship crown for the 250 cc class was about to change hands . . .

"We might have looked cool on the surface," said Read, "but underneath Jim and I both felt the pressure. Neither of us tried to show it in case we gave the other some sort of advantage. But I think we both wondered how long we could keep it up. The racing was really fierce, but enjoyable."

The series now moved to Ireland for the eighth round—the Ulster Grand Prix at Dundrod, a pure road race circuit set in a water catchment area outside Belfast. By this time, the two men knew all about each other's style. But this balance was upset by the Yamaha's outstanding speed. Read had no need to resort to trickery—he had picked up priceless points in East and West Germany and already held the trump card. Redman had had to struggle to gain second placings in his last three outings. He could rely only upon his superior experience and boundless bravery—but they were to prove no match for the faster pace of the RD56. A downpour, leaving the roads like rivers, did not make him any happier as he wheeled out the Honda, and he had little heart for the race that was to come.

Tommy Robb, back on home ground, led the race half-way round the first lap, followed by Redman and Bruce Beale, with Read literally in his wake. Redman went ahead—but only briefly, for Read soon splashed by him. Redman struggled manfully to get back on terms, survived two frightening slides, and stared through goggles that had turned into puddles at Read's fast disappearing figure. It was not his day and he knew it. He could not get himself into the right groove and he confessed later, in an outburst of self-criticism, that he had ridden terribly. "I don't think I have ever ridden so badly," he said dejectedly, "but the conditions were the same for both of us. The difference was that Phil got down to the job, worked out the conditions and rode a real good race to win. I wouldn't want to take anything away from him—he was more than a minute in front of me at the end."

Read commented: "It was my fourth Grand Prix win. Conditions were diabolical, but I just got my head down and went for the line. Once I'd passed the Honda it never came anywhere near me. But I was shaking like a leaf when it was all over. I suppose I stuck my neck out more than I would like to."

Honda now concentrated all their efforts upon a final bid to beat off Read's Yamaha. For the past three months, since the Isle of Man TT, they had been secretly developing a revolutionary six-cylinder 250 cc machine, code-named 3RC164. After the Ulster debacle, when their confidence was at its lowest ebb, their chief mechanic Aika flew back to Japan to help with its assembly. Redman was convinced that the new machine represented his only chance in an otherwise unequal contest, and urged the factory to hurry. He joined Aika in Japan in order to test the bike, to find that it handled appallingly. There was no time to make modifications. Despite the fact that it had been tested on the bench for only a few hours, it was pressed into service for the Italian Grand Prix at Monza, the super-fast circuit set in a park of faded splendour outside Milan.

Aika was red-eyed from lack of sleep three nights before practice started, having regularly worked through the night. Even then Redman was not sure whether he should ride the new machine. It certainly had the potential and was computed to have the speed, but its handling was still suspect. On the other hand, he really had nothing to lose—he knew that the four-cylinder had no chance even of matching the speed of Read's machine, especially on a circuit like Monza. And so he decided to take the risk and opt for the as yet untried 3RC164.

As soon as the six-cylinder arrived at Monza, crated and covered, all unauthorized personnel were banned from the Honda garage area. Two of the six pipes were removed to give it the look of a four-cylinder machine—and when it was not surrounded by mechanics, it was kept hidden under sheets. Redman and I were the closest of friends, but even though I had heard some of the rumours and realized that something special was about to be released, he never let me in on the secret. He merely winked and answered my questions with: "Just you wait and see—maybe Phil's in for a shock. It's about time I got some of my own back.'

When the new machine was pushed out at Monza for its first public appearance, the clamour had to be heard to be believed. From the back it looked like the trombone section of a dance band. Six exhaust pipes, angled three-a-side in a gentle v-shape, blared out such sensational engineering music that mechanics and officials came running from all over the place, attracted by the unfamiliar but exciting new sound. It was the sound of power.

Redman spurted from the pits to join the practice traffic already circuiting the wide and fast Monza track. His acceleration was exceptional, and the other riders hurried to latch on to his tail in a bid to seek out some performance characteristics. But Redman wisely kept the bike in check, giving away no clues as to its potential. As soon as he had motored back into the Honda pit area, a mechanic, poised like a matador with an enormous sheet, quickly covered up the surprise package before it was hurriedly pushed back to its lock-up garage. Tight-lipped yet inwardly delighted, Redman strode away, worried only by the machine's untried stamina.

Even in the comparatively cool atmosphere of the practice session, the Honda had started to overheat, although Redman had nursed it without strain from start to finish. As race day dawned, the temperature developed to an almost unsufferable heat, and it was this that effectively sabotaged Redman's hopes. When the race got underway, Redman, using only 16,000 of the Honda's 17,000 rpm, opened up a 3-second lead over Read by the end of the first lap. But by then the six-cylinder's temperature had soared to dangerous heights, and Redman could feel the engine begin to lose power. Responding only on three-quarters throttle, the Honda's lead was wiped out and Read's Yamaha flew effortlessly past.

"Even at that," Redman claimed, "I could hold Phil, but when the going got hard and the racing tougher, it was a hell of a job to resist opening the throttle to its limit. When I lapsed in the heat of the moment and opened it just that little bit too far beyond three-quarters, the engine would fade. The bike simply would not go until I shut down completely and turned it back again to three-quarters. It was crazy."

Redman needed to win in Italy and in Japan to retain his title—but his chances died off in the fourteenth lap at Monza, when overheating made it debatable whether he would be able to finish. Mike Duff sped by into second place as Redman strove to keep on the move and hang on to third place.

At the last Grand Prix of the season, in Japan, Redman beat Read out of sight on the six-cylinder Honda, but by then the contest was over. Read and Yamaha had won their first world title—the first of many. It was the first time a two-stroke manufacturer had made such a breakthrough. Signing up Read was indeed a turning point for Yamaha. Although he later became involved in an embarrassing and largely public difference of opinion with his team-mate Bill Ivy, and with officials at Yamaha, his worth to the factory in their early development as a Grand Prix entity was immeasurable.

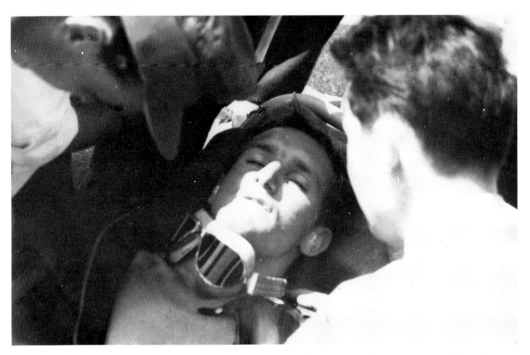

Mike Hailwood out cold after his spill in the 250 cc East German Grand Prix, 1964.

Triumph
for the Lightweights

During 1964, it was natural that Yamaha, well on their way to winning the world championship for 250 cc machines, should tend to lapse a little in the development of their 125 cc machine. But despite their emphasis on the RD56, Read's mount for the title, 1964 saw the entry of a new 125 cc model, the RA97, at the Dutch TT in June and later in Germany.

The RA97 closely resembled the bigger, more powerful RD56. Read steered it into second place at the Dutch TT, only 0.1 second or half a wheel behind Redman's Honda, on a course he had never ridden before. But he could not manage it a second time in Germany: he fell off in the rain and retired.

Yamaha were happy with the promise shown by the air-cooled two-stroke 125 cc model, and felt sufficiently confident to plan immediate further development for the following season. By now, water-cooling was well on the way as a viable proposition. The threat of seizures, the rider's nightmare, would largely be erased when the benefits of water-cooling were built into the temperamental two-strokes. Although the RD56 remained air-cooled throughout its active life, the RA97 was produced in a water-cooled version in late 1965 and stayed as such throughout 1966. Its maximum output, when it first emerged from the secret list at Yamaha, was said to be not less than 28 hp at 10,000 rpm—the same as the air-cooled type. The carburettor was a Mikuni VM25 and float chamber combined—the first time such a unit had been used by the factory.

The water jacket was a cleaning port cooled with mixed air. Water, cooled by the radiator, went along the frame on the left-hand side and was sucked into the water pump in the rear of the transmission. Cooling water from the pump was divided half-way and entered right and left separate cylinder heads—the two courses of water were fed out from the head front. It was then channelled to the separator in the central section and returned to the upper part of the radiator. The machine had nine speeds and weighed 100 kg. It enjoyed steady reliability and was the forerunner of a great new era of racing for Yamaha: the ultra-lightweight class of the Grands Prix was to become almost as exciting and as rewarding as the 250 cc division.

1965 was also to see the introduction of a brand new, water-cooled 250 cc machine—the RD05. At the end of the 1964 season, in the Japanese Grand Prix, Redman had beaten Read out of sight on his new six-cylinder Honda. After the race, Read told Redman: "I knew I was beaten and I let you get farther ahead so that Yamaha would work hard to match the speed of the six for the following season."

Though Read was not to know it, Yamaha were not anxious to rest on their laurels. Company director Takehiko Hasegawa recalled: "We realized that the new Honda Six, unveiled at Monza, was a serious threat to Yamaha for the new season, 1965. It was claimed to produce 60 hp and our RD56 was already near to its limit of power, even though the initial 40 hp had been increased to 54.5 hp. We did not expect its maximum output to be raised to a level of 60 hp and we decided on a new machine to replace it—the RD05. We adopted a V-four layout for this machine and wanted to raise the power output to around 70 hp. We weren't too interested in a square-four layout which had been unsuccessful with Suzuki's RZ racer—and the rotary disc mechanism did not allow the adoption of an in-line four layout.

"Our new development programme started right after the Japanese Grand Prix in October 1964. We had completed the first V-four engine before the opening of the 1965 season and the maximum power output was well in excess of 65 hp—with room for improvement and development as the season went on."

In fact, the new water-cooled 250 was not raced until late on in the 1965 season. And before the factory could get the machine to Europe, Read had already won the 250 cc championship—for the second year in succession.

Before the 1965 season began, Yamaha had decided to provide full back-up facilities for the team in the Isle of Man, Holland and Belgium. They would then withdraw the full team, leaving one mechanic. Before they pulled back to Japan the back-up team comprised Hasegawa, team manager; Masaharu Naito, chief engineer, experiencing his first season in Europe; and a money manager named Watanade. There were also three engineers and five mechanics drawn from the 30-strong racing department at the factory in Hamamatsu.

Read was to be the number one rider with Duff, once more, in support. Bill Ivy, who had been earning himself a tremendous reputation as a fearless competitor on England's short circuits, was given a two-race contract for the two TTs—the Isle of Man and the Dutch. Ivy was largely Read's choice. Read did not support suggestions that John Cooper, the tenacious, bespectacled Derby rider should be invited to join the team. In fact, it's doubtful that Cooper ever knew how close he had been to a coveted works ride for one of the most important and wealthiest teams in the business.

When the team got together in the Isle of Man in preparation for the 1965 TT, a race that Yamaha dearly wanted to win, they had an immediate background of success trailing behind them. Read and Duff, on RD56s, had taken the first two places in the 250 cc United States Grand Prix—even lapping the third rider. In Singapore, Hiroshi Hasegawa— the rider, not the team manager— had picked up first place in both the 250 cc and 350 cc classes and his team mate, Honbashi, had won the open race. Honda did not compete at the West German Grand Prix where Yamaha came first and second. In Spain, Read won and Duff was third. The Isle of Man brought Read and Redman together once more for a

Bill Ivy, given a two-race contract by Yamaha for 1965, covering both TTs.

confrontation that was an opportunity to settle old scores.

But it seemed that Read's burning enthusiasm to establish himself as the better rider trapped him into a tactical error—one that might well have been far more costly than it turned out to be. There was a race to be won: there was also the glory of being the first 250 cc rider to lap the island's terribly difficult course beyond the 100 mph barrier.

On the first lap, Read rode from a standing start straight into the TT record books by lapping at 100.01 mph. It was breathtaking stuff. By the time Redman brought his Honda back to the line opposite the timekeeper's hut, he was sixteen seconds down on the Yamaha. That sort of gap between Read and a man of Redman's calibre was almost unbelievable and there was a great deal of rechecking done on stop-watches. It was soon confirmed by the commentator—and there was no stopping Read. Or was there? Maybe Redman sensed that Read could be broken by his own eagerness, as he patiently and progressively chased the leader without overstressing his engine.

Read, it seemed, was determined to crush the Honda and embarrass Redman with the incredible speed of the RD56. But on the second lap, with Redman refusing to panic, the Yamaha died in its tracks. A crank pin had broken. Read was out.

Ivy then moved up to challenge Redman—but he crashed avoiding another rider in the mist at Brandywell on the fourth lap. He refused to quit and tried to restart his machine, only to find that the carburettors were hanging off. Even then, despite a painful hip injury, he manhandled his bike back to the pits for help—but instead, officials carried him into the first-aid headquarters for treatment. He was cheered every yard of the way—and found a special place in the hearts of the Yamaha team, particularly for Masaharu Naito, the chief engineer, whose affection for the little fellow kept pace with his enormous

After a fine start at the Isle of Man, a bad crash at Brandywell put Ivy out of the race.

admiration for him as a rider of great bravery and skill. Duff was left to carry Yamaha's hopes the rest of the way, but he just could not close the difference and finished in second place, behind Redman.

Rightly or wrongly, Read was heavily criticized for his flat-out eagerness, and was accused of a lack of caution that caused the Yamaha to break under stress. He was the first 250 cc rider to beat the 100 mph barrier—but Redman soon rubbed out that memory with a faster lap, 100.09 mph, before he settled down to a series of circuits that dropped below the 100 mph mark but conserved his motor for a Honda lightweight victory, the fifth in five years.

At the time, Read's defence of his break-neck speed was: "I set out to crack the 100 mph lap. I know that a lot of people have said that I was probably too hard on the bike and that's why it failed me. But that's not true. The snag that arose would have happened anyway.

"I had a wrong signal from my check point. It said I was second by 5 seconds with another Yamaha behind me. Whoever put that signal out was wrong. I thought "I'm not going to be beaten by one of my own team mates", so I opened up. At that stage I thought Jim Redman would slow me if I stayed with him. I'm delighted to be the first man to turn in the 100 mph lap—but I could not be more miserable at not winning."

Read, it appeared, was fated not to win that TT. He had given Redman 20 seconds start and still caught the Honda Six. Maybe his strategy was faulty, perhaps his zest was too rich, but whatever the reason for his dramatic collapse, Yamaha's backroom boys were not too happy.

Read did restore some balance, however, with a victory in the 125 cc race at the Isle of Man TT. This was an outing for the water-cooled RA97 and very many Yamaha hopes were pinned on it as a blueprint for the future. The machine behaved impeccably. Read rode superbly to beat the previous year's winner, the Swiss Luigi Taveri on a Honda, by 6 seconds. He showed, at long last, that he did have the necessary qualifications to win the world's most difficult race. I have the black and white garland he was awarded for that first triumph on a wall of my house: it is one of my most treasured mementoes.

With four wins in a row before the island disaster, Read secured his second 250 cc world championship at the Ulster Grand Prix. Redman was injured in a spill and Read led Duff to the line virtually unchallenged. That was the order in which the two team mates finished in the championship.

Although the question of the championship was settled, there were still two more Grand Prix meetings to go. And at Monza, Yamaha decided to reveal their latest development, the water-cooled V-four RD05. The thinking behind such a move so late on in the season was lost to many people outside the company. I suppose they may have felt that it was the right time to crush Honda psychologically.

The weather at Monza was foul. The rain came down like a dense, grey bead curtain, a thoroughly miserable backcloth for what should have been an exciting new move by Yamaha to counter the superior power of the Honda RC166. Honda had chosen to give the world its first showing of the six-cylinder 250 cc machine at Monza the year before; now it was Yamaha's turn to set the place buzzing. But it proved to be a sad anti-climax, and no doubt the move was later regretted by the Yamaha officials responsible.

Torrential rain caused the new machine to be withdrawn from the race: ironically because of over-cooling. It certainly delivered more power than the Honda, but its handling proved to be atrocious. At the last race of the season, the Japanese Grand Prix, it was again eliminated—this time by a crash at the half-way stage.

There was obviously a great deal more work to be done. Handling characteristics had to be improved, and it was also felt that the machine was too heavy. The engineers were instructed to reduce its weight by about 25 kg so that a more streamlined riding posture, for example, could be adopted.

Two new four-cylinder V-type engines were built at Yamaha's Research Department in Japan: one air-cooled version, and one water-cooled version for a machine designated the RD05A. The air-cooled version vibrated terribly in bench tests, but it gave out more power than the 65 hp that was expected of it. The water-cooled version was designed to decrease the huge calorific value, the temperature differences in the cylinders, and the total weight. As a result, it was 24 kg lighter than the air-cooled RD05 engine.

Overlapped rotary valves and a Mikuni VM25 carburettor were used on the RD05, which had a maximum output of 50 hp at 13,000 rpm. On the

RD05A, rotary valves without overlap and a Mikuni VM27S were used. The RD05A, with a 44 mm bore and 41 mm stroke, had a total displacement of 249.5 cc and a maximum output of 60 hp at 14,000 rpm.

The cylinders of the RD05A were arranged in a V-shape, fitted with crankshafts that were independent of each other. The opposed engines were thus reversed from each other. It had eight-speed transmission, through the dry multiple disc clutch from the idler shaft side. The transmission was dry sump, the same, in fact, as on the RD56 and all other Yamahas.

The water-cooling courses were designed to decrease the temperature differences in the cylinders. Cooling water, to each horizontal cylinder

Suzuka, the last Grand Prix of the 1965 season. Read gets his new RD05 Yamaha off the line a few yards adrift of Hailwood, who was riding the Honda 250-Six for the first time.

from the lower part of the radiator, went to the left from the lower side of the crank case; it was then pumped by the trochoid pump, mounted on the rear of the vertical cylinders, and transmitted from the vertical cylinders to the radiator. Synchronization of the four carburettors was by a forced switching system between the throttle grip and the drum under the fuel tank; four wires to the carbs operated through the drum.

Two tachometers, mechanical and electrical, were carried on the RD05A, placed above and under the tank, respectively. Yamaha felt that the electrical version excelled in accuracy and response, but the mechanical one had the advantage in indicating vibration and heat. The frame was the feather-bed type. The immense force that it was subjected to by the power of the engine was evidenced by the wide down tube and reinforced head cone. The front brake was a double-panel, two-lead type and the rear a single-cam. The RD05A had a front brake diameter of

260 mm, and a rear brake diameter of 220 mm. The RD05 air-cooled model weighed in at 145 kg, and the RD05A at 125 kg.

For the 1966 season, Yamaha put forward the best possible pairing—Phil Read, the previous year's 250 cc world champion, and Bill Ivy, who was now given a full-time contract. And with water-cooled equipment to draw upon, their chances looked distinctly good. But handling was still a problem, tending to negate the efforts the engineers had made to consolidate stamina and maintain performance. Yamaha began the season with the air-cooled 250 cc twin and later switched to the water-cooled V-four, but the new model was still plagued by handling problems and big-end breakages.

Results for 1966 were unremarkable for the Yamaha men, despite courageous efforts to salvage as much as they could from machinery that left them unhappy and lacking in confidence. Back at the factory, with a racing department now 35 strong, designers worked long hours in a bid to solve the problems. In the front line, led by team chief Nagayasu and chief engineer Naito, the two British riders struggled through what was for them a catalogue of failure. That they still managed to make a race of most Grand Prix rounds stood to their credit, but they were almost

Phil Read leads Mike Hailwood in the 1966 250 cc German Grand Prix, with Redman trailing in third place. An unusual configuration for 1966!

Honda's challenge to Yamaha for 1966: Hailwood and Redman discuss the vastly improved 250-Six.

helpless in the face of the challenging combination of Mike Hailwood, newly signed by Honda, and the vastly improved 250 Six. As if it was not enough to contend with Hondas in seemingly perfect order, they faced Hailwood at the very pinnacle of his form.

In Spain Ivy won the Maytime 125 cc Grand Prix—but both riders retired their RD05s from the 250 cc event. Read made third place in the French Grand Prix on the water-cooled 250 cc, and Ivy won the Dutch 125 cc TT with Read third; in the 250 cc class Read was second and Bob Anderson, a former car racer riding a Yamaha, fifth. At the Belgian Grand Prix, Read made a tremendous race of it with Hailwood, but the 250 cc Honda beat him to the line.

In East Germany at the Sachsenring, some 300,000 people saw Ivy take third place in the 125 cc class and Read manage second place ahead of Mike Duff in the 250 cc race. A week later in Czechoslovakia, Ivy was again third on his water-cooled 125 cc. Read came second and Duff fourth on their 250s. Finland saw Read beat Luigi Taveri to the flag by a few inches in the 125 cc event. And when the Isle of Man TT came round, Ivy was first and Read second in the 125 cc race, with Duff fourth. But in the 250 cc race both Read and Ivy broke down.

At Monza in the Italian classic, Ivy was third and Read fourth in the 125 cc race. Luigi Taveri, the little Honda ace from the German-speaking half of Switzerland, picked up the world championship title. By the time the Japanese Grand Prix was due, Honda had established a record by collecting every solo class in the world manufacturers' awards. They withdrew from the final title round on home ground, leaving Yamaha to pick up first and second places with two modified RD05s. In the individual titles, Ivy was second in the world 125 cc championship, with Read fourth. Read was second in the 250 cc championship, with Duff ninth. By Yamaha's standards, it was a disastrous year. They still had a long way to go to reach the sort of perfection they needed. But the little 125 cc RA31, the water-cooled four-cylinder machine, was nearing this state. And, indeed, it was to take Ivy to his first championship title in 1967.

Only a year after being flown to Japan and invited to sign a full-time contract, Ivy, the flamboyant little Londoner with a limitless taste for steak and chips even in the grandest gourmet restaurant, gave Yamaha the return for their money they wanted. Not even the race team bosses could have expected Ivy to do so well in his second full season. But then Ivy was a unique character, a seemingly carefree man who, on the outside, appeared to worry little. In fact his reckless appearance, his hippy style of dress and his love of flashy, noisy American sports cars, belied his feelings of responsibility. In that respect he was very much akin to his great Honda rival, Mike Hailwood. Off the track, apart from a brief breakdown of mutual affection, they were inseparable and, indeed, Hailwood was much closer to Ivy than was his own team captain, Phil Read.

Outsiders seeing Ivy and Hailwood chatting and laughing and generally enjoying life to the full, with Read somewhat in the background, would have believed that the Yamaha team captain was a man alone. I suppose he was in many ways. For Ivy spent more time night-clubbing and mischief-making with Hailwood than he did in the rather more serious confines of Read's company. When it came to racing, Hailwood put Ivy in precisely the same category as Read, that of rival, of man to be beaten. And a lot that was good about Hailwood rubbed off on his little companion. He learned much from the man he considered the absolute maestro of racing, and cared little for Read's views.

The 1967 season started well for Ivy. He and Read came first and second in Spain's 125 cc title round, while Read won the 250 cc class. At the West German race both riders crashed whilst overtaking the Italian Walter Villa, lying in sixth position. (Villa was to hit the heights of achievement for Harley-Davidson in the 70s, in both the 250 cc and 350 cc classes.) That incident deprived them of any points for the 125 cc event—but in the 250 cc event Read managed second place to Ralph Bryans on a Honda, after Ivy had quit with transmission problems and Hailwood had pulled out with engine trouble.

At the French Grand Prix, Yamaha had its finest ever result sequence. In the 125 cc race, Ivy was first, followed closely by Read. And in the 250 cc class, even though he was hindered by transmission difficulties, Ivy steered his machine ahead of Read. At the Isle of Man, Read won the 125 cc TT after Ivy had broken down when a carburettor fell off, and he collected second place behind Hailwood's Honda in the 250 cc class.

The Dutch TT was next. Here, Read led Ivy to the line in the 125 cc race. The little man was second in the 250 cc class after Read had withdrawn, and he went one better with a first place in the 250 cc race in Belgium the following weekend. He did it again in East Germany in the 125 cc class, with Read second. In the 250 cc race Read and Ivy were first and second. Ivy won the Czechoslovakian Grand Prix at Brno on his 125 cc, then slipped back to second place behind Read in the 250 cc event. The water-cooled RD05As were showing that absolute reliability was quickly becoming a reality.

At the Ulster Grand Prix, Ivy and Read were first and second in the 125 cc class. Ivy made it into third place in the 250 cc race after Read had fallen off; Hailwood was first and local man Ralph Bryans second. It was certainly on the cards for Ivy to win: his RD05A was quicker than Hailwood's RC166, but the Yamaha developed a misfire that soon put paid to his chances of victory.

In Italy Ivy was hit by heating problems when the radiator of his 125 cc machine sprang a leak, but he still managed to outdistance Hans George Anscheidt for a win. And in Canada, on an unpopular, short and bumpy track, he took his over-the-counter ultra-lightweight machine to victory three laps ahead of the second man. A willing back-up rider for Read in the world 250 cc title chase, Ivy was second to his team leader in the Italian Grand Prix and forced Hailwood into strenuous effort in the Canadian. Elated by Ivy's three-lap advantage in his 125 cc win in Canada, the Yamaha pair brought the best out of Hailwood and his

Honda. On the last, dramatic lap, Ivy, neck and neck with the great man, had to drop out with engine trouble. This let Read in for second place ahead of Bryans, but by then his chances of a second world 250 cc title had reached a borderline of controversy.

The final race of 1967 was in Japan, over the short course of the Fuji International Speedway. Honda had now withdrawn from the 125 cc class, leaving Suzuki to fight it out with Yamaha. Ivy won, Stuart Graham was second on a Suzuki RS67 with a two-stroke V-type four-cylinder engine, and third man was Hideo Kanaya on a Kawasaki KA 2, another two-stroke V-type four-cylinder machine. And the world 125 cc title was safely in Ivy's grasp.

It was a different matter altogether for Read in the 250 cc class. He was locked with Hailwood at the top of the championship list; each man with the same number of points. This was by far the hardest class to win. In fact, I would say that in the history of racing, and even after those hard-fought days of the mid-sixties there was never a more difficult title. It was a tricky situation for the FIM. They resolved it by awarding the title to Hailwood, who had a greater number of victories in his points tally. Read, therefore, was placed second. Third came Ivy, making it a year of great personal satisfaction for him. The manufacturers' awards were split

Read's fiercest adversary throughout 1966 and 1967: Mike Hailwood, flat out on the tank of the 250 cc Honda-Six.

The winners' rostrum at Brno, Czechoslovakia, 1967, after the 250 cc race:
Bill Ivy, Phil Read and Mike Hailwood.

between Honda, who took the 250 cc title, and Yamaha who were given the 125 cc honours.

It is not generally known that when the schedule for the 1968 season was thrashed out, Ivy was instructed to bid for the two world championships titles that most interested Yamaha—the 125 cc and the 250 cc. He already held the 125 cc title, but the 250 cc title, once held by Read, was in the hands of Hailwood and Honda. These team tactics formed one of the main reasons for a prolonged dispute between Yamaha's two top riders: having won a world 250 cc title, Read apparently wanted to win the 125 cc championship as well. In fact, their dispute became so well publicized that Yamaha's president, Kawakami, instructed his team manager to get it sorted out. Angry telex messages and cables flew from the president's office in Japan, underlining the need to get the two men to cool down—the company could not afford to have personal squabbles aired so widely. It was also embarrassing to those of us in their circle, who were alternatively invited to criticize one rider or the other—according to which one you were talking to at the time. The rift was obvious—even after Kawakami's chastening action.

It was felt at Yamaha that Ivy was consistently quicker than Read, that he had more potential and, because he was younger, he was a better long-term prospect. The fact that Read was beginning to prove himself as one of the world's finest tacticians did nothing to sway Yamaha's plans. For, in addition to these factors, there was a strong relationship between Ivy and the Japanese. They held him in high esteem and felt great affection for him. Contrary to popular belief, the Japanese are sensitive in this way and tend to behave accordingly. Perhaps it was because they could easily identify with Ivy; he was open, candid and good at describing the problems associated with the setting up of the machines. More than that, he was incredibly brave.

Read was a rather more distant, diffident sort of figure than the outgoing Ivy. He objected vigorously to the idea that he should play understudy to Ivy's star part. An ambitious man, with a fierce drive which never left him throughout his racing career and, indeed, in his business life, Read wanted to take the titles for himself. He decided to defy team orders. He felt he had some justification; he had helped Yamaha through their roughest patch and given his best, and he wanted whatever glory was going when things were getting a little less difficult.

The taste for being world champion had never left him. He enjoyed the benefits it accrued and the fame that surrounded it. And he told anybody who cared to listen, presumably Ivy too: "If he wants to be world champion he'll have to beat me to do it." He had thrown down the gauntlet and Ivy was happy to pick it up. But it was a formidable challenge and an especially difficult task for Ivy, facing a team mate of Read's skill and firm resolve. The relationship between the two men soon hardened into one of mutual—and open—dislike.

This vexed question of team orders upset the policy makers of the FIM in Geneva, Switzerland. They did not like to believe that riders were to allow team mates to win or to share places according to their status with their company, and felt that it was bad for the public to be let in on the secret. But as everybody appreciated, team orders were vital and very much part of the game when such vast returns were at stake.

Read's wrath at Yamaha's decision drove him to a rather surprising reaction—he wrote to the FIM, pointing out what was going on. The sport's controlling body acted quickly. They chastened Yamaha for doing what everybody else with works teams was doing, and criticized their tactics. What happened afterwards is not so clear. It would seem that Yamaha relented and granted Read the support to bid for the 125 cc title while Ivy went for the 250 cc championship. But by the end of the season, after a great deal of bickering between the two riders, Read had won both the titles that had been earmarked for his colleague Ivy.

Read was determinedly single-minded in a way that suggests he never made a move without having first considered every angle. He was always prepared to make a stand on an issue with which he disagreed—whether it be safety or money. His lack of enthusiasm in following orders that seemed to do little or nothing for his personal ambitions had got him into trouble once before—at the Isle of Man TT, when his bid to be the first man to cross the 100 mph barrier for 250s ended with a 'broken' engine. Whatever disenchantment Yamaha felt for him probably stemmed from this rather fraught period of their partnership—even though in the end the product of the disagreement was to be a magnificently achieved double world championship for Yamaha. And, of course, for Read.

Yamaha's long quest for perfection in the lightweight division of motor cycle racing was finally rewarded in 1968. They had been at the threshold for so long, but at last they had achieved the degree of development they wanted. The exciting breakthrough they sought came with the trimline V-fours, 125 cc and 250 cc, that Ivy and Read raced that year. The earlier lessons had been clear—water-cooling and scaled-down pots were the answer to the problems of durability. The disc valve V-fours of 1968, with their sophisticated water-cooling system and advanced technology, were supreme.

The RA31A 125 cc machine pushed out 44 bhp, had nine gears and revved to around 18,000. The 250 cc RD05A bustled along at about 15,000 rpm and produced some 73 bhp. The smaller machine was, according to the Yamaha designers, superior to the 250 cc model in construction compactness; the frame and complicated steering head reinforcement were similar to the RD05A, but improvements were to be seen everywhere else.

An oil pump and distributor with twelve outlets, three oil pipes going to each cylinder—the inlet port, the rotary valve and the big end of the connecting rod—were installed above the transmission and in front of the water pump. Each brake had a 200 mm drum; the front was double-panel, two lead, the rear a single cam. The magnesium alloy panels had air scoops. The main fuel tank held 16 litres and there was room under the seat cowl for another half litre—and the whole plot weighed less than 100 kg, a tiddler of a challenger. Although the cooling system was similar to that of the RD05A, there was a trochoid pump and crankcase combined as one unit—the cooling capacity was roughly the same as that of the 250s. The bubble remover, for cooling water, was attached to the radiator inlet, as on the tried and tested RA97.

Bolstered by huge injections of money for development, Yamaha's boffins were bordering on what they firmly believed to be an absolute thoroughbred in racing terms. But moves were being made behind the scenes, in that mystic land of intrigue called officialdom, to curb the threat of runaway progress by the Japanese. Ideas were being formulated that would mean the withdrawal of Honda, Suzuki and, later, Yamaha, as works entities. The Japanese were so far ahead of the rest in their technical development that the Grand Prix scene was becoming a three-horse contest—with the rest merely also-rans, lumbering clumsily in their shadows.

Honda, the great pioneers of motor cycle manufacturing in Japan, were the first to drop out when the FIM, the controlling authority of the sport, cut loose with their revolutionary plan to baulk the exciting trend established by the Japanese. Then Suzuki and then Yamaha. But first there was the 1968 season, a superb year for Yamaha. It was full of vintage racing from their two stars, crammed with effort and spectacular results and, indeed, a truly magnificent finale before what was the first—enforced—surrender to the authorities who put a stutter on development.

With Honda gone Yamaha had little to beat; there was no Hailwood around, no Bryans. Redman, too, had gone. Read and Ivy had the field largely to themselves.

With bitterness growing between them, Read and Ivy went to the Isle of Man for the TT in 1968, with nothing except each other to worry about in a racing sense. The eyes of the Grand Prix world were cast towards that 30-mile-long rock in the Irish Sea. Those who were there were privileged; those who could not be were envious. The two lightweight events, the 125 cc and the 250 cc, were high points of drama, raw courage and fine achievement. They were also platforms of awesome effort, when all the bitterness came to a head, and when open dislike turned into a public tantrum of contempt in a bid to embarrass a team mate.

Ivy, agressively determined to wipe out any vestige of a threat from Read, threw himself into heartstopping moments of defiance of the course's terrible promise to anybody who took liberties with it. Behind the fearless little man lay a bewildered trail of opponents, a legion of spectators hardly able to believe what they had seen and a lot of walls, kerbs and hedges scarred with the marks of his kicks to fend them off. He made a nonsense of the lap record, sent it soaring over 100 mph for the first time on a 125 cc machine, cast all caution to the winds and left a stunned Read somewhere down the road behind him.

But then Ivy, leading a race that was scheduled to be won by Read, according to revised team orders, suddenly stopped his little 125 cc

Yamaha in front of a startled crowd of spectators. Looking back up the road, he asked them pointedly where his team mate was. It was Ivy's way of blasting back—the most cutting reply he could devise as a professional racer aiming to devastate a team mate and put the final flourish on a disagreement.

When he had made sure that everybody around recognized that he had established his superiority, only to surrender it willingly, he allowed Read to win without even trying to rebuild his incredible lead. It was a remarkable performance and it left him with a lap record of 100.32 mph. Years afterwards 500 cc men were still trying to top the 100 mph lap. It will probably stay forever as a 125 cc record. The memory of his impudence certainly will—no man had ever done what he did.

The mood was surely upon Ivy that week, for he rode like a man possessed, no doubt stirred to even greater acts of bravery by his feeling of being robbed of his dues by Phil Read. Four days earlier he had hit record levels on the 250 cc machine, powering it to a splendid win, again on the slippery brink of safety, with a final best lap of 105.51 mph—still a record in 1978 and likely to remain unbeaten for years afterwards. Little wonder that the Yamaha racing personnel admired Ivy almost to the point of hero worship. He was to them a figure of legend and in the Isle of Man, the place that really mattered then, he reigned supreme. The course held no terrors for him. He and the machines given to him conquered it without demur, with little or no regard for caution, and with splendid panache and flair.

But it was Read, the man from Luton who had been taught to ride by his mother, who collected the real battle honours—the two world titles. It was Read's third 250 cc title and his first 125 cc crown, which he took from Ivy, his team mate. The stocky little man who had become such a hero to his mechanics would not be around to contest the title again, for he was to be killed in a tragic accident before the next season really got under way.

The close of the 1968 season was the end of an era for Yamaha, for they would not be fielding a full works team in the next Grand Prix season. It was an era distinguished by the great tradition set by Read, and quickly taken up by Ivy, in establishing Yamaha as the ultimate authority of the sixties. Read's double crown was in many ways a fitting end to this era, but the blistered hands, the heart-in-the-mouth moments and the sheer fright both men had experienced at times when their machines had suffered waywardness of handling, had all been badges of courage.

The Age of the Privateer

At the end of the 1968 season, Yamaha were all conquering, having successfully sorted out the contentious issues of handling and weight. It was thus a bitter disappointment to find their machines outlawed by the new FIM regulations, which in effect forced them to pull out of Grand Prix racing. Understandably, they felt that the FIM were simply aiming to suppress Japanese manufacturers, who were enjoying vast technological advantages and a more discriminating use of materials.

Under the FIM's revised competition plans, the criteria for Grand Prix racing were as follows: machines in the 50 cc class were to be limited to a single cylinder, six gears and 60 kg weight; in the 125 cc class to two cylinders, six gears and 75 kg; and in the 250 cc class to two cylinders, six gears and 100-plus kg. The new rules were to be applied in 1969 for the 50 cc machines, and in 1970 for the others.

It had taken Yamaha eight years to mastermind their way first of all onto equal terms with Honda and Suzuki, who had both started before them, and then ahead to the pinnacle of success in world championship contests. There was widespread disappointment among race enthusiasts when the FIM announced their strictures, and, I have no doubt at all, great annoyance at Yamaha headquarters. Many riders also regretted the FIM's moves—specifically those who had hoped to be able to cash in on the continuing success of the Japanese factory.

Yamaha withdrew their factory team from the international races scheduled for 1969 and the balance of power now tilted away from teams with direct factory support to dealer-backed set-ups. In this instance Yamaha were fortunate enough to have had a parallel development of production racing machines. These had been rolling from the assembly lines as early as 1963, when the TD1, based on the YDS2 street machine, had been marketed for the growing numbers of men who wanted to go racing on competitive machinery.

The 250 cc TD1 and the YDS2 had the same frame, crankcase and bore and stroke. The racer version, the TD1, had to have winkers and a headlight to be approved for marketing. It had a two-stroke parallel twin engine with piston valve suction, giving out 22 hp at 7500 rpm, and accelerating to a quarter of a mile in 15 seconds. It weighed 114.5 kg and cost around £500 ($1000 dollars). It was very quickly transformed into racing trim by removal of the street model accessories, and lightened by the use of a special cylinder, cylinder head, expansion chamber and carburettor with separate float chamber. When it had been trimmed down the TD1 was giving 35 hp at 9500 rpm and its weight was only 95.5 kgs. It was a tremendous success abroad.

There was also the TE1 with a displacement of 255 cc and a bore enlarged by 1 mm. An export-only TD1-B, another street machine that could easily be turned into a road racer by the removal of the safety parts, followed in 1966 and was marketed until the year after. It was given a 246 cc engine with a bore and stroke of 56 x 50 mm. It returned 35 hp at 10,000 with much greater durability than its forerunner.

It was plain to the economic and marketing planners at Yamaha that there was an enormous catchment area of eager customers who wanted to go racing with fast, reliable machinery, put together and backed by huge factory resources, at a cost well within the range of men with not a great deal of money to spare. There was hardly a race track in Europe and Central and South America that did not have a TD1-B hurtling round its curves and straights. These machines formed the basis of a lot of racing technique for riders who would otherwise have been operating on slower, inferior equipment.

Later Yamaha produced an improved version with five ports and 36 hp at 9500 rpm. The clutch was relocated to improve its reliability and the durability of the plates, and to cure potential oil seal problems. The five port system overcame the snag of residue gas. With two more transfer ports available, the fresh fuel surged into the cylinder through four

Just one illustration of the size of the market open to Yamaha: a small part of the crowd at a European race meeting.

passages and the burnt gases were cleared completely. The result, naturally, was that the engine delivered far more power over a wider range of speed.

Then the TD2 came along. Two-stroke and air-cooled as usual, its bore and stroke were 56 x 50 mm and it had a compression ratio of 7.6. Maximum power was said to be 44 hp at 10,000 rpm. The frame was feather bed, high tension steel tube and designed along the same lines as the proven RD56. The front fork was the Ceriani type and a high strength box section type of swing arm was used. In January 1971, the TDB2 was introduced. This incorporated upper and lower crank case sections, with five ports for more effective scavenging flow, replacing the octopus type. Bore and stroke were also changed to 54 x 54 mm.

To satisfy the great demand for a full-sized machine in the 350 cc class, the TR2, based on the marketed R3, was developed. The engine and crank case were the same as the R3 but the capacity was considerably different. The piston valve twin had five ports and a bore and stroke of 61 x 59.6 mm. Engine displacement was 348 cc and returned 54 hp at 9,500 rpm. There was a 1.8 litre oil tank under the sea cowl; petrol was mixed at 30:1. It was equipped with Auto-lube, a wet multi-plate clutch and five gears, like the R3. The frame was double cradle, in keeping with other Yamaha models, and was interchangeable with the TD2. The machine was improved with Ceriani forks, box type swing arm, large-diameter brakes made of aluminium—and breathtakingly fast. It was to give Agostini's all-conquering MV-Agusta a thorough testing in the 350 cc title chase, and it enjoyed large sales to private entrants throughout 1970.

Though they marketed both a 250 cc and a 350 cc production racer model, Yamaha held back on selling a 125 cc version—even though they had the basic requirements in the AS2, the machine that formed the main element of their own factory racer. The YZ623 124 cc machine was built in accordance with the FIM's ruling—an air-cooled six-speed model that weighed only 75 kg. There was also a watercooled version, the YZ623A, but neither had the usual double cradle feather bed type frame. Instead the diamond frame, with its thick back bone, was used.

Thus, despite the FIM's virtual shutdown on progress and the subsequent withdrawal of Yamaha's factory-entered machines, the company's name was still being inscribed on trophies and written in record books around the world, wherever there was racing. The age of the privateer or sponsor-backed rider, with highly sophisticated, ultra-fast machinery, opened up as a grand new era in the history of motor cycle racing.

Among the first men to endorse Yamaha's confidence in the production racing machines was Rod Gould (now the company's public relations chief in Amsterdam, Holland). In 1967 he and Bruce Cox, a friend from Banbury, Oxfordshire, set off for Southern California, where massive amounts of Japanese money were being poured into American-style racing. "It wasn't so much that the money was going towards

Europe—rather into the USA," said Gould, "and we went to meet up with it. We thought we'd like to get in on the action."

After a meeting with Tony Murphy, the racing manager of Yamaha International, Gould bought a TD1C Yamaha engine, not available in Europe, and built it into a Bultaco frame. He raced at Daytona without success in 1967 but in 1968 things started to go right for him. He decided to invest £2000 in two new Yamahas—a TD2 250 cc and a TR2 350 cc. And in 1969 he made a run-in to the world championships in Europe, gaining a third place at Daytona on his 250 and a fifth place on his 350. He shipped the bikes back to Europe where he joined the Swede Kent Andersson in a newly established team supported by Yamaha NV, Holland. For the rest of that season, Gould shared the same sort of snags that were wrecking the hopes of many Yamaha riders on the production racers—the machines just weren't sufficiently durable. In the short-dash races, the bikes were fine. In England, Gould picked up eleven wins from thirteen starts on his 350 cc, while the 250 cc gave him twelve victories out of fourteen starts. But the Grands Prix, with their long,arduous circuits, presented immense problems, and he finished only twice on the 250 cc.

Although things went wrong, Yamaha liked what they saw of the young rider's style and combative abilities. Gould, really, was the pioneer of the bright leathers that are so much a part of the racing scene today. He decked himself out in garish gear and painted his machines Candy Apple blue with white streaks, inevitably catching the eye of a duller European race scene. It was a self-promotional gimmick that quickly caught on, and rightly so.

In 1970 Yamaha's faith in Gould was rewarded when he won the 250 cc championship racing a TD2 production machine, again under the banner of Yamaha Motor NV. The year before, the championship had been won by a great friend of Gould's, the Australian Kel Carruthers, aboard an Italian Benelli. For 1970 Carruthers switched to a Yamaha TD2 as well, and between them the two men were to provide a memorable season of close racing in the 250 series. Now approaching the veteran stage, after a career of being almost there but not quite, Carruthers was a typically tough-nut Australian, whose happy-go-lucky manner belied his awesome determination. He and Gould were equally suited to the job in hand, and each wanted to make sure that their friendship would survive the battle ahead. Gould in particular was anxious to preserve the status quo.

The night before the Italian Grand Prix at Monza, when there were only two races to go, Gould called on his arch rival. The two men were running neck and neck in the championship, and Gould knew that to win the race in Italy would mean his first ever world title—at the expense of his friend Carruthers. "I just wanted to see him to make sure we could stay friends whatever the outcome," said Gould later. "It was as important to me as winning the world title." Standing in front of the Australian, he asked tentatively: "Tomorrow's result won't make any difference to us, will it? We'll still be friends afterwards?" A firm

Rodney Gould's partner in the Yamaha NV team, the Swede Kent Andersson. He was nicknamed 'the Swan' because of his habit of sticking his neck out, and this photo, taken at Assen in 1974, shows just why.

assurance from Carruthers sent Gould away a happy man, and brought the pair of them to the start grid in the right frame of mind.

They crossed that seemingly endless divide between the final curve and the finish line almost wheel-to-wheel, each staring hard at the other's front wheel spindle to see who had won the advantage. They had made it a race to remember, but neither man could honestly say which one had won. They hurtled round their lap of honour, almost at racing speeds, to get back to the start-and-finish point to find out who had been adjudged winner.

Gould recalled: "I just didn't know whether I'd done it or not. But I knew it was mine as soon as I motored back into the pits and saw the look on the face of my mechanic Randy Hall—he was split from ear to ear in a massive grin. I had hardly got off my machine when Kel was by my side wishing me luck, shaking my hand and hitting me with congratulations. That's just what I needed to round off a really perfect day."

Rodney Gould after clinching the 250 cc world title at Monza, 1970.

Kel Carruthers finished as runner-up in the class. He achieved the same position in the 350 cc championship, taking his Yamaha TR2 into second place behind the fabulous Agostini. Although Agostini collected nine Grand Prix wins out of ten starts, he was hard pressed all the way by the determined Australian.

Andersson and Gould also competed for the 125 cc championship, but without success. In 1971 their YZ623s were well and truly beaten by Dieter Braun's little Suzuki, the Kawasaki of Dave Simmonds—the world champion in 1969, and Angel Nieto's Derbi from Spain. Andersson finished ninth in the world 125 cc championships and Gould was twenty-fourth. In the 250 cc championship Gould lost his title of the previous year but at least managed to make second place—behind privateer Phil Read and his Yamaha, and ahead of the sensational newcomer to Grand Prix racing, the Finn Jarno Saarinen.

In 1971 Read was on his own in the championships, no longer the great star treasured by Yamaha. He told me that he had invested all the money he had, some £10,000 ($20,000) to buy machines and spares in his bid to secure the title. This was Read at his best, back to the wall and fighting for his very survival in racing. He made sure of the 250 cc championship, his fifth title, at Jarama, outside Madrid, at the Spanish Grand Prix. Afterwards we shared a bottle of champagne at a rather second-rate hotel where most of the Grand Prix line-up was based. "I have done it all on my own," he stressed, "I gambled every penny I could and it's paid off. I had only myself to look out for and worry about. Everything will be okay from here on in—I'm champion again." Before the race, Read had seemed strangely calm. He had so much money at stake that he felt it was his last throw of the dice. Yet these fraught circumstances seemed to affect him in exactly the opposite way to what one would expect—just one more puzzle about the man who always seemed to slip easily into the role of an enigma.

There can be little doubt that Phil Read's old rival, Bill Ivy, would still have been a major part of Yamaha's planning, had he lived. But his taste for the high life, a part of his character which had made him such a vibrant character, had caught up with him.

His motto had been to spend as fast as he could, to enjoy himself and gather around him all the good things in life. The upshot of that ambition, however, was that he was left struggling for money. He was trying to mix car racing with bikes and that was something else that was costing him a fortune. He needed money fast and he accepted an offer from the Czechoslovakian Jawa factory to race their machine in East Germany. The bike was a notorious 'seizer', not that he worried about that. All he thought about was the £5000 ($10,000) they had offered him and how far that would go towards buying an aeroplane.

The tragedy was that he did not even get to race it. In practice at the Sachsenring, he was motoring slowly into the action, his helmet on—but unfastened. A passing rider saw him leaning from the saddle, looking down at the machine as he toured along with only a few miles an hour hardly stirring the needle on the rev counter. Suddenly the bike seized and threw him off, onto his head.

He died very quickly—to the great disbelief of everybody attending the East German Grand Prix. Ivy had seemed so indestructible; he had so much vitality and so much to live for. It was an enormous tragedy that stunned all those at Yamaha. They had seen him survive so many moments of daredevil riding on the track and so many hair-raising adventures off it.

Two world champions: Bill Ivy and Mike Hailwood in East Germany, the scene of Ivy's tragic crash.

A week later, at a party in Brno, Czechoslovakia, I was with Frankie Stastny, the former Jawa works rider who had organized this race for Ivy. It was a party he had planned long before little Bill's tragic crash and he was determined to go through with it; but he lasted only an hour before he broke down in tears. He was inconsolable. He blamed himself.

The Japanese are often wrongly accused of feeling no emotion. They were grief-stricken by Ivy's death. Yamaha's race directors, engineers, technicians, team members—all had been able to identify with Ivy; that he was also amongst the world's greatest riders, was just the icing on the cake. Victory without any rancour along the way and a general lift in morale had seemed to follow naturally whenever Ivy was around. From the time of Ivy's death to the signing of Jarno Saarinen, the spectacular Finnish ice-rider who was to dominate the Grand Prix scene in 1972 and 1973, all at Yamaha felt something of a void.

But just as Ivy had done before him, Saarinen was to bring a new dimension to Yamaha's racing schedules. His verve and vitality, his fearlessness and will to win were to grow in parallel with a rebirth of exciting new developments behind the scenes at Yamaha. It seemed inevitable that their paths should cross.

Jarno Saarinen
and the Monza Tragedy

The time was 3.17 pm; the date Sunday, 20 May 1973. The 38 riders in the 250 cc Italian Grand Prix sweated to push and bump start their machines in front of the crowded grandstand at the Monza Autodrome, near Milan.

Less than two minutes later, Jarno Saarinen, the young genius riding for Yamaha, was dead. So was the Italian veteran Renzo Pasolini. And in the horrific chaos and confusion that surrounded their deaths more riders went down, machines and wreckage lay scattered like grotesque lumps of twisted shrapnel, and the memory of it all had been stamped forever in the minds of the men who saw it but somehow survived.

Hidden in trees high above the Curva Grande, a flat-out bend about 1 kilometer after the start, two Italian photographers witnessed the scene with growing shock. Back at the grandstand, an excited audience still awaited the return of the riders from the first of their 20 laps. A thin spiral of smoke, curling upwards on the still air, hovered like a spectre over the shrub-lined spot. But nobody, aside from the two photographers, knew what had happened.

Other riders who had got through unscathed went about the business of winning, in the manner men of their vocation have. But two Englishmen who had escaped, Charles Mortimer and Mick Grant, ran back up the track, waving their arms to slow down riders who had rounded the Monza circuit and did not realize how bad things were. And only then did the full impact of the disaster begin to bite. Mortimer limped for first-aid treatment for a gashed leg to the caravan of his friend Jack Findlay, almost speechless with shock. Grant was too upset to speak.

And the German, Dieter Braun, who had survived violent avoiding action, went off quietly to his caravan. All this while officials tried to unravel the awful mess—and the mystery of the cause of the crash that was really no mystery at all.

The events leading up to the most disastrous pile-up in Grand Prix history had been normal. Saarinen, aglow with hope of the 250 cc world title, had already notched up enough points to give him the lead before he went to Monza for the fourth Grand Prix of the season. He had snapped up the big money prizes in the prestigious Daytona 200 in America and the Imola 200, and had emerged as one of the truly great riders of all time. On 20 May, he had only one thought in mind, to amass more title points to answer his responsibilities to Yamaha. His confidence was at a peak and, as always, his cheeriness was infectious.

His lovely wife, Soeli, a slender Finnish girl who had been with him when he was an impoverished privateer trying to make ends meet,

Jarno Saarinen, the spectacular Finnish ice-rider. He was given a full works contract by Yamaha for 1973, but was tragically killed only halfway through the season.

Renzo Pasolini, one of the best loved Italian racing stars, who was killed at Monza in the same crash as Saarinen.

realized Jarno's need for isolation as he made his final preparations. She kissed him lightly before he followed his mechanics into the sunshine and strode off towards the grid; then she melted into the mass of people on their way to watch the race and joined Rod Gould in the shady cool of the Yamaha pit area.

Any rider who was not employed tried to find a place in the crush of spectators or climbed onto the already over-populated pit walls. I was standing on the roof of the Dunlop VIP box, enjoying a glass of champagne and looking forward, like all the others up there, to a race that had all the makings. But we had seen a trickle of disaster and hoped that a warning had gone out to all those riders grouped around their machines to our left, down the broad Monza straight.

Oil—the dread enemy of all racing men—lay in a treacherous streak along the racing line of the 250 cc men. It had seeped and then gurgled from the Italian Walter Villa's works Benelli in the previous 350 cc race—and nobody seemed to have done anything about it. As Villa sped by, it was plain to me that he was leaving a trap behind him—the lifeblood of the Benelli was pouring out. In fact he opted to pull into his pits on the last lap but one—but was urged to go out again by his mechanics, so that he could finish and total some points. He managed to score a fifth place behind Agostini, Tepi Lansivuori—Jarno's friend and countryman, Kent Andersson and John Dodds.

Racing margins are thin enough, but when the track has been smeared with oil they are swallowed into non-existence—and that was the threat that lay ahead of Jarno and Pasolini and the others.

When the flag dropped, the field fled the grid with that familiar buzz-saw din made by two-strokes under stress; and when we were receiving only echoes of the machines and the wispy blue smoke had cleared, Pasolini and Saarinen were, as expected, out in front, neck and neck. Soeli and Gould craned their necks to follow the fast disappearing mass and Soeli thumbed on her stopwatch. Above their heads the illuminated progress board at the end of the grandstand registered the news that the 250 cc men had left the grid. At 120 mph Pasolini was first with Saarinen five or six feet behind him, the rest of the riders peeling and swooping in line astern . . . watching . . . watchful. Pasolini had his head down. So did Saarinen. Racing, not oil, was on their minds.

One and a half inches width of slick lay ahead along the right-hand bend called the Curva Grande. Pasolini heeled his Harley-Davidson into the bend, drifted a little, found the oil and felt himself sliding sideways, out of control. Saarinen was right behind him, precisely where he should have been if he wanted to win.

Saarinen can have had only a split second in which to recognize the problem, forecast what would happen and decide upon his action as he watched Pasolini's machine slither to the left. For suddenly the Italian's machine left the oil; its back wheel gripped and he was pitched over the top at 120 mph. By then Jarno was already in dire trouble. Instead of taking up the usual 1 foot or so of the track, the sliding Pasolini was monopolizing about 6 feet and there was nowhere for Saarinen to go. Whatever God-given skills Saarinen had been blessed with, he was helpless to do anything to save himself or avoid hitting Pasolini. And behind him, bunched together, came a pack of men, all travelling at about 120 mph.

Jarno, tragically and inevitably, rammed Pasolini's machine. Suddenly, bikes were crashing; petrol tanks were falling off and catching fire, setting the straw bales alight; men were being flung onto the track or hurled into the steel barriers. Others simply closed their eyes and managed to swerve their way through to safety. The figures of Saarinen and Pasolini and the other fallers were hurtling upside down through the air, bent into gymnastic shapes, vainly throwing out hands in a bid to protect bodies that were slamming into the barriers or onto the track at high speed. There was no run-off area on the Curva Grande—you were either riding . . . or in the barrier. It was as simple as that.

Rod Gould made enquiries in Monza at the time of the fatality, and told me later: "Both riders hit the barriers—and both came back onto the track. Had there been a run-off area it is almost certain they would have been hurt, maybe seriously, but I don't believe they would have been killed. Renzo died from severe concussion, after hitting the guard rail. Jarno died as a result of full facial impact from a motor cycle."

Gould discovered that Saarinen bounced off the guard rail and back onto the track, into the path of the follow-up riders. "For all we know he may have had only a broken leg. He managed to sit up. A rider told me as much. But there was a rush of 25 riders coming up, all at 120 mph, and the track was a mess of spinning bikes, petrol tanks and bodies. An impossible situation.

"It was obviously a matter of chance that anybody got through, particularly those in the first ten. Skill really didn't come into it. Faced with these difficulties it was impossible for riders, however good they were, to take avoiding action. At that speed and on a corner it was odds on that Jarno would be hit. It's a great tragedy but that's how it was; and, ironically, it happened to be a great friend of his (a Swedish rider, who was so shocked by the accident that he has since stopped racing).

"I know precisely how the man felt. It happened to me at Mallory Park in 1965. A guy went down in front of me and I hit him. He died, and there was not a thing in the world I could have done. He was right there under my wheel. It's just part of racing I'm afraid, accepted by everybody."

Back at the pits it was pretty obvious that something had gone terribly wrong. Riders were slowing down, Italians were talking animatedly, and the whole of the crowd in the grandstand was straining to see down the straight to the Curva Grande. The yowl of ambulances began to rent the air.

Anxious for news but desperate not to leave Soeli's side, Gould looked around for help, for information, for anything to allay his fears. He told her: "Jarno's crashed—but we don't know what's happened. We're trying to find out for you right now." He knew instinctively that something extremely serious had happened. He had heard that Pasolini had been killed and he knew that Jarno must have been hurt, at the very least.

Alberto Pagani, Giacomo Agostini's former team mate in the MV team, realized that Soeli, Gould and Yamaha probably needed help. "He was great," said Gould. "I don't know what we would have done without him. He came along right away to see what he could do—then he took us to the first-aid post. But they didn't know anything. Soeli by now was getting quite worried—but she was trying hard not to show it. She was very brave. We were told by the first-aid men that the riders who had been injured were still at the corner. Then we heard from one rider that he had seen Jarno sit up. That was the biggest hope we had. It gave us cause to relax a little. But I still wasn't sure."

Then Gould discovered that Jarno had been taken to hospital in Monza. Pagani sprang to help once more. He commandeered a police car, virtually hi-jacking it by yelling at the driver: "This is Jarno Saarinen's wife—get us to the hospital." Then he kept his hand on the siren all the way in to the hospital.

When the party arrived Soeli's composure had broken, she was upset and crying. But at the hospital, with Pagani still acting as interpreter, they were told: "We don't know anything." It was then that Gould, standing with Pagani and Soeli in a state of bewilderment near the hospital reception desk, caught a glance from a surgeon. "He shook his head as if to say 'It's finished, it's all over.' And I knew then that he was dead."

Soeli did not notice the doctor's terrible message and Gould, with no idea how to break the awful news about her young husband, said: "Let's go back to the hotel, then we'll check what's happening." Gould himself was terribly upset but he managed to hide it. "I had to," he recalled, "I had to for Soeli's sake. She didn't know what was happening—she hardly knew where she was. She was being rushed here and there in the hope that she could get some good news. In the end there was no hope. And I had to break it to her."

In her hotel room, amid the untidy bundle of Jarno's belongings, casually thrown down before he set out for the race that was to kill him, Soeli listened as Gould told her: "I'm afraid Jarno's dead. I'm afraid it's all over." She did not break down or even cry. She kept all her feelings bottled up inside her for the next 24 hours—and then it happened.

It was a different story with the Japanese hierarchy from Yamaha. Purely by chance, they were all assembled at Monza, having gathered in Italy to meet up with the Yamaha outboard motor importer. They went to Monza for a social weekend, in order to see a highly-prized capture add to his world championship status by winning, as he undoubtedly would have done, on one of their machines.

They were devastated by Saarinen's death. When the helicopter whirred off the parkland at Monza, carrying what was then Saarinen's body to hospital, they anxiously grouped around for news. When they discovered he had been killed they sat in total isolation in an officials' enclosure, bewildered by the suddenness of it all. And they did not know what to do, what action to take.

Their reaction was understandable, for it was the first time one of their factory riders had been fatally injured. Gould, so close so often to such a tragedy, was able to bring some stability to the situation. He was sharing a room with team manager Naito, a great admirer of Saarinen both as a man and as a rider. "He simply could not believe it," said Gould. "He was terribly shocked and deeply upset; he spent three hours on the telephone to Japan every night over the next few days."

In the meantime the Yamaha outboard motor importer in Italy made arrangements through the Finnish embassy to have Saarinen's body returned to his homeland—and Soeli phoned her relatives with the news.

Yamaha offered to arrange a flight for her and her husband's body, but she declined and said that she wanted Jarno's two brothers, both in the undertaking business, to take him back overland. It took them two days to drive from Finland to Italy in a hearse to collect Jarno's body. Soeli waited for them, and then travelled back to Finland in the hearse, despite the gruelling nature of the journey.

Gould, Naito and Kuratomo—one of the top executives in Amsterdam, returned to Amsterdam. There was little doubt in their minds that Yamaha would put a stop to factory-backed racing for that year at least, despite the immense investment they had made. Within ten days the President had endorsed their opinion that Yamaha should withdraw.

Gould explained: "We could, I suppose, have found another rider—but we did not want to appear to be hard-hearted, merely using riders as a means to an end. You know . . . when one goes, just wheel out another. The Japanese are not like that. And they felt they owed it to Jarno's memory, anyway, to pack it in. I agreed. I was sick at the loss of Saarinen, just like everybody else who knew him. None of us could believe it—even days after it had happened. The enormity of the investment Yamaha had made in Grand Prix racing in support of Jarno did not matter one jot to them. And even though it was early in the season they had no hesitation in cancelling the team."

In the bitter aftermath of the crash the organizers at Monza came under fire. The stature of Saarinen and Pasolini—one of the best-loved Italian racing stars, made a popular outcry inevitable.

Gould offered this view: "The organizers said that the machines, our Yamaha and Renzo's Harley, must have seized. Before the official track engineers examined the machines, we and Harleys agreed to allow each other's mechanics to examine the bikes. They came to see ours; we went to see theirs. And there was absolutely no evidence of seizure. Incidentally, the Harley was using Yamaha pistons.

"We felt, and still do, that the organizers were not blameless. We pointed out the need for greater track security and safety. We felt that the lives of riders were being put in jeopardy quite senselessly."

Gould's anger at the crash and the subsequent findings was supported by race journalist Volker Rauch, who issued a booklet containing his own investigations. It was called *Documentation of an Accident*. It was stark and it was hard hitting. And it was supported by Yamaha who, opposite a dramatic last page photograph of a twisted body cartwheeling into the tarmac of the Monza track, wrote:

"Yamaha Motor Co Ltd would like to thank Mr Volker Rauch for his research and effort in compiling this report of the events of May 20, 1973.

"Yamaha Motor Co Ltd hope that this document will be studied by all people concerned with motor cycle racing.

"Motor cycle racing always will involve an element of danger. It may be said that danger is necessary to bring out the qualities of a champion, when man and machine are striving for the ultimate performance. Unnecessary and senseless danger can, and should, be eliminated as a duty to the competitors. It is never too late to improve.''

Certainly Rauch knew exactly where he wanted to point his finger as the following excerpt demonstrates:

"The Autodrome of Monza was built more than 50 years ago. In its long history it has witnessed many serious accidents, the most tragic having been the one where Count Berghe von Trips and 17 spectators were killed.

"Improvements of the track were effected several times, but they were never of a decisive nature. As a result of demands by automobile racers following the accident of Count Trips, a steel barrier was constructed along the entire track. On several places hedges were erected to protect the racers; this took place, however, behind the steel barriers. The necessary improvements of the track surface were carried out shortly before the '73 Gran Premio delle Nazioni, but these were effected in a very superficial manner.

"Thus, in the Curva Grande there was a difference of several centimetres in the track level. Moreover, another type of material was used for track improvements.

"Jarno Saarinen protested against it energetically to the management of the event after the first practice session. However, this fault could not be corrected for lack of time.

"In the race of the class up to 350 cc which preceded that of the 250 cc class, Walter Villa drove a works Benelli. Toward the end of the race the motor of this machine lost oil so rapidly that Villa decided to pull into his box in the last lap but one.

"Already before that, everybody could see him riding around the track with a strong oil-smoke behind him. It is normally the duty of the organizers to take the rider out of the race immediately under such conditions. This did not happen. Villa, who came to the box out of his own initiative, was asked by his mechanics to continue the race in order to finish. Villa ended the competition in the fifth place.

"Comment by Pino Allievi, editor the Milan journal *La Gazzetta dello Sport*: 'I happened to be in the Benelli box during the 350 cc race; in the last but one lap Villa came in, but the mechanics shouted at him—go—go—only one more lap.

" 'Villa continued in the race. Subsequently he showed me his Benelli and said—'Look, it is full of oil'.

"French journalist Christian Lacombe watched the race from along the track. He too saw the Benelli losing oil, which gathered on the road surface. He talked about it to a marshal posted there and asked him to show the oil-warning flag.

"But the marshal reacted differently; he called several policemen to the spot and all of them threatened to remove Lacombe from the track by force.

"Two of his colleagues, F. M. Dumas, a contributor of *Moto Revue*, and Alain Kluchnikoff watched the scene; they too had seen the oil.

"Immediately thereafter followed the race of the 250 cc class. An urgent intervention by John Dodds asking the organizers to postpone the start and clean the track was rejected.

"The first bend after the start is the Curva Grande. It is approximately 9 meters wide, ie very narrow for a close field of riders.

"On the side of the track there is a steel barrier, which was covered by straw bales. Pasolini, in whose slipstream drove Saarinen and Kanaya, lost control of his machine at the beginning of the bend. Saarinen could not get round him any more and fell over him.

"Kanaya was just able to get around, but crashed into the straw bales with full force. Of the following closely knit field of drivers, 12 others came to fall and suffered considerable injuries.

"Saarinen and Pasolini died on the spot. After a prolonged period of indecision the organizers decided to stop the race.

"On July 8 a national race of juniors took place in Monza, the first event after the tragedy. Before the start, a doctor of medicine, Costa, of the Moto Club Santerno, Imola, demanded that an ambulance should be posted at the Curva Grande. His request was not accepted.

"In a mass collision in the Curva Grande three drivers lost their lives. It took 20 minutes before an ambulance arrived at the place of the accident."

Rauch's findings were simply yet dramatically presented. Photographs were assembled into blocks in the shape of a cross, while the text was reproduced in white on a black background. Although his booklet was widely distributed, he did not leave it at that. He also interviewed some of the world's most famous riders for their views on the incident.

Hideo Kanaya: "Before the 250 cc start I was told there was oil on the track. I had a good start and was lying neck and neck with Jarno. Pasolini was in front of us.

"When we reached the Curva Grande we were all three very close together, one just behind the other, with a distance of about half a meter between us. Pasolini was first, Jarno second and I was third.

"I saw Pasolini's bike slide under him. Jarno could not do anything. He crashed, I forced my bike to the outside and hit the straw bales. Immediately everything was on fire.

"I had seen Jarno crashing to the left side, but later his body was lying on the right side of the track. The next day I went to this place and could still see all the oil lines."

Victor Palomo, the 1976 FIM Formula 750 cc champion and a Spanish lawyer: "After the start I was lying behind the Italian, Bonera. Pasolini went into the corner on the left side. I did not know where Saarinen was. Suddenly Pasolini's bike went over and immediately there was a wall of fire. I don't remember how I managed to pass through, but then I crashed right after.

"I don't exactly know what the reason was. I didn't see oil on the track. I think—but I don't know it for sure—that Saarinen and Pasolini were side by side before they crashed."

Charles Mortimer, the British Grand Prix star, married to a Finnish girl, described the scene this way: "I arrived at the Curva Grande in about tenth place; I didn't see any oil.

"I crashed at the beginning of the bend, I don't know why; my bike was sliding far away, nearly to the end of it. Before I crashed I saw a body lying on the right side, I thought it was Jarno. Later I rushed to Borje Jansson to care for him. It was obvious that he was hurt."

Kent Andersson, the Yamaha team rider from Sweden: "During the end of the 350 cc race I was duelling with John Dodds. In the last two laps before the finish, my bike sometimes slid away at the rear.

"In the Curva Grande I could see nothing but blue smoke and a black shiny oil line. Then Dodds passed me and pointed his finger, meaning that the rider in front of us was causing the trouble.

"We were both very careful now, riding on the outside of the corners. In the last but one lap I caught up with the smoking bike and saw that it was Villa on the Benelli.

"After the finish I went to the Yamaha garage and told Jarno and Kanaya to beware of the oil on the track. Probably Pasolini was not informed about the oil—in fact he had also raced in the 350 cc, but he had pulled out with some trouble at half distance. The only way to prevent accidents like this in the future is to build broad safety zones around the circuits and to remove—or at least place farther back—the steel barriers."

Giacomo Agostini, the most influential of all the voices raised in protest, added his weight to the discussion: "During the 350 cc race I noticed an oil line in the Curva Parabolica. I didn't see Pasolini after the race, so I was not able to speak to him about this.

"My opinion about safety on racing tracks is as follows: We are racing with modern and ultra-fast motor cycles on sometimes outdated and antiquated circuits, which were built many years ago and thus planned for much lower speeds than we have today.

"In the last few years some new and very modern circuits have been constructed, most of them with safety zones, yet we also have to race on old circuits. It would be rather easy to reconstruct old circuits, to make them suitable for the speeds of the modern racing bikes. The most important thing is to remove the steel barriers from the trackside and erect them, if at all necessary, behind a wide safety zone."

Agostini later became an ardent campaigner on the issue of safety. Despite his magnificent showings and expert knowledge of the Isle of Man TT, he refused to race the mountain circuit from the early 70s.

What effect Rauch's interviews and his Yamaha-backed booklet had is difficult to assess. I am sure that at the time many men felt bitter enough about the deaths of Saarinen and Pasolini, and critical enough of the Monza track, never to race there again. Memories, however, are short and such censures are rarely upheld permanently. In 1977 the Italian Grand Prix was once again moved back to Monza after a four year lapse . . . Had Saarinen and Pasolini escaped death and recovered sufficiently to continue racing, they would probably have been among the first entries for the Italian Grand Prix at Monza in 1977. That is the strange thing about these men who go racing—they bear so few grudges and are reluctant to apply sanctions against circuits, organizations, countries or rivals, however terrifying or bitter their experiences.

Rod Gould agreed with me: "Yes, it really is odd that Monza should be allowed to stage another Grand Prix—there are so many better tracks, much safer, than that place. Imola, for instance, is superb. It has a great record and most of the riders really like the place. But I know that Renzo and Jarno would both have been in there with their entries had they lived through that dreadful nightmare."

Gould and I were lazing in the early winter sunshine of North Africa, during a splendid Yamaha promotional trip for 65 journalists from all over Europe. A chartered jet had flown us in from Amsterdam and at a cost of around 065,000 we were being entertained at a lavish hotel near the old market in Marrakech. Test riders were churning up the dust of the surrounding countryside, riding deep into the Atlas mountains and the nearby desert, on a new range of motor bikes. When he had seen them safely on their way, Gould joined me to talk about Saarinen, the man he had helped to manage in his capacity as public relations chief for Yamaha in Holland and the rest of Europe, and against whom he had raced in the late 60s and early 70s.

Gould first met Saarinen at the Austrian Grand Prix in April 1970. Saarinen, then 25 years old, was riding for a big Finnish dealer, Arwidson. He had been Finland's national champion and was the best ice racer in the country. Now he was out to show that he was a world class rider in Grands Prix. Gould continued: "Kent and I were contracted to Yamaha NV—then the only works contract going, aside from the MVs. We had a big tent with a work bench and all the other necessary trappings. Suddenly this guy came in and started jabbering away to Kent. I couldn't understand a word of what was going on—but Kent seemed to know him. I asked Kent: 'What does this guy want? Let's keep everybody out.' I thought he was just another paddock scrounger, and I didn't have too much patience. I had things to do and I wanted to get on with them. But it seemed this fellow wanted some chain. I said that all the chain we had taken off was in the rubbish bin and if he liked he could sort through it and keep what he found. That's just what he did—and he used it on his bike." Smiling with embarrassment despite the gap of years, Gould said ruefully: "Of course, it was Jarno. And he never let me forget it. He used to rib me about it years later; he said I was patronizing."

Gould did not see Saarinen too often in racing situations, at that time. Then at the top of his form, he was more often pacemaker than follower and Saarinen, though good, was rarely higher than fourth or fifth.

"Because of that I didn't worry about him too much, nor did I think about his style. I had, of course, seen him—but not a lot. Round about that time there was a lot of talk about him. You know, when the riders get together in their caravans and have a gossip. I can remember, round about 1970-1971, guys coming into the van and saying 'Did you see that Finnish bloke . . . what's 'is name? He's mad. It's only a matter of time.' Nobody could even pronounce his name. But they all knew him and most

Rodney Gould, racing under Hostettler Yamaha colours, on his way to victory in the 250 cc Swedish Grand Prix, 1972—his final year in racing.

said 'There's only one place he is going to finish and that's in a box.'

"My feeling generally is that every rider, every really successful one, that is, goes through a hairy stage at some time or another. And that, really, if we had stopped to think objectively about him, it could only mean one thing: he was on his way to the top. That was pretty obvious by the end of 1971 and I, among others, was not too happy when he was sponsored by Yamaha as I was."

In 1971 Yamaha fragmented their system of sponsorship and spread it among dealers. Gould was instructed to have 'Hostettler, Switzerland' painted on the fairing of his machine; Andersson was allotted to Hegner of Norway; and Saarinen, because of his growing reputation and the need for dealer growth in Finland, was entered by Arwidson. These moves were all decided by Yamaha NV, Amstelveen. The riders had no choice, in some cases being allotted rides under the banners of men they had never met. All the support was factory based. Gould never met his dealer, Mr Hostettler: "I don't know why we were spread out in this manner," he told me; "I suppose it was all to do with media values. Individual connections between men and their machines with the countries concerned was presumed to be of good publicity value. And who's to argue with that? The machines were rolling advertisements for the dealers and importers."

1971 was the year in which Gould was beaten into second place by Phil Read's private Yamaha in the world 250 cc championships. And in the 350 cc championships, Saarinen achieved second place, beaten only by Agostini. At the start of the season, Agostini had realized that he was facing an almost terrifying adversary. He simply could not come to terms with Saarinen's willingness to stick his neck out, and was rarely happy to follow the same line at the same speed as the spectacular Finn.

In 1972, Saarinen won his first world championship—the 250 cc. This was a title Gould had dearly wanted to win himself. In April, he had been told that he was to be put in charge of Yamaha's public relations the following year, and he quite naturally wanted to end his racing career at the top. He admits now that he thought the team top heavy, and was not happy with the support Saarinen was given. "When we were racing against each other, we were not enemies," he told me, "but we were not exactly friends. We had crossed swords once or twice—and we didn't mix at all socially. I'd rather he had raced for another sponsor at the time. But despite the fact that we were all under the same banner of Yamaha, it was all systems go and every man for himself. He was certainly a man to be reckoned with."

British fans had particular reason to remember Saarinen's name in 1972. He entered nine races in the country and won them all. At the time, he regarded it as his most important breakthrough, for he beat many foreign riders as well as the best British stars. He also picked up a good deal of prize money, which he banked carefully, as was his usual custom. At about this time, he hinted that he was thinking of retiring from racing altogether. But by the end of the season, as the reigning 250 cc champion, he was receiving offers thick and fast and saw a way to make enough money to achieve his aim of getting married and having children. At last, he reasoned, after all the tough spadework of sleepless nights, working on his machine as a privateer, he could enjoy the comforts afforded a works rider.

First over the line: Saarinen and his 350 cc Yamaha at the end of the 1973 Daytona 200-mile classic.

It is not widely known that Saarinen was almost tempted to join Benelli for the 1973 season. He was invited to the factory at Pesaro, in the north of Italy, and promised a fat contract to ride their 350 cc and 500 cc four-stroke machines. Benelli fussed over Saarinen with the loan of a fabulous De Tomaso sports car and the promise of more world titles under their care. He was uncertain . . . and Yamaha, stirred by Benelli's action, moved in quickly with an offer that matched his ideas of what he was worth.

Yamaha hired Saarinen as their top works rider for the 1973 season. They paid him just about the same money—£30,000 ($60,000)—as Agostini at MV, principally to ride their new and highly secret 500 cc machine. He had been earmarked for the job in the middle of 1972; indeed, it was felt that he was the only rider on the Grand Prix scene who could be relied upon to beat the superbly gifted Italian champion in the big class. Saarinen quickly repaid Yamaha for their interest and support with a win at Daytona, probably the most glamorous race in the world. It was the first time a Yamaha had won at Daytona, and he achieved it on a down-power, 350 cc machine, against all the beefier 750s. He followed that up by another win at Imola, Italy's 200-mile classic equivalent of the

Saarinen in Victory Lane, Daytona, with the runner up, Kel Carruthers. It was the first time a Yamaha had won at Daytona.

American race. He knew that Yamaha would develop the new 4-cylinder 500 in time for the Grand Prix season and was left in no doubt that this was his primary target. There was enormous sales potential behind the Grand Prix model, and endless publicity to be earned by pushing MV off its perch.

Gould described how Saarinen went to Japan for his first test ride of the 500: "On only his third lap, he lapped the circuit a full second quicker than anybody had ever done there before. It was quite fantastic. He took to it like something he had lived with all his life. He and the 500 were the perfect combination."

The racing world waited with mounting excitement as the clash of the two giants of racing drew nearer: Agostini, the long established and much respected champion with his tried and proven MV Agusta, against the brash new-comer Saarinen, with the unknown quantity of the secretly developed 500 cc Yamaha. The arena chosen by Yamaha for their first battle for the 500 cc championship was the Circuit Paul Ricard. Set on a dry and dusty plateau at Le Castellet, on the fringes of the Cote d'Azur, this sandblown circuit had been custom-built for Grand Prix racing, with a bewildering variety of flat-out straights, dashes, swoops and dead-slow corners. Yamaha were ready. The product of long winter months of planning and secrecy, and gruelling test sessions in Japan was to be on public view for the first time.

Hideo Kanaya, a young and hitherto unknown Japanese with a ready grin and easy manner, had been brought in to help Saarinen tackle the formidable but far from friendly MV twosome of Read and Agostini.

Hideo Kanaya's big Yamaha chased by Phil Read, MV Agusta, at the Paul Ricard Circuit, France. Note Read's neater, tucked-in-style.

The first public outing for the 500 cc Yamaha: Saarinen on his way to victory at the French Grand Prix, Paul Ricard Circuit, April 1973.

There were to be 35 other starters on that late April afternoon in 1973, but Agostini knew that to preserve his title he would have to look no farther than the numbers 3—Saarinen, 4—Kanaya, and, of course, 2—Read. In fact, a fall prevented Agostini from making it to the end of the 20-lap race. But he had plenty of time to see Read fight a losing battle against Saarinen, who set the fastest lap only three circuits after the start, and hung on to second place against Kanaya by only 2.1 seconds. Both Agostini and Read had reached deep into their reserves of experience and bravery to stay with Saarinen's Yamaha, but they were outpaced. It was as simple as that. Talk about the immediate and long-term effects of the race went on in the MV camp until the early hours. This was clearly no flash in the pan, and some quarters of the racing fraternity were already hailing Saarinen as the next world champion, even though this had been the first test.

I recall talking to Agostini about the combination of Saarinen and the new Yamaha shortly before the next round, at the Salzburgring, Austria, on 6 May. "Together they are fantastic", he said. "It looks like a perfect marriage. We at MV will have to do something. We cannot hope to compete. Yamaha have built a beautiful machine."

Not even the freezing rain of Austria could halt Saarinen's progress. The new Yamaha never faltered in its victory path as Read's and Agostini's MVs fell out. Saarinen clocked the fastest lap again—on lap three—and Kanaya made it into second place ahead of the New Zealander Kim Newcombe, by 30 seconds.

Saarinen and the sensational 500 cc Yamaha winning the Austrian Grand Prix, 1973 . . .

. . . and wearing the victor's laurels after the race.

But Austria was to be Saarinen's last 500 cc Grand Prix win. In the heat of Hockenheim, West Germany, in front of a massive crowd, his rear chain broke, forcing him to withdraw. Agostini also went out, leaving Read to rejoice and cross the line in first position. When the Grand Prix teams assembled again, it was in the bustling autodrome of Monza . . .

I asked Gould how Saarinen's worth really revealed itself to Yamaha. "By his total commitment," he replied. "He gave his all and he only ever thought about winning, an achievement that became as regular as clockwork. Was he dangerous? No, not really. Racing is selfish and you have to appreciate that fact. It's every man for himself.

"His style was certainly different, but who was I, for instance, to complain? Personally, I don't believe any style is wrong. It makes me laugh when people talk about the purists, the classical lines and form of a rider. It's how you feel on a bike that's important. What makes a man comfortable and at ease at racing speeds is the best style for him."

Saarinen had the severest of drops to his handlebars, straight down so that the grips were almost vertical in his fists. This style, and his habit of moving about on the saddle, was largely the result of his experiences racing on ice in Scandinavia. Ice riders always seem to be about to fall off—the machines buck and slide at impossible angles, forcing the riders to adopt greater mobility. Saarinen's riding was characterized by violent shifts of his body—right or left, on or off the seat. Sometimes, when his bike was heeled over hard, it appeared to be riderless—he was so far over the other side. In a report to the factory, a rather worried Yamaha observer once said: "Saarinen's ability to maintain stability at high speeds and in cornering is strange and appears to be violent." This style probably accounted for his reputation amongst many case-hardened professionals as a dangerous rider, one to be avoided at all costs. But any mention of this to the fair, spiky-haired Finn was received with blank-faced, wide-eyed astonishment—and then with gales of laughter.

Compared to the flowing, graceful heeling over of stylists such as Derek Minter, Geoff Duke, Phil Read and Mike Hailwood, flicking their big 500s through a series of sharp Ss, with little or no movement about the saddle save the occasional knee-cap peeping from behind the fairing, Saarinen's style did seem rather messy and overly aggressive. But it was undoubtedly effective—and set a new fashion which was quickly taken up by many of the top riders.

Saarinen's courage was also outstanding. Gould told me: "He never shrank from a corner—never. It wasn't in his make-up. I can remember racing at Clermont-Ferrand in 1972 in the 250 cc class. We had all climbed up, got our heads down, and made for the first right before going down the mountain. I was about fourth through a series of hairpins, real tight stuff and not to be played about with. I suppose the only way to pass at places like that is when somebody really gets onto their brakes and then you can shoot past. But generally to overtake is just ridiculous, you either fall off or settle for going round in a queue at the same pace as the others.

"Not Jarno. Oh no! He swept past three of us—not on the track, but off it. Between the track and the armco barrier, right over the white paint line. It was the most amazing thing I'd ever seen. I couldn't believe my eyes. There was dust flying everywhere. He was on the outside, cranked right over, hanging off the seat, rounding us all and apparently not worried in the slightest. I can tell you I was shocked! I viewed it then as the act of a madman. I was convinced that it was impossible for him to last—but he did, right through 1971 and 1972. So, I suppose, you must assume that he was in full control.''

Saarinen's other great quality was his supreme confidence. "It was total,'' said Gould. "He never had any doubts about his own ability. He was hard, and he never gave a quarter to anybody—but he was fair, too. He wouldn't hurt you, wouldn't set out to do you any damage—but he wanted to win with all his heart. He used to get himself into some spectacular slides but I don't believe they were anything he couldn't control. In fact, he once told me that he had never frightened himself and that's quite something coming from a man who earned his living on the Grand Prix scene. He always maintained that he had a safety margin. I remember him saying that it might be very small, but it was there. My safety margin was bigger, much bigger . . .

"His initiation in Europe was quite a long one really; he was around for some three years before he was really noticed for anything other than his rather lurid style. He was riding in GPs often and he knew the circuits very well. That way he built up his Grand Prix knowledge and circuit know-how until he had a greater knowledge than most even before he threw his leg across a bike.

"Most times he was a very quick learner, but for some strange reason he didn't learn Ontario, the Californian circuit where the Champion Spark Plug classic was held. It's a flat, difficult place with a lot of infield turns and it's a problem to remember the sequences. You can't see them, so you just *have* to remember them. But Jarno failed completely to get them into his head.

"On the third lap, he was going faster than he probably should have been over a circuit he didn't know. He came off and cut his leg quite badly. You see, he wanted to ride just one way—to win. He could not bring himself to ride to finish tenth, or anywhere outside first place. If he felt he was not going to win he would just go faster. It was as simple as that. And if he could not win he would rather not have ridden at all. Imagine being up against that level of determination! It made him extremely difficult to beat.

"He took up a lot of room on the track with his habit of getting off the saddle. On some twisty sections of a circuit, when you are up against a neat, packed-in sort of rider like, say, Phil Read, there is a foot or so of room left so that you can at least get up alongside. But with Jarno, it was a whole deal different. His wheels could be a foot or so out from the kerb or the white line, but this body would be completely off the bike, blocking any chance of getting through. Unless you tapped him on the shoulder and asked him to move over, there was no way to get by. Towards the end

Lansivuori swoops the big 500 cc monoshock Yamaha into action. For evidence of how far he leaned his bike over, look at his right foot: the leather is worn right through to his sock!

of his racing career, this didn't matter too much anyway, as he was usually far ahead of the field.

"I am sure he did not go to the Isle of Man TT because he felt he could not learn the course quickly enough to win in his first year there—and 370 miles is a long way for anybody to remember. He didn't want to race for a second place and he could not restrain himself enough to take it slowly."

Saarinen had a finely developed sense of economics and preferred to live austerely rather than splash his hard-earned thousands on flashy hotel living and fancy foods in high-priced restaurants. He opted to live with Soeli in a caravan at the circuits and travelled around in a Volkswagen that had seen better days.

"He wasn't mean," Gould explained, "but he was very careful with his money. He made sure he spent none of it unnecessarily. He worked on his world championship bikes on his own in 1972, solved his own problems and then rode the machines in the style of a superstar. He didn't go partying or drinking a lot, but he liked a good laugh. He certainly wasn't miserable, though he was a bit more serious than the run of the mill rider.

"He gave good value for whatever money was paid him by organizers. He hardly ever had rows about the cash he was paid to appear at various circuits, even when he was in the top line. At first he organized his own arrangements for start money and then I took over the haggling with officials in 1973.

"He was careful to salt his money away in the banks, building all the time towards the engineering business he so wanted to start. Jarno raced with tomorrow in mind, again unlike so many other top rank riders who ride and race only for today. Jarno had everything worked out; he even knew precisely when he was going to pack it all in."

His shrewd approach to money matters was beautifully in evidence when he raced and won gloriously at Daytona in 1973. This was the first of his truly big wins, when the cash bonanza for the day reached a record pay-out. He collected US $15,800 (£7900), including a thank-you bonus of $1000 from Yamaha International. And he took home more money than the winners of the next two Daytona 200s through the simple expedient of not paying any tax.

His planning was faultless. Before the race he painstakingly plotted which companies would pay the richest bonuses and used their stickers on his machine. He changed his helmet allegiance, setting up a special one-off contract with Bell, USA, even though he had ridden with a rival firm's helmet in Europe, and haggled a fat bonus. "There was absolutely no question in his mind that he was going to win Daytona," said Gould. "He was so confident, the race was as good as done. It was academic, a foregone conclusion. And everybody believed him." His next move was to get out of America as quickly as he could. He had a car waiting to whisk him to Daytona airport where he was due to fly to New York and

Saarinen flat out at Daytona. Note the almost vertical position of the handlebars, producing a push and pull method of steering.

on to Helsinki by Finnair, the only airline he would fly with. He held his bagful of dollars in his hand. He almost had heart failure at Kennedy Airport when a call went out for him over the tannoy system. He refused to answer in case it was the Internal Revenue Service.

The American Motor Cycle Association had warned him that he had to pay tax on his earnings in the USA. But he was the big winner, he had struggled hard for his money and he certainly was not about to hand any of it back if he could possibly avoid it. In the end, when the tax authorities challenged the AMA, they had to pay it for him—and afterwards they made sure that every prize winner was taxed at source.

It was at the Daytona classic that the curious behaviour of Saarinen as an engineer first came to light. He refused to believe that any man could build as good an engine as he could—and he had, after all, won a world 250 cc championship on that basis. "He would not leave the workshops when the Yamaha mechanics were working on his machines," Gould recalled. "At Daytona he had with him a very good mechanic, Vince French, a chirpy little Englishman who had lots of experience among Grand Prix riders and was certainly a man who knew his way round an engine. Jarno didn't try to do anything and he didn't tell Vince what to do—he had a great deal of respect for him and didn't want to upset their relationship. But there was no way he would leave the workshop until Vince had finished. It was as if he just wanted to be there, to know that everything had been done. He would help a little maybe, perhaps check a crank or help lift an engine out of the frame, but no more than that.

"Sometimes, just to make him feel more comfortable, Vince would say to him 'Jarno what about this? What do YOU think?' And that would make Jarno really happy. He'd weigh in with a suggestion that Vince had already worked out. It was all designed to give Jarno peace of mind.

"Pete Shick, the racing manager at Yamaha International in America, could't believe it. His guys would get off a machine, shout that it needed this or that and disappear. But not Jarno. He would sit on a toolbox in the workshop, sometimes fall asleep, and stay until two in the morning. Maybe he didn't want Vince to feel that he was leaving him alone, leaving all the work and responsibility to him—even though Vince could handle it and knew what to expect. His interest in the job was complete. I suppose that's why they liked him to much at Yamaha . He didn't veer away from anything and he was always, and I mean *always*, ready to give his opinion and to test and retest until they were happy with things.

"He quickly formed a bond with the rest of the staff who dealt with him in the racing department. His personality and readiness to smile came over to them. They had tremendous respect for his knowledge as an engineer and as one of the greatest riders of all time. It was easy to see why they all felt so sad when he was killed.

"I suppose when he died at Monza it was if a script had been written for him, one that was not typical of his character or accomplishment. It seemed to me, and to many others, too, after his early wildness in Grand Prix racing, that the only way he was going to be killed or injured was as a result of somebody else's mistake, somebody else's carelessness. And that's just the way it was."

Hideo Kanaya, Dieter Braun, Charles Mortimer: three men who survived one of the most disastrous pile-ups in Grand Prix history: the 250 cc race at Monza, 1973. Mortimer and Kanaya were injured, but all three continued their racing careers.

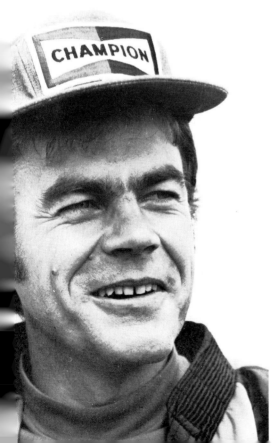

Giacomo Agostini, Superstar

As a works entity, Yamaha had finished for the season after Monza. Shocked by the loss of Saarinen, they would not admit publicly that they were considering a return to racing in 1974. Saarinen's oldest friend and fellow countryman, Tepi Lansivuori, carried the Yamaha banner for the rest of the season, on a borrowed machine. He performed so well, in a convincing triumph over the great personal doubt that had beset him since Saarinen's death, that Yamaha later rewarded him with a lucrative works contract. But when Yamaha decided to resume their struggle for the title they wanted most, the 500 cc championship, they needed something more. They needed someone with presence and charisma, to complement the sort of ability and skill that could virtually ensure success. Although there was no obvious contender amongst the riders, there was plenty of speculation around the paddocks and among men ambitious enough to take Saarinen's place.

This was the way the conversation turned when Rodney Gould climbed into the MV truck in the pits at Assen, to talk to Agostini. It was one month after Saarinen's fatal crash, and Gould, now Yamaha's publicity chief covering the whole of Europe and Scandinavia, had no ulterior motive in mind: just the need for old friends to chat in a calm oasis, amid the hurly-burly of practice for the following day's Dutch TT. Gould recalls that Agostini, as usual imperiously ignoring the clamour of girls around the olive green truck, finished their half-hour conversation about nothing in particular half-jokingly: 'Don't forget, Rodney, my contract with MV expires at the end of this year.'

Phil Read won the Dutch TT. At the Belgian Grand Prix a week later, Agostini beat the Englishman to second place, picking up his first big class victory of the season. Agostini was now well on the way to losing the world 500 cc title he had held for so long. Even worse, his always tense relationship with Read was deteriorating rapidly. The bitter differences between the two men were now being aired both publicly and privately, and the atmosphere in the MV camp was becoming intolerable. Agostini, for so long the hero and idol of all Italy, felt he was being squeezed out and that Read, the rider brought in to support him, was being given the best machines. He was conscious of internal pressures building up around him, and his mood sank lower as each Grand Prix came and went.

At Francorchamps, high in the beautiful forests of the Ardennes and above the busy little town of Spa, Agostini's mind was focused solely on beating Read, the man who had usurped his authority with MV and who was invading his jealously guarded championship title. In the 500 cc race

Giacomo Agostini, idol of the Italian racing world, aboard an MV Agusta—the team he left to join Yamaha.

he determinedly set new lap and race records, to win by more than one minute in the oppressive heatwave. Afterwards he singled out Gould, to tell him in all seriousness: "Don't forget what I said about my contract . . ." It was obvious to all but the blind that he wanted to get away from MV as soon as he could, after honouring his arrangement with them for the 1973 campaign.

The season ebbed away. In spite of another win to Read's second place at the Czechoslovakian Grand Prix at Brno, with it went the title he had assumed from the great Mike Hailwood. He managed to secure the lesser honour to him, the 350 cc world title, as he had done for the previous five years. But the one he wanted most, the one he had won six times before, in 1972, -71, -70, -69, -68 and -66, passed to Read, the rider he could not get on with. It seemed that a split was inevitable.

There was no further conversation between Gould and Agostini before the publicity boss caught a Tokio-bound Jumbo jet from Amsterdam, for a sports festival and a meeting of the Yamaha Race Committee at the factory's headquarters at Hamamatsu on Japan's main island.

It was mid-August, 1973, and the Grand Prix season was drawing to a close, when Gould faced all the Yamaha race executives to discuss the oncoming season. For the first time, Gould realized that the factory would be returning in full strength for the 1974 season. Everything before had been guesswork. Hata, the head of the racing department, attended the meeting with his second in command, Naito, who was a little closer to

Mike Hailwood, once wanted by Yamaha and by just about every other team in the sport. He last rode the terrifying Honda 500 (right) in 1967: a pensive Agostini lines up beside him on an MV.

the engineering side of the business, and, finally, Nishamoura, the top administrator. At the top of their agenda was the need for a rider—not just any rider, but one who could beat Agostini. For in their minds, he was still the tops in the business.

One or two names were suggested and discussed—Dieter Braun, the German, and John Dodds, the promising young Australian among them. But it was generally agreed that they did not quite match up to Yamaha's needs. Then Gould suggested: "Why not Agostini?" After lengthy discussions, the race executives decided against this possibility. They thought it would be contrary to the good principles of racing to *buy* the best—that would be like buying success, and Yamaha did not, and would not, do business that way. As long as Agostini was number one in the world, he was the one man they would not attempt to lure on to their pay list. To me, this seems strange reasoning. But it would have embarrassed Yamaha to have to suffer the accusation that they could only win by virtue of a huge cheque book. Agostini's name was scratched out.

One other name did excite the Japanese: that of Mike Hailwood. The former world champion, who had last raced the terrifying Honda 500 cc in 1967 before switching to racing cars, was not enjoying a happy time in Formula One. Gerry Wood, Yamaha's workshop manager in Amsterdam and an old friend of Mike's, had sensed that he might be interested in a return to two wheels. Wood had been staying with Hailwood at his home in Maidenhead, Berkshire, and the talk had got round to motor cycle racing. Hailwood admitted that he still had a hankering for the sport (incidentally he still had the fearsome Honda 500 standing in the dining room of his mansion!). Wood delightedly reported the news back to Yamaha NV, Amsterdam.

Gould immediately phoned Hailwood, inviting him to Paul Ricard, France, for a highly secret test session. It was all fixed. The machines were readied and mechanics, including Mike's old Honda helpmate, Nobby Clark, were put on stand-by for the long journey from Amsterdam to the Riviera. But meanwhile, Hailwood went on to America and delayed his return beyond the time he was expected at Paul Ricard. The test session was postponed, and everybody returned, rather disappointed, to Holland. Gould phoned Hailwood on his return to Berkshire, asking him: "Well, are you interested or not? Are you serious about the test?" Hailwood's zest for four-wheel racing had returned. In America he had sorted out his problems and arranged sponsors. He therefore declined the chance of a comeback to motor cycle racing.

Personally, I had my doubts about a return to motor cycle racing for Hailwood. He was an old friend of long standing, and I felt the need to help him decide. Despite his undoubted genius for the sport, I felt he had been too long out of racing to come back as immediately competitive as he would have wanted. The operative word here is *immediately*—there is no way that Hailwood could have been patient in his wait for success. His way was to win and return full value for the responsibility others heaped on his shoulders. (By a strange irony, four years later Mike did make a comeback—and with Yamaha. His boredom with a life of choking mundanity in New Zealand, far removed from the challenge and excitement he had lived with all his life, finally edged him out of retirement for a TT return in June 1978. Despite his 11-year lay-off, Yamaha readily provided him with three machines through their United Kingdom importers, Mitsui.)

The final consensus of opinion was that the only man who really fitted the bill was Agostini—but Yamaha would not open negotiations for him while he reigned as number one. And so Tepi Lansivuori got his reward. He was told that he could have factory 350s and 500s. Phil Read was not even discussed as a contender—years before, he had upset Yamaha because of his highly publicized verbal exchanges with his then team mate, the late Bill Ivy.

That seemed to be the end of the whole issue as far as Gould was concerned. But when he arrived back in Europe the picture had changed completely.

The Read versus Agostini battle was ablaze, and everybody in racing knew about it. Read was MV's blue-eyed boy—Agostini had slipped out of favour and even the Italians were cold shouldering him. It was quite evident that Read was being given preferences that the Italian had been used to enjoying, and he made no secret of the fact that he felt a change of loyalties would suit him. Yamaha needed a man of Agostini's promotional qualities, for despite his fall from favour in the MV camp, he was still the world's most attractive proposition. Now it seemed as if they were about to suffer for their principles. Honda, for so long rumoured to be returning to big time racing, made highly confidential approaches to the upset and bewildered Italian.

Back in Amsterdam after the inconclusive meetings in Japan, Gould received a telephone call from Volker Rauch, the German journalist and photographer who was an old friend of Agostini's. He confirmed that Honda were stealing in behind the scenes in a bid to persuade Italy's national hero to sign a contract with them. One thing was uppermost in

Agostini in familiar pose. At first Yamaha would not open negotiations with him while he reigned as number one.

the anxious Gould's mind: Honda must not be allowed to beat Yamaha to Agostini's signature. A representative for the Mark McCormack organization, world wide promoters who handled big golf names like Arnold Palmer and Gary Player, had taken Agostini's moves in hand and was acting as middleman in the deal. Agostini himself had made no attempt to contact Gould. "We certainly could not afford to allow Honda to get him," said Gould, "and I was determined not to be beaten. He was the best in the world. I knew it would be a fight but I was sure I would persuade him to ride for Yamaha."

Gould tested the seriousness of the Honda offer with Rauch, his vital link with Agostini. And Rauch stressed: "It is serious. They *do* want him." After urgent talks with Japanese executives in Amsterdam, he dictated a letter to Yamaha headquarters in Japan, outlining his moves and underlining the need to move quickly. By now, Rauch had contacted Agostini and warned him that Yamaha were making firm moves to sign him, and that he should hold any decisions until he had met them to discuss their offer. Agostini stayed at home in Bergamo, northern Italy, thinking about the Honda possibilities and wondering about the machines he had been told they had built, a three cylinder 500 two stroke and a 250 twin. Although the machines had been readied and tested, they did not seem too promising and a lot more work was needed to make them competitive.

Gould's green light to go ahead and approach Agostini came by return letter, and he contacted Rauch for Agostini's unlisted Bergamo number. Agostini was with his girlfriend, Lucia, when Gould called from Amsterdam. He came straight to the point. "You're leaving MV?" It was more of a statement than a question, and Agostini admitted that he was— but that he did not know where he was going to sell his talents. They arranged a meeting in Milan, and the agonizing saga of the chase for the Italian started.

Japan handed the responsibility for the signing over to Amsterdam and Gould. Agostini's name was taboo. The switchboard girl at the Yamaha NV headquarters in Amstelveen, Amsterdam, was not even given the name of the man who answered the phone at the number she had been given in Bergamo. Agostini was instructed to say only "Hello". In fact, only half a dozen people at Yamaha knew what was happening. Gould's secretary arranged a flight to Milan for the meeting and attended to the tickets at every stage. When Gould left his office for this most crucial get-together, he did not reveal even the country to which he was going, and left no telephone number. Even his wife Linda did not know where to contact him.

Agostini welcomed Gould at the gates of his home and they stayed up most of the night drinking coffee and wine. Lucia hardly said a word throughout. She listened intently as the stocky little Italian quizzed Gould on every aspect of the deal. "He was interested, okay," said Gould, "but he wasn't sure. Remember he'd been most of his racing life with an Italian factory, MV, and he understood everything about their ways. Now a Japanese company was after him, and he was, naturally, curious about the ways they worked. He had what seemed a million questions to ask. How they treated riders, how they looked after their mechanics, the bikes, the problems with getting parts, would they do exactly as he wanted; just about everything you could think of, he asked. But it did not end there.''

It became clear that the bitterness that had eroded the Read-Agostini partnership, fired by the apparent preferential treatment of Read by Rokki Agusta, the MV boss's playboy son, had alienated Agostini beyond the point of no return. Why this should have happened (apart from Rokki's recognition of Read's great skill) is not clear. But people close to the centre of activities at MV have suggested that Rokki did not take too kindly to having all attention focused away from him and on to Agostini, whenever the Italian group gathered in the usual haunts of the jet-setters. When Read was felt to be in need of a tonic before an important Grand Prix, he was invited to join up with Rokki and his followers aboard his yacht at Portofino: no such invitations went out to Agostini as his days at MV drew to a close. But then, Agostini had his own clan, and they did not always get on with the wilder, champagne-squirting bunch who rolled along in Rokki's wake. By the time Rokki's guiding hand on the world's circuits had been removed from the MV team, Agostini had gone.

Gould was commuting to and from Milan. He had made his fourth trip in three weeks when he heard from a friend that his rivals at Honda were to make a decision as to whether they would resume racing again, after a lay-off since 1968, within a week. The McCormack man was still trying to effect a tie-up for Agostini at Honda . . . The seven-day deadline spurred Amsterdam to phone Japan. They told him to get Agostini to Amstelveen at all costs—and to get him signed. A contract was quickly drawn up and Gould once more boarded the breakfast-time jet to Milan. Only this time,

Rodney Gould, the man responsible for signing Agostini, chats to the Italian superstar at a press conference at Imola, 1974.

the preliminaries were over, and the hard negotiation had to begin.

In the event, when Agostini was presented with the contract, he took issue with only a few points. He was of course still interested in the Honda deal, but he disliked working through a third party, the man from McCormacks. He much preferred the personal touch of dealing directly with a company and with Gould, a man he knew and whose integrity he could trust. Agostini's alterations to the contract were carried back to Amsterdam in Gould's briefcase. There had been no talk about money— just general discussion about the machines he would ride and the sort of support he could expect. The final act was to be played out in Holland, ten days later. Once again, the fair-haired girl on the switchboard plugged a call to the mystery man in Italy, and Gould said simply: "Get the 12.30 flight to Amsterdam. I'll meet you." A gruff "okay" crackled down the line and Gould knew he was on the very brink of success; only that familiar, tightly written upward scrawl of a signature was missing.

Just off the E37 route to Assen in the north of Holland, not far from the superb track where the Dutch TT is held, Gould and Agostini booked into a hotel room, reserved in the name of Yamaha. The two of them agreed that it would have been madness to stay in Amsterdam and risk being seen together by somebody who could add a Yamaha presence to an Agostini arrival, and total it up to a sensational pairing of racing names. Secrecy was the keyword. Any Yamaha move leaked to Honda, or even to MV, could have spelt disaster for Gould, and he knew it. He was joined at tea-time by Tanaka, who had known both Gould and Agostini since his days in racing, and by Nagaoka, Yamaha's managing director in Amsterdam. The big guns were being wheeled in . . .

But when they all went into the hotel's lovely old dining room for dinner, and sat in a quiet corner—the Englishmen, two Japanese, and the world's most famous motor cycle rider—six swarthy Italian faces, smiling recognition, stared excitedly from behind the waiters' partition. Every one of them knew instantly that Agostini was in the restaurant with, of course, the men from Yamaha. So much for secrecy. "In all Holland", said Gould, "there could not have been more than six waiters from Italy—and there they all were in our hotel." Whatever exhortations were made to the Italians, they forgot them five minutes later and blurted out Agostini's name whenever they served a fresh course, clasping their hands to their mouths in theatrical self-admonishment.

The following day Agostini and Gould booked out and motored to a house owned by Yamaha at Vinkeveen, ten miles or so from Amsterdam and within easy drive of the offices. This house, with its own jetty on to the big lake at Vinkeveen, a yacht and a motorboat, six bedrooms and a boardroom, is a meeting place for Yamaha VIPs and a stayover for honoured guests. It is also used by factory employees, however lowly their status, as a weekend retreat and holiday break. Here Gould—by now feeling a little harassed—talked over the contract with Agostini and told him that Nagaoka would be back that night with his number two, Kuratomo, to settle the details and prepare the contract for signature.

Agostini was a shrewd businessman, who fully understood and appreciated his own worth. He felt he should ask for about £75,000 ($150,000) a year. Gould argued that he was asking for too much, and suggested that he lower his demands. My understanding, based on conversations with friends close to Agostini, is that he agreed and lowered his price to around £55,000 ($110,000)—a figure closely related to his earnings with MV after his bonuses for fastest laps and Grand Prix wins.

That evening, the two Japanese directors crunched up the deep gravel drive under the weeping willows and sat themselves down in the lounge, with its panoramic view overlooking unsuspecting boaters. They had not come to haggle. They knew full well that commercial exposure through Agostini's undoubted race-track performances would provide a vital link in their bid for world-wide markets. After asking him his price, they conferred for a few brief moments, speaking quickly to each other in Japanese. Then Nagaoka smiled and replied: "Okay." It was as simple as that. The greatest name in motor cycle racing had joined forces with a factory that wanted only value for money to complement the awesome determination they demonstrated in earning success. Everybody shook hands. The Japanese went to their homes in Amsterdam, and a weary Gould gave Agostini a lift to the airport for a flight back to Milan and returned to the wife who had seen hardly anything of him for weeks.

A few nights later, Gould was off again, taking the final contract to Milan—two copies, one English, one Italian, drawn up at Agostini's request in the simplest of terms. The contract specified the number of races, Grand Prix and International, he would be required to attend. All it needed was the closing act of the signatures of all the principals. Nagaoka flew in, signed and flew out again. After exactly six weeks of dealing and persuading, of secrecy and worry, Gould watched triumphantly as Agostini added his name to the contract and gave the world of motor cycle racing its biggest story in years.

For the first time in months, Agostini felt happy and relaxed. His burning determination to get away from MV and join forces with Yamaha, their main rivals in the 500 cc struggle, was emphasized by his reluctance to try to squeeze more money out of the Japanese. He wanted to stress the fact that Yamaha were not paying him any more than MV would have paid him to stay and ride for them—despite the difficulties. He summarized the change round at MV by saying: "Read won once or twice—and suddenly I am a nobody in their eyes. I don't have any trust in MV any more. All I want to do is win races. I want to show them that I can win on anything—not only MV."

Whether Yamaha beat Honda to Agostini's signature, or whether Honda merely dropped out, is still one of the big mysteries of motor cycle racing. Jack Findlay, the great Australian rider who won the world 750 cc superbike championship in 1975, reckons that Honda did intend to make a big return—and that they had even fitted out mechanics with overalls. Why the comeback failed can only be guessed at. The obvious answer to that riddle is that the machines would have been out-performed, and that

Honda realized this and shelved the scheme. Whatever the answer, Gould had certainly chalked up an impressive victory for Yamaha—probably his most valuable achievement since he won them the world 250 cc championship.

Ironically, as I write, Read and Agostini are still locked in mutual dislike. Stranger still is the complete turn around by the two men. Read left MV a disillusioned man—after winning the world 500 cc championship for them in 1974, he relinquished it to Agostini the season after. Then Agostini's new employers, Yamaha, withdrew from racing and the Italian returned to riding MVs—this time as a private runner under the Team Agostini banner, but with seven works mechanics as helpers. Read, having been snubbed by his former bosses, became a freelance, riding private Suzukis and Yamahas. What a strange, unpredictable world motor cycle racing is.

Once Gould had dealt with the immediate problem of the contract, he had to deal with the Swiss-based Marlboro cigarette company, for whom Agostini, a non-smoker, worked under sponsorship. He flew to see them in Lausanne, where he was forced to let them in on the secret. Marlboro were happy to help and, indeed, assisted in keeping the secret a little longer by organizing, publicizing and paying for a Press conference in Milan, to announce "their man" Agostini's plans for the oncoming season. For Agostini's sponsors, the conference was a natural move. The surprise, for the pressmen who bothered to attend, was to be the announcement of the tie-up between the world champion and the massively influential and successful Japanese company. As a little subterfuge, the Italian Yamaha outboard motor importer, Cianferoni, booked the hotel for the conference—Yamaha NV, the umbrella name for the motor cycle racing section of the business, were determined to keep their name out of it right up until the last minute. They even refused to allow the hotel to include their name in the heading on the lunch menus—that was left purely under the auspices of Marlboro and Agostini.

"There was rumour, of course, and plenty of it," Gould told me later. "My phone hardly stopped ringing. And it was really hard to put off people I had known for years, good friends, contacts and business associates. But that was the way it had to be. We didn't want it to leak out before the right time." In fact Gould had to play his own version of the game of cat and mouse, making phone calls all over Europe and saying: "Hey, have you heard the rumours about Agostini? Who's he signed for, do you know? I don't know a thing, I wish somebody would tell me. I've phoned all over the place trying to find out, but nobody's talking." Said Gould: "It was the only way I could take a little bit of heat out of the situation. I had to swing things back on the questioners and hope it fooled them."

But despite his efforts, Gould was beaten by the inventiveness of one Italian journalist, Pino Allievi. He pressed Agostini, an old and revered friend, to let him have the story. Agostini, eyes wide in a face deliberately blank, denied all—but Pino was not satisfied. He went back to his office and worked out a plan to break the story. He sent identical telexes to all the major factories: "Have you made a contract with Agostini for 1974?" They all replied—except Yamaha. And Gould was not around to dictate a reply. He was still operating his cloak and dagger moves in Milan. Allievi tracked him down at Cianferoni's offices and Gould, admitting later that this was the biggest mistake he had made all along, agreed to meet him at a discreet cafe close to the offices of his newspaper in Milan's city centre.

Gould and Yamaha wanted to have the maximum amount of world-wide publicity in one shock announcement. As all newspapermen will testify, one exclusive release tends to nullify all else, and no newspaper likes to follow up a story that has been broken elsewhere. A general release, at the Press conference, with Agostini present and ready to answer questions, was thus vital to their plans. This was uppermost in Gould's mind as he walked into the cafe shortly after 6 pm. Allievi flashed him a triumphant grin and Gould immediately had the wind taken out of his sails. Allievi announced that he had already written the story and that it was going into the paper that night. Knowing that he could only have found out by accident, Gould was in no position to confirm the Italian's suspicions. Anyway, he reasoned, he might be bluffing. All he could do, in order to avoid upsetting other important journalists, was to ask Allievi not to write that he and Gould had met and talked, or even that he had seen the Yamaha man in Milan. Allievi agreed, accepted the non-committal Gould as having substantiated his story, and ran it under screaming headlines the morning after—coincidentally timed with the Press conference. Even then, because there was no official confirmation, not even from Agostini, the story had the look of yet another piece of sensationalism from an excitable Italian reporter . . . To anybody who was not familiar with the cool and seasoned Allievi, one of Europe's most respected motor sport writers, that, at least, is the way it would have looked.

At the conference Gould hid himself in the bar, watching reporters file in and out of the big room where the announcement was to be made, until he was joined by Agostini. When they walked in together, the whole place came alive, and Allievi smiled with satisfaction. "Giacomo Agostini has joined Yamaha" confirmed Gould, and the two of them sat back to listen to the welter of questions thrown at them in half a dozen different languages. And enjoy the astonishment on the faces of the men who had had no idea of what had been going on behind the scenes.

The conference started at 11 am. At 2 pm that afternoon, Gould and his newest colleague were booked to fly to Rome to catch a jet for Tokio, via the southern route. A 10 am conference in Tokio had been planned. Agostini and a friend at Alitalia—one of the directors, had planned the tickets—another way of keeping Yamaha's name under wraps. So fine was the planning for the cover-up that even the Alitalia man failed to realize just why his illustrious friend wanted to fly to Japan. The schedule was a tight one. There were only 15 minutes between the touch down of the domestic flight from Milan and the take-off on the international jet to Tokio. A car was to be standing by on the tarmac to whisk Agostini, Gould and their luggage across the airport to the waiting aircraft. Halfway through what had turned into a hectic and noisy Press conference in Milan, Cianferoni leaned across to Gould and whispered: "The airport at Linate is shut down. No more flights from there today."

Across the other side of the world, with another conference planned for 10 am the following day, the Yamaha hierarchy patiently awaited the arrival of their world class star. Everything there was planned to the minute and Gould knew it; he knew, too, that for the prestige of his company, it all had to go smoothly in Tokio. Unpunctuality is the greatest sin in Japanese business. A little puzzled as to what would happen next, Agostini then sampled his first taste of Yamaha's readiness to overcome any problem swiftly and decisively. Gould worked fast. He hired a private Lear jet to fly to Rome with their precious cargo. The bill, about £700 ($1400) for the half-hour flight, was small change compared to the trouble it could save. The conference was drawn to a premature close and Agostini and Gould fled to Milan's alternative airport, the trouble-free Malpensa.

Ironically, the MV complex sprawls alongside the airport. As the white jet nosed up towards the clouds, Agostini had a panoramic view of the factory that had been his life, but whose chiefs had not even attempted to persuade him to stay. He had given them glory, success, and world-wide stature, in the great traditions established before him by riders such as world champions Mike Hailwood and John Surtees, and men who might have been, like John Hartle and Gary Hocking. But he had been hurt that not even the aristocratic, autocratic Count Corrada Agusta, the man who had inherited the factory's leadership, had invited him to stay with MV. Read, of course, was. They were, it seemed to Agostini, glad to see the back of him. A sight that became familiar to them later on. Oddly, the mechanics with whom he had developed his racing career were saddened by his departure. When he later began to win on the Yamahas, they were as warm in their congratulations as if he had scored such impressive victories on one of the machines they had prepared. They could not and would not hide their feeling for him. And this was something Read came to resent, probably as any man would who was not afforded quite the same adulation as the man who switched loyalties.

Agostini was due to stay in Japan for three days. Mindful of the fact that it was only November and that his contract with MV did not terminate until 31 December, Yamaha announced that he would not be riding any machines whilst he was in Japan. But Agostini's persuasion was greater than Yamaha's resistance. He wanted to get aboard a machine just as soon as he could. After the Press conference, he and Gould went to Hamamatsu where two Yamahas were waiting. Mechanics at the factory had already heard about the 350 cc world champion's preferences, and they had worked out a shallower slope on the handlebars. On the gleaming new 500 cc and 750 cc machines, they had also switched around the gears and the brake, to the right and left foot respectively. All he had to do was climb aboard. After ten laps he sat down with Naito, the engineering wizard at the factory. Speaking in fractured English, the Japanese and the Italian got down to sorting out exactly what he wanted the factory to do to the bikes.

"The Japanese", said Gould, "were extremely impressed with Ago's mechanical and engineering know-how, and his feel and sympathy for the machines. In no time at all he had virtually designed a new gearbox.

Agostini beside Yamaha's test track at Hamamatsu. He should not really have ridden the machine at all—his contract with MV had another month to run.

He knew what he was talking about and Naito appreciated it. He organized new ratios and combinations on each of the gears." The suspension, too, came under Agostini's scrutiny and this notorious blind spot in Japanese engineering had to be developed to his liking. He also asked for the engine to be moved slightly forward, and for some readjustments to the footrests. All this was after only ten laps' testing. Feeling that he had left them with enough work to be getting on with, he went off to his hotel for an early night.

It was his turn to be astounded when he turned up at the test track the next morning. Everything had been done. The mechanics had stayed up throughout the night, working on his ideas and suggestions, and the bikes were exactly as he had specified. He of course had not dreamt that the job would be done in 24 hours, thinking it would take maybe a week or so. "I could not believe it," he told me later, "the machines were ready to go and all the work had been done. And it didn't matter if nobody had any sleep for two or three days or for how long it took for the job to be finished."

Rested after his trip, and excited about the preparation of the machines, Agostini did the mechanics proud by lapping a full second faster than the brilliant Jarno Saarinen had done the year before when he had first joined Yamaha. It was the first time Agostini had been on a two-stroke—Saarinen had never ridden anything else. If he had nursed any secret worries or apprehensions about switching to two-strokes after almost a lifetime of racing four-strokes, he never voiced them to anybody at Yamaha. All he wanted to know was the symptoms of seizure on a two-stroke, the old Yamaha rider's fear, which was much less of a threat with water cooling. He accepted, without demur, that he would simply have to relearn his techniques, though, as Gould points out, racing is racing whatever the machine. "I had raced against two strokes throughout 1971 and 1972 and I knew they were extremely fast", said Agostini. "But my feeling was, and I found it to be true, that it needed only a slight change in technique from racing the MV to racing the Yamaha."

For example, on the MV he had never had to use the clutch to keep the revs up on the slow corners—he just rode through the corner, turned his right wrist back and let the engine power flow on. With the Yamaha, the two stroke would not allow him that sort of leeway and he had to learn to operate the clutch to keep the revs up. The power band started at 4000 rpm on the Japanese machine—on the MV it was 6500 rpm.

He had two complete days of testing—and enjoying himself aboard the super-fast machines. By the time he had finished, the racing department knew precisely what to do to the machines to get them to Agostini's liking for the first race of the oncoming season, the fabulous Daytona 200 in Florida.

"The impressive aspect of his testing", Gould explained, "was that he could actually explain, in terms everybody could understand, what was needed. We soon realized that we had captured not only a fine rider but a great technician too. Saarinen was an engineer, had been all his career,

*Agostini at speed on the new 500, during his secret 10 lap test. He had cut
the MV insignia off his leathers.*

but he could not give us the answers that Agostini did. He had the
experience, the feel and the know-how, and because of his standing he
was not afraid to point out what he wanted. We began to learn from him.
He had not even raced a Yamaha and already the factory was able to feel
the power he had and the value of his views. Tepi Lansivuori was another
man who could not help out too much in setting up machines. He was a
brilliant rider but, and I suppose it may have been because he could not
speak English, he could only say 'It's good . . . not so good'. And that was
all. No real clues as to what might have been done to the bike to make it
better. He simply could not explain it any further."

Gould's great pride in having been instrumental in getting Agostini to
join forces with Yamaha was shared by nearly everybody who came in
contact with him. Lansivuori was one exception, however. He could not
quite understand Agostini's value in terms wider than those of racing and
winning. In Gould's words, "We felt we needed some prestige. In
Agostini we got exactly what we needed. He was not only a winner. He
carried himself with poise, he was composed, well-behaved and admired
all around the world. He was, to us, a winner on and off the tracks."
Lansivuori objected to Agostini's selection as number one rider—riding
for second place was not for him. I have been assured that nobody in
authority ordered Lansivuori to run second to Agostini—but it was
obvious that he should. Later, when Agostini had been hurt in a crash
and Lansivuori had to assume the number one role, I believe he may have
overstretched himself by asking for a bigger salary increase than Yamaha
were prepared to pay him. (Previously, his earnings had been about a

Tepi Lansivuori, former ice rider and great friend of Saarinen. A fierce competitor in his own right, he was inevitably overshadowed by his flamboyant partner in the Yamaha team.

quarter of Agostini's.) Then his feelings got the better of him, and he was eased out of the team. When faced with that kind of problem, Yamaha were known to be ruthless. When Phil Read and Bill Ivy squabbled over who should win what world championship, Read slipped from favour and, despite the championships he had won them, Yamaha made it impossible for him to have any works machinery in later years. Lansivuori faced the same sort of difficulty when Yamaha pulled out of racing in a full supporting role in Europe in 1975. Agostini was offered works bikes on a private basis; the Finn was not.

From the outside, it never seemed to me that Lansivuori was enjoying his service with Yamaha, particularly when Agostini was around. The slight, moustached Finn would sit silently, almost morosely, in a corner of a hotel, taking no part in the conversation going on around him. When the crowds flocked around the Yamaha entourage, it was mainly to stare at Agostini. When the cameras came out, they were invariably focused on Agostini. Autograph books were waved under the Italian's nose, and the less forthcoming Lansivuori—struggling against an insuperable

language barrier—was left out in the cold. There can be no doubt that once he had got over the terrible shock of his friend Saarinen's death, Lansivuori turned into a fierce, determined competitor. He was spectacular, too, with that backside-off-the-saddle style of racing that had suddenly become so popular. A star in his own right, he must, understandably, have felt slighted by all the attention lavished upon his Italian team mate. But the more Lansivuori edged away from the limelight, the more certain Yamaha were that they had taken a vitally important step in signing on Agostini.

After two years of close alliance with Agostini, at the time when Yamaha withdrew their full support at the end of 1975, Gould's original assessment of his protege remained unaltered. "He was always well behaved, no childish pranks, and therefore no embarrassing incidents to apologize for the morning after some celebration or other. His reliability, his attitude to people in authority, and to those in lesser jobs, too, was a joy. Everybody liked him and enjoyed working with him. Whenever there was an office party to attend, he always turned up on time—and well dressed. I never saw him scruffily turned out all the time we worked together. He had too much respect for his own position and the feelings of others to come dressed like a hippie. He realized that's how people who knew no better would expect a professional motor cycle racer to dress. He disappointed them in that respect—or, rather, gave them a pleasant surprise."

Gould continued: "I don't suppose that my ideas about what he would be like altered at all from what he turned out to be. From the racing standpoint, he was such a quick learner he hardly seemed to have to try. It was his great strength—I had discovered that to my cost when I used to race against him. I mean, he went to the Isle of Man for the TT and set the place alight the first time. And he knew more about that course, a terribly difficult one to learn, after one or two visits than most other riders did in ten years of real hard study."

If Agostini had a prediliction for anything that was not racing, it was women—and they for him. At around 5 ft. 8 ins. he was short and stubby, but devastatingly handsome in a matinee idol sense: a well shaped head black curling hair and a proud swagger that appeared to lend him more height than he really had. He had an unwavering, slightly bewildered stare that seemed to promise sincerity and concentration. The bridge of his nose carried a slight scar, the result of a spill—the only flaw on a face women found unashamedly fascinating. "Of course I knew about his enjoyment of women—and the way they went for him", said Gould, "but he never allowed them to interfere, in any way, with his racing. That was his love and he professed it at every opportunity." In truth, Agostini was almost contemptuous in his treatment of women. He has even kicked them out of his bedroom, when he felt it was time to concentrate on a race. Yamaha never had to fret about his love life. The night before a race— whether a Grand Prix or a comparatively unimportant national meeting, he would slip quietly away to his room at around 9.30 pm. It did not matter how successful the party, how much fun the company, or how attractive the women—Agostini would turn his back and leave it all behind. His personal life was wrapped up in a girl called Lucia, who left her husband to live with Agostini in Bergamo. She knew when he needed affection and love, and when he did not. She lasted throughout—when other, more attractive girls, younger than her 38 years when Agostini was 34, had been cast aside.

His flamboyant lifestyle gave rise to one amusing myth, never corrected by Agostini because it really did not matter to him. People thought that when he went around the world racing and living it up in the plushest suites in the most exclusive hotels, he was taking Yamaha for a financial ride; that the Japanese company was being foolishly generous in picking up his trail of tabs. Nothing could be further from the truth. For under the terms of his agreement, within that sizeable annual pay-out, he bore the responsibility of transporting himself to any track in Europe where a race was being run, of keeping and feeding himself while he was there. Private expenses—hotels, meals, planes, were all borne by him. There was a different arrangement for trips outside Europe.

Yamaha could not have cared if he had walked or travelled by pogo stick to any race they were contesting, just so long as he was there. It did not matter whether he lived in luxury or in a chickenshack, provided he was fit, ready and able to race. It was their responsibility to get there with machines and a full back-up team and supply centre. It was his to get himself there. How he did it was his business. They did have a rider written into their contract. It was a penalty clause that stated that if Agostini, for any reason that was his own fault—for example, racing when they had not sanctioned the event, failed to start in a championship round, he would forfeit £3500 ($7000). The same figure would be forfeited at each subsequent race he missed. By the time the contract came to a close two years later, Agostini had not lost one penny under those terms.

Yamaha agreed to insure his life for a premium of around £6000 ($12000) and supported him with medical and health cover to the tune of £3500 ($7000). He also received many fringe benefits and sponsorships, which nearly trebled his earnings: AGV helmets, API petrol, Marlboro cigarettes, tyre companies, and even flights with Alitalia. In fact, even before he fired a machine into life, by merely sitting on the start line with that impressive array of advertising scrawled colourfully across his back, legs, chest and helmet, he was worth about £100,000 ($200,000). In the end, naturally, he had to do his stuff in order to keep that sort of support. Yamaha were often offered sponsorship for their highly successful machines. Never feeling the need for it, they always turned down the offers, that were at times mind-boggling in their size. They did not mind Agostini enjoying the benefits—but nothing was to be stuck on their machines that would detract in any way from the makers, Yamaha. Agostini was allowed to keep all the prize money he won, and to negotiate the best terms he could get for appearance money. Unlike many other factory teams, who insist their riders put the prize and start money into the team pot, Yamaha let Agostini keep it all. But they did not pay him anything extra for winning the championships of the world. Little wonder that Agostini, with fifteen world titles won by the start of the 1976 season, laughed off suggestions that he might fancy a switch to Formula One cars.

We were talking in an hotel on the Adriatic, when I put the point to him: "You have had offers, you have done just about everything on motor bikes, why not a change?" "I would be mad", he replied; "this is a short life and you have to earn as much as you can while you can. If I went into motor cars, who could pay me anything like the money I get to race motor bikes? Nobody. And I would have to start right at the bottom again. No. It used to be the ambition of every bike rider to move *up* into cars. Not any more. And in many cases it is a move *down*. Why should I take a drop in pay to start to learn another trade when I'm at the top of the one I enjoy most?" He cited his old rival and former team mate, Mike Hailwood, who had just announced his intention to go into business in New Zealand. After a bad crash in Formula One in Germany, Hailwood had finally decided that he could not race again. "Look at Mike. He could have earned hundreds of thousands of pounds if he had stayed on motor bikes. When Honda quit, he quit too, except for a brief flirtation with bikes later. He could now have been right at the top. It was too early for him to change—but he felt he had done everything on bikes and he wanted cars. He was not nearly so successful in Formula One—though he did have a lot of bad luck. I still rate him as the hardest man to beat. And the money we were racing for in those days was nothing compared with what we can earn today. I'm not saying that big money makes you race any harder but it makes you aware of your responsibilities, and when that happens you naturally race harder. But I'll stay where I am for the moment. When I do quit, it will be overnight. Just like that. One night I'll go to bed a racer. The next morning I'll wake up and retire. No arguments. And no going into four wheel racing."

In 1978, Agostini confounded this philosophy utterly when he did in fact switch to motor car racing, to the astonishment of everyone in the racing world. Sadly, this volte face owed more to force of circumstance than to any fundamental change in attitude. Even so, it really is rather strange how one man's firm intentions regarding his career can change so dramatically. There can be no doubt at all that Agostini meant every word of what he was saying to me: at the time, motor car racing, despite the interest shown in him by Ferrari and other famous marques, was as far from his mind as retirement altogether.

The first major challenge facing Agostini, after he had signed on with Yamaha, was the American classic—the Daytona 200. Over in England, one man in particular was especially excited by the news that Agostini

Agostini with Enzo Ferrari at Imola, 1974. At that time, not even the grand maestro of car racing could persuade him to switch from two wheels to four.

would be competing against the best American riders in spring 1974. His name: Tony Mills, the leader of the tyre development and research department at Dunlop, Birmingham, in the industrialized Midlands of England. Mills was an outgoing personality, with an infectious laugh that belied the deadly seriousness of his concentration when it came to tyre issues. He had enjoyed a long understanding and association with Yamaha. When he discovered that Agostini, another old friend, was to ride a new 700 cc superbike at Daytona, he phoned Gould in Holland and suggested a get-together to sort out the tyres.

Daytona presents enormous headaches for tyremen, with its freak heat and stress factors that are harsher than any in the world. Dunlop had had very little experience with the immensely powerful 700s, and Mills felt he needed to trade ideas with the factory, and with the rider charged with the unenviable responsibility of tackling the 31 degree banking and the fierce infield turns. Mills had worked on tyres for a 750 cc Suzuki for the 1972 Daytona, but the contour had been a failure. The shape was not right for the job, and there had been a lot of distortion with the heat build-up that the Dunlop boffin could not master. In fact, everybody had tyre problems in the 1972 event. Manufacturers were baffled by the stresses that were thrown up by the awesome thrust of the big machines. In September 1972, Mills set to work to develop new tyres for the 1973 Daytona 200 miler. To his great pleasure, these tyres won a safety award from the American Motor Cycle Association after the earlier Talladega races. "We felt we had the tyres for the job in 1973", Mills told me, "but when we all got to Daytona and set up our contracted machines with our tyres, we were left without a final answer to the question of whether they were okay or not. Every one of the machines on our tyres broke down or packed up—not because of tyre failure, but for a variety of reasons. So we had no proof that our tyres were suitable for the excessive demands of Daytona. We were left in limbo and in doubt."

That was the situation when Mills asked Gould to arrange a meeting with Agostini and Yamaha. The Japanese welcomed the idea, and Mills began to prepare himself for a trip to the Orient. (A stickler for the type of old world courtesy that had existed at Dunlop for many years, he first cleared the trip with Dunlop Japan.) When he boarded the 11 am jet for Tokio at Heathrow, London, he was carrying eight differently patterned tyres as hand baggage—twenty more had been sent ahead by airfreight. His final destination, after a quick visit to Kobe, for the Dunlop factory call, was Hamamatsu. It was Mills' second trip to Japan. He had been to the Fuji circuit in 1967 for the last Japanese Grand Prix, trying to win contracts with Yamaha, Kawasaki and Suzuki. He was not to know it then, but it was the start of the biggest triumph of his career.

Mills was yet another expert who was happily surprised at Agostini's grasp of technicalities. "The more I got to know him, the more I began to appreciate his value as a man who could express himself and explain what he needed, what he felt should be done and what improvements he felt might be made. We talked for ages and what he said technically made sense. He did not volunteer advice or even try to enforce his ideas—but he gave clear impressions of the reactions he was getting from the various things we were trying. And if you asked him to do something, he'd do it. He didn't look for excuses not to, or put on the big-time act and refuse. More importantly, he could *listen* to advice. He realized that what we told him was for his own good, in his own best interests. And he told me in return that he felt he could trust us; he was happy with us. When you have that sort of relationship, it is not difficult to work and understand each other's problems. I'd never spent so much time with him before and every day I seemed to learn something new about him. He was amazing."

Though the test track in Japan was in no way a replica of the Daytona circuit, having no banking, the infield did have certain similarities and Mills and Agostini were able to form some idea of the sort of compromise tyre they were seeking. They needed the best grip for the infield while, at the same time, they could not lose sight of the need for safety around the terrifying banking. They also had to try out tyres for the longer European Grand Prix season.

As Mills pointed out, "Daytona is a very important race on the calendar of international events. The prestige it brings is endless. It's the first race of the season. Everybody who is anybody is there and the eyes of the racing world are focused on that resort in Florida. The extremities of the weather, humidity, heat, temperature, together with the stresses, leave you operating on a dangerously narrow margin of safety. It is a great test bed—and it costs Dunlop a lot of money to attend, a small fortune. The only worthwhile return is success, and every tyreman is looking for that as some sort of justification for all his sweat and his company's massive

Dunlop tyre designers Tony Mills (right) and David Buck, comparing a 'Racing 200' tyre designed for use on American banked racing tracks such as Daytona (right), with a standard racing tyre used on European road circuits (left).

cash investment." Mills admitted that Dunlop had learned a lot from Daytona and had been sending men to the race since 1964. But there could be no half measures, no cutting corners. Safety, stamina and durability were the watchwords.

With all of these factors in mind, Mills and Agostini worked together, piecing together the missing parts of the jig-saw that would lead them to success. In contrast to his first test session in Japan, when his lap times had been faster than Saarinen's, Agostini returned to the test track to circulate even slower than the test rider. "But he never panicked", said Mills. "He didn't worry that people were looking sideways at him, wondering what had gone wrong with the great champion from Europe. He couldn't even get round as quickly as the factory test rider! You could see what they were thinking. But he was just getting the fit of the machine right, making sure it was as he wanted it."

In the restaurant at the track, after he had tested the 350, 500 and the 750, Agostini had a big blackboard set up. Then he, Mills and the Yamaha team manager, Mizo, a dominant character with plenty of patience and an endearing nature, all wrote down their tyre preferences on a one-to-five marking system. Handling, grip, compound, and wear were all graded in order of suitability for each of the three machines. For the 350 there were two types of front tyre, two rear. For the 500 two types for the front, three for the rear; and for the 750 two types for the front and three for the rear: 14 types of tyre in all. When all the marks were totalled up, the ones with the highest grading were selected—and Mills knew exactly what his task was in preparing covers for Daytona. "It was the simplest way of all", said Mills. "This way we all had our say and we reached a democratic agreement. Smashing."

Mills did not get much sleep on his return journey to England. He spent most of his time working over the conclusions that had been reached in the most rewarding test session he had ever attended. He explained: "To me, and to many other people, I suppose Agostini was a great rider. Just that. There was no time before I met up with him in Japan when I had been led to believe he was anything else. What a surprise I got! He was so serious about it all that it was no problem to get down to work. He played only when all the work was done to everybody's satisfaction."

The next time the two of them met up was in Daytona itself, the Atlantic resort that bursts at the seams once a year with the craziest assortment of motor cycle fans you could see gathered anywhere in the world. Mills endured gnawing doubts in the furnace that was the Daytona speed bowl. The sun baked men and machines alike with blistering ferocity, and the problems that face men who work with tyres came bubbling to the surface of Mill's mind. But little seemed to disturb the Italian. As at the test session back in Japan, Agostini motored round at his own pace. He was unhurried, unruffled, but certainly aware of the criticisms that were inevitably being levelled at him. He was happy to be the slumbering giant . . .

Then, on the qualifying day, which is almost a replica of the race itself, Agostini exploded from his apparent lethargy, to confound those who had written him off, appearing as a long shadow over every other rider's ambitions. "That", said Mills, "was the touch of the master at work. He did it when it was most important. He wasn't out to impress, he was there to do a job—and to do it on the right days. He wasn't there to please people. He was there to win. And he did. By Christ, he did! He was fantastic. It was like a fairy tale for me. There he was, on our tyres, riding a two-stroke for the first time in a race, hardly knowing the machine at all, in the premier event of the season—and he bloody well beat them all. I don't mind telling you, it was the most important moment in my life. The high point. It took him 45 minutes to get to the winner's rostrum. He collapsed. That's how hot it was. It was bloody baking, but the tyres held up. All the work we had gone through was worth it. If there were any doubters about the place, they must have all crawled underground afterwards."

For Agostini, it was the perfect start to the year. After the ignominy of his split with MV, his bickering with Read and his disappointment at losing his world 500 cc title, Daytona was a pinnacle of achievement. "You can't do better than that", said Mills. "We had always been tied up with Yamaha, and together with Ago we all knew we were on to something really big, something outstanding and exciting."

One of the prizes Agostini collected at Daytona was a brand new Camaro sports car, a gift from General Motors. Kenny Roberts, the American number one road racer, was given one as well. Later, Agostini was invited to Manila with the Italian film actress Gina Lollobrigida and eighteen others, for a ten day holiday of unbelievable luxury. There were private jet trips around the islands, governments receptions, banquets and barbecues . . . A few years ago, all this would have been outside the social sphere of a racing motor cyclist. But this was the manner of man that Yamaha had on their side—no other enjoyed that sort of charisma.

Gould summed him up this way: "He behaved as a leader, and as a man, should."

Agostini setting up the big 750 cc Yamaha in Japan for Daytona, 1974.

Agostini and mechanic Nobby Clarke taking a break from practice at Daytona, 1974. The first outing, and the first victory, for the Yamaha superbike.

There was an interesting side issue to Agostini's win at Daytona. Under a controversial and bizarre ruling by the American Motor Cycle Association, a claim backed by a statutory $5000 (£2500) in cash could be made by anybody for the first-placed machine within thirty minutes of the end of the race. The owner had no choice. He had to sell. There were methods, of course, to combat a prospective buyer. Friends or associates could be recruited to make counter bids, for when there was more than one offer the referee, appointed by the AMA and stationed in the victory enclosure, placed them all in a hat and drew one out. Under such circumstances, the chances were that the genuine bidder would never get his hands on the victorious machine. Naturally, no successful works team would ever want to contemplate the thought of its formula for success being spread around for a handful of dollars—a fraction of the development costs.

But at Daytona someone did make just such a bid—Patrick Pons, a little known Frenchman, who rode a Yamaha under French sponsorship. He took the Yamaha team by surprise. Agostini had collapsed in the pits with sun stroke and was in no state to get to the referee with a counter bid. Rodney Gould had armed himself with a written bid signed by Agostini before the race and was carrying a sackful of money—dollars, guilders, marks and francs, but the referee insisted that Agostini had to present himself. Time was running out. A police car, sirens howling, brought Agostini to the enclosure, stll in his sweat-soaked leathers. But it was too late—the machine now belonged to Pons, or whoever had put him up to it. Security officers from the speedbowl's own force held back the Yamaha mechanics as they moved to unscrew the fairing from the 700. Agostini and Gould watched in amazement as it was quickly loaded onto a truck.

The error of his ways hit Pons some time within the next two hours. He turned up at the Howard Johnson Motel, opposite the track, where Gould was staying and pleaded with him to take back the machine and return his dollars. It does not take too much guesswork to figure out that the young, ambitious Frenchman had realized that he had far more to lose than to gain in upsetting the vast Yamaha organization. Gould agreed and the machine was wheeled into his ground-floor bedroom, where it spent the night propped up against the ventilation system.

The Frenchman Patrick Pons getting down to action. After the Daytona 200, he had the temerity to claim Agostini's 750—but he later regretted it.

It was the first time since 1968 that anybody had made such a bid. Later, the AMA revised the regulations, making it a less attractive proposition. For $4000 (£2000), only the engine, gearbox, carbs and exhaust pipes could be claimed, while the rest of the machine, if somewhat skeletal, remained the property of the original entrant.

With Daytona so triumphantly behind him, all Agostini's attention was now focused on the ensuing Grand Prix season, and the biggest prize of all—the 500 cc world title. Throughout 1974 and 1975, the tug o' war for the championship was to be completely dominated by two men, Agostini and Phil Read. The role of the other Grand Prix riders seemed to be reduced almost to that of bit players, propping up the main drama. Such determined competition between two men presupposes an element of mutual dislike, almost hatred, and there was certainly plenty of that between the former team mates: they had struggled to find harmony even when they were racing for the single cause of MV Agusta's fine reputation. Now there were no holds barred, and accordingly any confrontation between Agostini, newly signed by Yamaha, and Read, who had stayed with MV, was guaranteed to fill the world's Grand Prix circuits to capacity.

The two protagonists grew further apart as the season drew on, frequently giving vent to public displays of slanging, insults and jibes. When they lined up against each other at the Italian meetings held early on in the season, so vital for the national championship and the prestige that went with it, the Englishman was delighted to hear the home crowd booing and jeering their former hero for leaving MV. It may have upset Agostini, but he was experienced enough not to show it. His sole aim was to wrest back the 500 cc world title that Read had snatched from him after a seven-year domination of the class. Suzuki, too, moved in with what was rumoured to be an 180 mph four-cylinder two-stroke and a bright young man called Barry Sheene to ride it; but their challenge faded away as the season developed into a dog fight between Agostini and Read.

Read gave Agostini a taste of what was to come in the Grands Prix at an international meeting at Imola. More than 50,000 fans packed around the circuit watched an absorbing tussle explode into a sensational finish, as Read overtook Agostini in the final few hundred yards and held him off right up to the chequered flag. From that moment on, there was never any doubt that the 1974 season would see some pretty heated competition.

At Clermont Ferrand, a dizzying, twisting circuit set high in the Massif Central, Read won the French Grand Prix—but only after Agostini had broken down on lap 9 with an 8 second lead and a new lap record. The West German Grand Prix at the Nurburgring ended in chaos when the mainliners refused to start: the organizers had refused to make the circuit as safe as the riders wanted it to be. The following weekend, in Austria, Agostini came back in fine style with a great win in dreadful conditions on the terrifyingly fast Salzburgring circuit.

But back at Imola, for the Italian Grand Prix, Agostini hit a blank spot in his pursuit of points. It could not have happened at a worse place for

Barry Sheene, then a newcomer to international Grand Prix racing, chases Agostini. In 1974 Suzuki's challenge was entirely overshadowed by the Agostini/Read battle.

the Italian, anxious to please his supporters and reawaken lost affection from his fellow countrymen. The race distance was increased by two laps to meet the FIM's minimum 45-minute race time for GPs. With no time to get bigger tanks set up, Yamaha were forced to take a risk and hope that the thirsty multi would hold out with the petrol it had aboard. But the pace of the race was so quick—much faster than Agostini had anticipated, that Yamaha's bluff was called. As it swept across the line for the start of the last lap, well in the lead but still hotly chased, Agostini's brave 500 spluttered to a halt. Lap records were scattered in his shadow and a massive crowd had risen to his dash and daring, but his championship tilt had been sabotaged. Read, recovering from 'flu and feeling desperately ill, motored in for a 10-point third place.

At Assen, in the north of Holland, 120,000 people paid to see Agostini and Lansivuori come home in first and second places. Agostini became the first rider to round the track in under three minutes and finished with a record race average as well. But Read was still grimly hanging onto his crown and came in third. And the next race was the Belgian Grand Prix at Spa, a circuit tailor-made for Read and his MV. As if Read did not have enough going for him, Agostini made the mistake of choosing to ride a brand-new, slim-line lightweight 500. It was far too slow, and no match for the sheer brute speed of the MV. The upshot was a total wipe-out of

Kitted out in a wet weather suit over his leathers, Agostini feels his way through a downpour at the Salzburgring.

the Yamaha challenge. The 8-mile-long circuit at Spa became the stage for Read's rise back to the top of the world championships. He also established a breathtaking new lap record of 133.34 mph, the fastest in the world.

In Sweden Sheene and Agostini went down in a heap and hurtled into the catch fence in a cloud of dust and wreckage. Read escaped the pile-up and dodged through, as the air around the stricken fallers resounded with accusation and blame. Agostini's injuries kept him out of the next round in Finland, where Read made sure of his title with a start to finish victory.

Agostini went back to his home in Bergamo to think out his plans for 1975. He knew that Read was becoming disenchanted with the set-up at MV and that there was some disagreement behind the scenes—so much so, in fact, that Read had flown to Japan to test the new Suzukis, despite the fact that his friend, Barry Sheene, was hoping to be signed again as their number one rider.

The fortunes of the two men began to change. The Yamaha operation was smoothness itself. Agostini was now master of the two stroke, the elementary errors of the previous year were behind him and his determination was in full flood. Read, on the other hand, was experiencing difficulties at MV, the machine did not seem to be running

1000 cc's worth of racing machinery: Agostini ahead of team mate at the time, Tepi Lansivuori.

well and he wanted changes. Nor could he find satisfaction in his dealings with some of the personnel at the factory and in the team.

Read's hunger to outdo Agostini saw him hurtling down the St Moritz Cresta Run, while on holiday, in a desperate attempt to better a time set by the Italian shortly beforehand. He succeeded, by two seconds. He felt great elation in beating Agostini's toboggan time, but admits to not telling his boss, Count Agusta!

Read was not to have the same success on a motor cycle in the 1975 season. His bid to collect a hat trick of 500 cc world titles collapsed almost before it began. A tumble during a practice session in France aggravated a finger injury to his braking hand and left him struggling for points. A win in Belgium and a second place in Sweden, after Agostini had pulled out with a puncture, gave Read a brief appearance as leader in the

Agostini piloting the experimental lightweight 500 cc Yamaha during its disastrous outing in the Belgian Grand Prix, 1974. He was forced out with engine trouble, but by then the Yamaha was well beaten anyway.

championships. But by the time the pair arrived in Finland, Agostini had logged three firsts and one second place, against Read's single win at Spa and a mixture of seconds and thirds.

Read knew he had to win the Finnish Grand Prix at Imatra, near the Russian border, if he was to stave off the attack on his world title. Halfway through the race, when he was heading his rivals, his magneto failed him: although it was the first time that the MV had not finished in the first three, it was a costly breakdown. Read realized deep down that the one slender thread that held him to the 500 cc crown was the skill of his team mate, Gianfranco Bonero. But Bonero fell off and the title was Agostini's, provided only that he finished somewhere in the first seven at the Czechoslovakian Grand Prix at Brno. Knowing precisely what he had to do, Agostini rode a beautifully controlled race at Brno. Although Read won the Grand Prix, taking his number of points to 96, Agostini comfortably secured the greater glory with a second place.

It was Yamaha's first 500 cc title: the culmination of a great deal of ambition, planning and hard work, and the ultimate accolade for

Agostini leads Read at Hockenheim, West Germany, during one of the finest of all 500 cc races, 1975.

The first three: Kanaya and Agostini (Yamaha), and Lansivuori (then with Suzuki), after the 1975 West German Grand Prix.

Tyre boffin Tony Mills and other Dunlop competition managers, past and present, celebrate Agostini's 500 cc title. Left to right: David Shaw, Derek Carpenter, Roger Sanders, Tony Mills (now in the USA for Dunlop), and Paul Butler (now with Yamaha in Amsterdam).

Agostini, who had given new life to the project that had faltered when Saarinen was so tragically killed. As Agostini said, "It's been hard work, but I really wanted to win back my title. Yamaha gave me the best possible chance, and though it's been a tough two seasons I feel it has all been worthwhile."

Sadly, 1975 was to be Agostini's last 500 cc world title. In fact, little more than two years later, after two disappointing and at times frankly uninspired seasons, the Italian would announce his retirement from motor cycle racing altogether. In retrospect, it is even possible to recognize the beginning of Agostini's decline in 1975, his year of triumph. For if 1975 was the year in which he reclaimed his 500 cc title, it was also the year in which his 350 cc crown was snatched away from him by a young and hitherto unknown Yamaha rider—the Venezuelan, Johnny Cecotto.

Agostini on his way to his only victory in the 1975 350 cc championship series: at Jarama, in the Spanish Grand Prix.

Naito greets Agostini as he arrives back at the pits.

When he was just nineteen years old, Cecotto arrived on the international racing scene with his Venezuelan based team, Venemotos, and proceeded to set that world back on its heels with a staggering third place in the 1975 Daytona 200. He then went on to Europe and on his first outing, at the Paul Ricard Circuit in France, won both the 250 cc and 350 cc championship rounds, leaving a massive 140,000 crowd to go home wondering if they could believe what they had seen. By the end of his first season in Europe, Cecotto had registered four wins in the 350 cc championships and walked away with the title. Agostini, the defending 350 cc champion, managed only one first place in the title round—at Spain, where Cecotto came second.

Cecotto's racing career had been nurtured on Yamahas. This familiarity, combined with an abundance of natural talent and a certain measure of good fortune, was enough to eclipse Agostini's vastly superior experience. It is possible that the Italian found the transition from the 4-stroke MV to the 2-stroke Yamaha more difficult than he cared to admit. The change in power characteristics and the reduction in weight all served to trouble him and favour the precocious young pretender to his throne. Despite his mastery of the more demanding 500 cc, and the magnificent victory it brought him, in the 350 cc class Agostini was quite simply humbled and outpaced.

Johnny Cecotto, the 19-year-old Venezuelan who hit the big time in 1975. At Daytona (left), he cut his way through from the back of the 65 rider pack to an astonishing third place.

A contrast in styles: the fluid grace of the master—Agostini aboard a 350 at Jarama, near Madrid . . .

. . . and a snappy gear change from Cecotto, the precocious newcomer, aboard another 350 cc Yamaha at Spa, Belgium.

The defending champion and the young pretender to his throne: Cecotto and Agostini together at the start of the 350 cc Grand Prix in Finland, 1975.

*Cecotto's first year in international racing was not all plain sailing . . .
Shortly before the Champion Classic Formula 750 cc race at Assen, he
looks at his big Yamaha superbike (with mechanic Vince French, in
cap) . . .*

Things start to go wrong—at 100 plus mph.

He's in the ditch

A marshal wades in to help as the big Yamaha steams—and Cecotto fumes.

More helpers lift Cecotto onto the banking.

He's carried away on a stretcher.

The burnt-out 750 has been dragged clear.

Compare it now with the photograph taken just before the race . . .

What is left is wheeled away. The fairing looks in good shape, but underneath all is wreckage.

Developing the Heavyweights

To the outside world, 1973 to 1975 were years of high drama on the Grand Prix circuits, dominated by the personalities of Jarno Saarinen and Giacomo Agostini. But behind the scenes, at Yamaha's research department in Japan, these years were no less momentous. They saw the development of the 500 cc and 750 cc machines that were to provide these two riders with the sheer power they needed in order to trounce their rivals. Just as the sixties had seen Yamaha gain the advantage in the lightweight classes, culminating in Phil Read's magnificent double victory with the RA31A 125 cc and the RD05A 250 cc, so the seventies were to see them wrest supremacy in the heavyweight divisions—first with the OW20 YZR500, and then with the 700 cc production racer and the 750 cc OW31.

Although the 500 cc machine was not raced publicly until April 1973, at the Circuit Paul Ricard, it was on the drawing board at Yamaha's R & D Department in Japan as early as November 1971. Naito, who was to form a close alliance with Bill Ivy, Jarno Saarinen and Giacomo Agostini, was put in charge of the project, assisted by his designer Takasi Matsui. Significant developments in the use of lighter metals and water-cooling techniques, and expertise gathered in the lighter weight divisions of racing had given the men an unrivalled background knowledge. It hardly seemed possible that they could fail: and they did not.

They started work in November 1971 and the engine—two 250 cc's doubled up—was first run in July 1972. They could hardly wait to get it onto the track and in September—in great secrecy, with only six members of the racing department present—the new YZR500, code named OW20, was put through its paces. The veteran tester, Motohashi, Yamaha's longest-serving rider, climbed up onto the slim-line 500, tucked his legs around its narrow waist, and pointed it into the light wind that was taking any warmth out of the bright early morning. It motored like a dream. "It was perfect first time out," recalled Naito, "We got it right from the very beginning."

Giving 80 bhp at 10,000 rpm, this exquisitely balanced machine had a top speed of 165 mph. It incorporated Yamaha's new seven-port torque induction system, with V-type induction valves, as tested on the motocross machines. A considerable improvement on the conventional five-port system, the new design increased exhaust efficiency for higher output, and eliminated the possibility of a blow-back. The cylinder block was square, bore and stroke being 54 x 54 mm. Total displacement was 494 cc. The crankshaft pushed power to the idler shaft in the centre by helical gear.

There were six gears and four Mikuni VM34SC carburettors, with four cables connected to the end of the throttle grip. The igniter determining the inner rotor magnet and ignition timing was positioned at the other end of the clutch. The frame, changed from the usual feather bed type adopted by Yamaha, was given more rigidity. Monocross suspension—the first year it had been used—reacted well on bumpy, uneven surfaces, with long cushion strokes. To counter the enormous power, there was a double disc brake on the front and a single disc on the rear

There can be little doubt that had Saarinen lived through the 1973 season, he would have won the world 500 cc championships, by a substantial margin. Posthumously, he finished seventh. In a sad, final line to the confidential notes assembled by the racing department after every Grand Prix, an anonymous engineer wrote: "The name of Saarinen will be transmitted from generation to generation for a long time." It was an emotional departure from the usual clinical assessments of the team's progress.

As we have seen, for the remainder of the 1973 season, Yamaha withdrew from racing. Back to Japan went the machines that had given such a startling return for Yamaha's investment. The men at MV breathed a sigh of relief. Neither Agostini nor his team mate Phil Read,

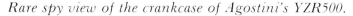

Rare spy view of the crankcase of Agostini's YZR500.

on what were then the world's most successful 500s, had been able to cope with the combination of Saarinen and the OW20. As Phil Read said: "With Saarinen, it was so incredibly quick, it was almost unbeatable. It certainly had the edge on the MVs, and Agostini and I had our work cut out just trying to keep up with it."

Although the YZR500 undoubtedly took the racing world by storm, it represented only one stage in Yamaha's rapid development of the racing heavyweights. There was more to come: specifically, the Production 750 cc racer—really a 700 cc, and later the OW31, the fastest machine ever made.

Midway through October 1973, Yamaha's policy makers met at Hamamatsu to discuss the need for an entry into Formula 750 racing, a class that was to be afforded the status of a world championship four years later. It took the board of directors hardly a day to agree unanimously that development of a 750 cc machine was essential. With their reputation as two-stroke manufacturers, Yamaha wanted a big capacity machine as flagship to their otherwise successful squadron. At a time when big, beefy motor cycles were hitting peaks of demand, world-wide publicity in this field was vital.

Developed by Naito and the team responsible for the 500, the 700 cc racer was breathtaking. Catalogued the TZ750, it was closely allied to the YZR500, modified to increase only the piston displacement. The four-cylinder engine, with seven ports and a suction system with a piston reed valve, consisted of two cylinder blocks. The bore and stroke was 64 x

Yamaha's test rack at Hamamatsu: proving ground for some of the most exciting developments ever seen in motor cycle technology.

54mm, similar to the TZ350. The engine was equivalent to that of TZ350 doubled up, and the crankshaft, piston and other parts were all similar to those of the TZ350, although these parts were not interchangeable.

The transmission system was similar to the YZR500's, using a gear in the middle of the crankshaft. Power went through a dry sump to the six-stage transmission through the driveshaft and the dry multi-plate clutch. The engine rotated counter-clockwise for forward direction, because power was transmitted through the idler shaft. The magneto, water pump and oil pump for the transmission—situated on the left side of the bike—were all driven through the idler shaft.

The primary stage reduction was reported to be 2,609 and the secondary stage 2,167. Gears had the following ratios: first, 1,722; second, 1,286; third, 1,042; fourth, 0,093; fifth, 0,808; and sixth, 0,750.

At 10,000 rpm the bike was said by technicians at the time to be giving better than 90 bhp and a speed in excess of 175 mph. In fact, it was capable of returning 130 bhp, but the tyres and chains could not stand the excessive strain this put on them and so Yamaha were forced to detune it.

It was typical of Yamaha that the bike was made to undergo a severe testing on race circuits before it was marketed. The Yamaha policy of using the track as a proving ground was still firmly upheld. In March 1974 Agostini, by now signed by Yamaha as a works rider to replace the

The TZ750 superbike production racer.

Gene Romero, known as 'the hard man' of racing and a Yamaha International rider. Scraping the fairing of his big Yamaha TZ750 on his way to victory at Daytona, 1975.

late Saarinen, won the Daytona classic in his first race aboard a 750 cc
racer. During the same race, Kanaya lapped the 157 kg bike at a
phenomenal rate, and was said by Yamaha personnel to have topped
190 mph in one section. Other riders included Akiyasu Motohashi—the
rider who had been the first to test the 500 cc machine, Kenny Roberts,
Gene Romero and Gary Fisher from Yamaha International. Indeed, at
Daytona that year there were 57 Yamahas out of 80 entries. After Daytona,
Agostini transported his powerful Yamaha back to Italy, stopping off at
Imola in the northern part of the country to collect the first prize.

The TZ750 was made available to the general public just before the
1974 Grand Prix season got underway. At around £4,000 ($8,000) each,
the ultra-fast superbikes were plainly a heavy investment for privately
entered riders—but if their skill matched the undoubted speed of the
latest flyers, they were assured a reasonably quick return for their money.
One such rider was Jack Findlay, the Milan-based Australian, and one of
the sport's genuine nice guys. At the age of 41, Findlay bought one of the
big Yamahas with the last of his reserve cash. With little or no help from
anyone, but with a good deal of restraint and clever riding in order to
protect his bike from needless wear and tear, he eased himself to the top of
the list of contenders, to win the unofficial title for the FIM Formula
750 cc.

The FIM, the controlling body of motor cycle sport, were loath to grant

*The TZ750 in action at the Champion Classic at Assen, 1976, ridden by
the Spaniard Victor Palomo. He won the race and the still unofficial
Formula 750 championship.*

the big formula an official world ranking. Even before Yamaha introduced the faster OW31 machinery, this seemingly archaic collection of legislators did their best to arrest the enormous interest aroused by the TZ750. Their attitude seemed totally at odds with the outside world—at a time when 750 cc racing was gripping the imagination of the racing fraternity. Thus, after a long career of hard-fought competitive racing, with success always tantalizingly just out of reach, Findlay failed to gain an official world title. With his limited resources, he was unable to repeat his success the following year, when the Spaniard Victor Palomo on a private Yamaha won the still unofficial title from the American Gary Nixon—the Kawasaki team rider, and the Suzuki GB rider John Newbold. I have always thought that when the FIM finally gave the 750 cc championship official world status in 1977, they should have made it retrospective, and honoured Findlay with a well-deserved accolade.

In October 1974 Yamaha produced an improved version of the TZ750. This was a full-size 748 cc model, with a top speed in excess of 175 mph. The works model, code named YZR750, weighed only 160 kg, 10 kg less than the production machine. Bore and stroke were 66.4 x 54 mm and it had a maximum horsepower of 110 in the works machine and 100 in the production bike, at around 10,000 rpm. The main area of improvement, other than in capacity, was in handling: the works machines were fitted with the new monocross suspension at the rear end, though the production TZ750s retained the standard suspension.

The improved 750 was water-cooled with seven-port induction and

The YZR750 works racer. Unlike the TZ750, this was fitted with monocross suspension.

four cylinders in line. Fuel tank capacity was 24 litres. The four mufflers were arranged in a one-up three-down layout in a bid to reduce the width of the power unit and help with better handling and reliability.

Yamaha had also been working hard to produce a street superbike at a viable price. But this project, codenamed the GX750, was ill-fated. The company found it impossible to meet the strict controls on emission enforced in the United States, and still provide an adequate level of performance. This, naturally, was the company's principal concern. Any bike that big just had to deliver the goods. And so, reluctantly, the GX750 scheme had to be shelved.

This period also saw improvements in Yamaha's lightweight racing models. The works YZR350 weighed in at only 97 kg, compared to the 115 kg of the production model, with a top speed in excess of 150 mph. This in-line, water-cooled twin had a bore and stroke of 64 x 54 mm. Maximum power was said to be 65 hp at 9500 rpm in the works model, and 58 hp in the production machine. The fuel tank held 23 litres. It was this machine that gave Johnny Cecotto his first world title in 1975, in the 350 cc championship series.

The works YZR250 also weighed 97 kg; 18 kg lighter than the production TZ250. It hammered out 53 hp at 10,000 rpm, compared to the TZ250's 48 hp. The top speed was in excess of 140 mph. Like the 350 cc machine, it was six speed with a dry multiple disc plate clutch, with disc brakes front and back. Bore and stroke were 54 x 54 mm and the

The 350 cc works machine, the YZR350, which gave Johnny Cecotto his first world title in 1975.

The TZ250 production racer: used by just about every lightweight championship challenger.

The production 350 cc racer, the TZ350.

carburettors were VM34SC, with the fuel-oil mix set at 15:1. As with the 350, the fuel tank capacity was 23 litres.

In 1975 Yamaha decided that the problems of emission and pollution had become so great that they would have to withdraw from full factory-supported road racing in the following season. Instead, they diverted much of their race budget towards experiment and investigation. They announced their decision officially on 5 November 1975—but by then they were well on the way to completing their small yet specular legacy for the racing world: the 750 cc OW31, the fastest motor bike ever produced.

From the outside, there was little to distinguish the OW31 from the TZ750s that had gone through the 1975 campaign. But in fact the frame was the centrepiece of a vast improvement in performance. It was a development of the monoshock skeleton on the 500 cc machine, used by Agostini to win back the world championship in 1975. Lighter materials had been used to give a considerable saving in weight—as much as 20 kg had been slimmed off, reducing the overall weight to 136 kg. Some 5 kg were saved on the frame alone. Alloy was used extensively on the tubing and bolts that held the accessories, more magnesium was used in the engine and almost every nut and bolt was made of titanium.

Internal modifications were few—great care had to be taken to ensure that there was no infringement of the homologation rules for Formula 750 racing. Thus like the TZ750 it was an in-line, four cylinder two stroke, with seven port induction and water cooled. Bore and stroke were 66.4 x 54 mm, and capacity 748 cc. The fuel tank held 24 litres. There was a six-speed gearbox with a dry multi-plate clutch. The carburettor was a VM34SC, and the fuel-oil mix was 15:1. Suspension was telescopic at the front, and monocross, swinging arm type at the rear. There were double disc brakes on the front, and a single disc on the rear.

The shape of the ports was modified, but the cylinder barrels were of the same casting. Improved exhausts were fitted integrally. These modifications were to result in staggering acceleration figures and vastly improved handling. The knack, really, was to reduce the weight without making the bike too fragile. In fact, Yamaha felt that they could have made it even lighter, although its endurance capability might have suffered thereby.

These dietry engineering techniques added nothing to the top end speed already achieved by the TZ750. Indeed, Yamaha officials told me that the new mufflers which had to be used in the early days of decibelization probably clipped a little off the flat-out performance. But in terms of acceleration and staying power the OW31 was supreme.

Yamaha made just five of these new machines, and they gave them to a select band of faithful servants—men like Kenny Roberts, the laconic Californian who was prepared to let his racetrack performance do all the talking for him; Johnny Cecotto, hailed a wonder boy at nineteen when he took the world 350 cc title from Giacomo Agostini in his first season of Grand Prix racing; Hideo Kanaya, the Yamaha factory rider who was one of the most valued support riders in the business; Steve Baker, who was to ride the Canadian Yamaha; and, finally, Agostini, fifteen times champion of the world.

When the OW31 was first unleashed upon an unsuspecting racing world, only Agostini failed to turn up: the race organizers were not prepared to pay him any appearance money or expenses, and so he refused to make the long, expensive journey from Italy. For the arena chosen by Yamaha for unveiling their legacy was Daytona—1976.

The Legacy of Five

It was late February 1976 and Barry Sheene was sweating profusely in the steaming heat of Daytona. His face was drained, his long hair matted with perspiration and his leathers crumpled and damp. His black, full-face helmet, bearing his lucky number seven and a cheery Donald Duck cartoon, dangled between his knees at the limits of its chin straps. He was looking into it deeply, as if searching for answers in the darker shadows of a crystal ball.

All his natural Cockney cheeriness had ebbed away. Shaking his head with more resignation than is normally in his nature, he turned to Merv Wright, the team manager of Suzuki GB: "Bloody 'ell, Merv, them Yamahas are about 10 miles an hour quicker than we are."

This had been plain for all to see at the practice session when, at last, the record entry of the 134 riders contesting the Daytona 200 Mile classic had been out on the twists and slopes of the speedbowl. This session was the race within a race, an opportunity to fill your opponents with so much respect for your skill and your machine's performance that they might suffer the erosions of apprehension and, doubting their own capabilities, allow you to snatch an advantage.

There must have been some 400 helpers, hangers-on and officials watching from behind the fencing at the nearest infield. Munching foot-long hot-dogs and chilling their stomachs with canned Budweiser and Schlitz, they waited for the familiar yowls of the big two-strokes to come within earshot. The men practising for the first international race of 1976, and for the £7000 ($14,000) prize that went with it, headed in an untidy bunch through the winding infield towards the terrifying heights of the slopes of the speedbowl. Chests were pressed hard onto petrol tanks, heads ducked down behind screens, and chins, wary of the uneven almost corrugated surface, tucked onto the sponge padding behind the flick-open filler caps.

On the long straight, after the first left and first right turns into the infield, the Yamahas accelerated away from Sheene's Suzuki as if it was marking time and they were being shot from a catapult. It was possible to see the distance between them streching by yards even as they approached the banking of the 3.87 mile circuit. Daytona's banking is impossible to scale on hands and knees. With 31 degrees of angle, the effect of two G-forces shoves the riders' heads deep into their shoulders, making eyeballs bulge as if struck by some malfunction of the thyroid gland. Here Sheene was passed as if he were parked.

One after the other, the four Yamahas swept past Sheene, battering his confidence and leaving him bewildered, frustrated and downright angry. Fighting off the pain of an injured leg, with knee ligaments hardly strong enough to keep his foot on the gear shift or get it back onto the peg, he was in an anxious state as the all-revealing practice session drew to a close. He felt that he had been let down by Suzuki and raged that as soon as Daytona was over he was going to Japan to stir them into action.

It was a sight that few watching in the 80-degree mid-morning heat could fully grasp. Sheene was having his first competitive outing for six months following his leg injury. He was the Suzuki team's number one hope, reputed to be earning at least £50,000 ($100,000) a season. He was also thought to be aboard one of the quickest 750s in the race and his fierce determination made him a formidable contestant. Yet the Suzuki, in keeping with all the other machines that were not brand-new, lightweight Yamahas, had been outdistanced so comprehensively that it was embarrassing. One could only feel sorry that Sheene's immense skill should be upstaged by the excessive speed of his four main rivals.

Sheene's backers argued a line of superior reliability—but he wanted more speed. He knew he could match anybody in a battle of wits and skill and no-one doubted his bravery. He was convinced that horse power held the key to Daytona. And one brand name, Yamaha, seemed to have the monopoly on that score. Suzuki, so much a 500 cc force during the previous season's world title campaign, had been caught resting on their laurels. Their 750 simply failed to come up to the Cockney's demands and ambitions for it.

After the practice session, the young Londoner leant dejectedly against the personalized Rolls-Royce Silver Shadow he had been loaned by the company's American agents. He estimated that he was travelling upwards of 176 mph when Kenny Roberts, crouched low and looking comfortable on the new 750 Yamaha, *sped* past him. "I thought I'd stopped," he added gloomily, "I nearly got off to see what was wrong." It is an old racing cliche but it has rarely been used more graphically.

There was silence all round, almost an embarrassed hush. To escape any silly answers, mechanics got their heads into the innards of engines or aimlessly polished bits and pieces that had already been cleaned. Even the other two members of the Suzuki GB team, John Newbold and the normally happy-go-lucky John Williams from Liverpool, were quiet. Merv Wright clicked his tongue and said, somewhat sardonically, "I reckon we must have the first 200 miles an hour bike up against us. I'll get the stopwatch on the Yams next time out." Sheene merely shook his head in disbelief.

In the slightly hysterical atmosphere of Daytona between practice and race day, it became a game to attempt to uncover the facts of what had been going on in Japan. There were stories, often dismissed as wild rumour, that average Yamaha factory test riders had been timed at a phenomenal speed of 187 mph on a Japanese track. In the event, because of the different gearing requirements for an all-round performance at Daytona, the four Yamahas did not *officially* reach that mark. I stress the word *officially*. Although trackside radar recorders registered nothing quicker than 182mph (by Roberts), other riders claimed that the

Kenny Roberts and his super-fast OW31 in the pits at Daytona, 1976. Seen here with his team manager Kel Carruthers, the former 250 cc world champion, who went to California to work for Yamaha International as an engineer and development expert.

Phil Read racing his privately entered 750 cc Yamaha, tuned by Don Vesco, at Daytona, 1976.

machines were going much faster through other sections of the track, which were bare of timing devices.

Yamaha may have pulled out of any official backing on a direct support basis, but their shadow was looming over the other riders as surely as if they had turned up with their usual £15,000 ($30,000) budget for a Grand Prix race. The four machines qualified in the first four places for the Daytona 200, and would, no doubt, have had fifth spot had Agostini made the trip. The clear favourite, Roberts, qualified at 111.456 mph; Steve Baker was next at 110.309 mph, then Kanaya at 109.271 mph and then Cecotto at 109.099 mph. Sheene came way down in seventeenth position, behind many riders of inferior ability, with a speed of only 106.108 mph to show for all his efforts. If any sceptics had any lingering doubts about Yamaha's ability to make a clean sweep at Daytona, and at the following international 750 cc races, they had only to look at that qualifier's grid.

More than 130,000 motor cycle fans poured into Daytona's concrete strip of hotels as the big day neared. Yamaha had no problems—the young hero, Sheene, had enough to share around.

He had fallen out with Phil Read, the deposed 500 cc world champion, and his dearest friend of 1975. No longer supported by MV Agusta, the Italian team he had served so well the previous two years, Read had bought himself a 750 Yamaha which was being prepared for him by Don Vesco, one of America's finest tuners. At Daytona the two of them hardly exchanged a glance. Read's opinion—and he was as outspoken as ever—was that Sheene was making more publicity mileage out of his 175 mph crash at Daytona the year before, than out of any real achievements. And, indeed, compared to Read's record, Sheene's was non-existent.

Then there was his troublesome leg. In an effort to get it put right, Sheene flew 250 miles to Miami to see the specialist who had originally cared for him after his crash. In the meantime, manager Wright had Sheene's mechanic, Don MacKay, build a three-inch block of foam rubber onto the seat, to help ease the pain. Sheene arrived back still limping. Dr Don Nevaiser had diagnosed inflamed tendons and damaged ligaments. He had given him jabs to draw off fluid and fixed him up with some painkilling pills.

His problems with his brand new machine were not confined to its lack of speed. As well as being slower than the two one-year-old Suzukis his team mates were using, it was beset by mechanical failures: a cylinder gasket blew, it sprang out of gear and the water pump drive failed. It is a great tribute to Wright's patience and MacKay's skill that between them they put the ailing Suzuki into good order in time for the gruelling 200-mile race.

With all these problems, who could blame Sheene for feeling that Suzuki GB might just as well pack up and go home? "It's bloody embarrassing," he told Wright, "I've no chance the way things are. You should see them Yamahas go! Jeez . . ."

On the opposite side of the complex of garages, Kel Carruthers, cool and composed in the familiar yellow and black colours of the American Yamaha team, went about the business of looking after Roberts' machine, squeezing out of it as much demoralizing power as was prudent.

"The new Yamaha is probably only about 6 miles an hour quicker than Sheene's Suzuki," one of the Yamaha mechanics told me, "but I suppose every single mile an hour over 175 mph must seem to be amazing—especially when you're on two wheels."

Before the race, the battle had been seen as a straightforward issue: Sheene's Suzuki versus the Yamahas of Roberts, Cecotto, Agostini—if he had bothered to turn up, and Baker, with Kanaya handily placed if not ahead of the Londoner. But with the arrival of the new Yamahas, it boiled

The two men who dominated the Daytona 200, 1976: Roberts and Cecotto. Their fierce duel was ended only by Robert's forced retirement with tyre problems.

down to a contest between the men who were fortunate enough to own one. Even though the new Yamahas were not reaching the 190 mph mark that Kanaya had achieved on the TZ750 the year before, the margin was still wide enough to cause widespread unrest and consternation.

Sheene was understandably uptight, and would remain so right up to the last minute, until the American anthem had been sung, until Evel Knievel, glittering like a pawn shop window with masses of heavy gold rings, bracelets and a watch as big as a frying pan, had completed his publicity rounds of a grid that could have done without it, until the starter's flag had fluttered.

It was plain that Sheene had to be patient in the early stages of the race, for amidst the accompanying clamour and thunder the four aces in Yamaha's pack made all the running, headed by Cecotto and Roberts who were continually swopping the lead. But soon that instinctive determination that separates him from the ordinary began to refuel his effort and sharpen the raw edges of his courage. It was to take him into third place and almost to second before his rear chain broke, when he had only three of the 52 laps to go.

The eyes of the American ace: Kenny Roberts at Daytona, 1976.

The race was completely dominated by the monoshock Yamaha—
until, one by one, they were picked off by tyre failure, victims of their own
superior power and acceleration. Baker went out on lap 10, his engine
seized. Cecotto and Roberts maintained the lead for the first 35 laps, rarely
more than a few yards apart. They were enmeshed in a tremendous high
speed duel, leaning hard on each other in the corners, fighting over every
yard of the track with the greatest ferocity. They pit-stopped together and
stayed in each other's shadows until Roberts' Yamaha developed a
terrifying habit of sliding and weaving. He slowed and headed for the pits
once more. When he pulled up alongside his team manager Kel
Carruthers, the pit crew could see that the rear Goodyear tyre was
punctured and almost worn out. They set to work to change the complete
wheel, as Roberts yelled: "I'm using the same tyre as Cecotto—why the
hell's mine worn out and his hasn't?" His frustration was
understandable.

Kanaya also fled to the pits to change his rear tyre—another big
Goodyear slick—and still Cecotto, oblivious to all the drama, piled on
the pressure and increased his lead. But his tyre, too, was being churned
into a capricious state. As it tried to trap him into wicked slides, the
Goodyear experts in the pits urged that he should be called in before
disaster overtook him. Scenting a great victory, Cecotto spurned the brief
respite offered by the pits, risking all in a stubborn gamble to make it back
to the chequered flag ahead of everybody else.

On the last lap the South American's machine, despite being eased off, was still weaving perilously close to the edge of adhesion. But he made it back, into the arms of a massive crowd of excited supporters, for a brave and memorable, if foolhardy win. Kanaya finished in seventh place and Roberts, the pre-race favourite who had for the third time found himself out of luck, managed to get into ninth position. It was a rather glum

Cecotto in Victory Lane, Daytona, 1976.

*Cecotto on his way to victory
at Daytona, after a brave ride
with the tyres of his OW31
worn down to the canvas.*

Roberts who said, amid all the celebrations, "That was one race I really did want to win." There was little celebrating amongst the Goodyear men.

In their first outing, the new OW31 Yamahas had achieved a magnificent double bill: Cecotto's record breaking first place—52 laps in 1 hour 52 minutes 47 seconds, at a speed of 108.77 mph, and a lap record taken by Roberts in the qualifying round. It had been firmly established that the new machines were light years ahead of their rivals in handling and outright performance. At Daytona, a circuit that relied almost entirely on horse power, no other machine had a hope of catching them until the freak intervention of tyre failure.

In quick succession, the Yamaha bounty hunters collected all the

Superb action shot of Kenny Roberts, his knee scraping the ground below the level of his ankle. He is wearing the number one plate as the top man of American racing.

major prizes in the following 750 cc races. Inside the first month of the 1976 racing season, the OW31 had earned for Steve Baker a phenomenal £20,000 ($40,000). He won the Venezuelan 200-miler, and then repeated his success in Italy at the prestigious Imola 200, beating an assembly of the world's finest riders—Agostini, Roberts and Sheene. He was beaten into second place at the Moto Journal 200, held at the Paul Ricard circuit in France, but his victor was another OW31 protagonist—Johnny Cecotto, showing full value for the £200,000 ($400,000) a year salary paid him by four sponsors.

At Easter, Baker and Kenny Roberts, his laconic countryman, arrived in England as part of the 8-man American team contesting the 1976 Transatlantic Superbike Trophy. It is estimated that it costs £65,000 to

For the second year running, Cecotto came to grief in the Formula 750 Champion Classic at Assen, Holland . . .

Here he walks away without a glance over his shoulder at the burning wreckage of his OW31.

stage this series, £25,000 of it being the cost off bringing the American team over to Britain. At the 1976 event, more than 150,000 people were to have the unforgettable experience of watching the new Yamahas perform on three tracks of varying quality—Brands Hatch near London, Mallory Park in the Midlands, and the pastoral Oulton Park in Cheshire.

In fact, Britain, with Phil Read as captain and Barry Sheene, Yamaha's old enemy, as the top home team performer, crushed the American challenge. But, with four victories to his credit, there was no doubt that the man and the machine of the whole series were Steve Baker and his red and black striped OW31. Roberts won one race, but was on the whole unable to cope with the immense power and troublesome lightness of his machine, falling twice at Oulton Park. This provided the background to

A 110 mph power slide: Kenny Roberts on the 750 cc twin cylinder dirt track Yamaha, in a 1 mile event in the USA.

one of the most amazing sights I have ever seen at any race meeting. Urging his machine out of a slow corner, Roberts showed rather more ambition than he could control, with calamitous results. His bike stuck its nose up in the air and almost somersaulted over his shoulder. Baker was lying just behind Roberts, and saw the whole thing happen. Despite such a graphic warning, he proceeded to hurtle his OW31 out of the same bend—and then wheelied past Mick Grant's 750 cc Kawasaki along the pit straight, in front of a jam-packed grandstand. At that moment, Baker was travelling at around 100 mph *on the back wheel*.

The OW31s' triumphs continued. Agostini took the laurels at Mettet and then again at the Norisring. Baker won twice on American soil—at Loudon and at Laguna Seca, California, and then recrossed the Atlantic to walk away with the Race of the Year at Mallory Park. Back in the USA, Roberts won the Riverside race. Finally, at the Indonesian Grand Prix, Hideo Kanaya—the last of the five men to be awarded an OW31, took the title.

I asked Steve Baker for his opinion of the OW31. "The OW? That's some bike," he replied. "It's so unbelievably quick. It's the fastest bike ever made, there's no doubt about that. I'd say it would do 190 miles an hour. It's the best bike I've ever ridden. It handles superbly, gets the front wheel up if you're not careful, but goes like a jet. It's a good deal lighter than standard 750 cc works racing models. And through 1976 it brought me a lot of success; it made it the best money-earning year I'd ever had in racing."

The legacy of five that Yamaha bequeathed to the racing world for 1976 was undeniably the most impressive assembly of motor cycle machinery the sport had ever seen. In one dramatic season, the OW31s had demonstrated their enormous potential, and swelled the bank balances of each of their five fortunate riders.

Return to Grands Prix

1977 saw Yamaha return to official works support for Grand Prix racing. The 750 cc class had at last been awarded Grand Prix status by the FIM, and Yamaha were also anxious to reclaim what was perhaps the biggest prize of all—the 500 cc championship.

Although 1976 had been a truly victorious year for the OW31, Yamaha's experience in the 500 cc class, albeit at one remove, verged on the disastrous. Like many other observers of the GP scene, I have always questioned the wisdom of their decision to withdraw direct factory support from that season's racing. I felt that in so doing, the company lost the initiative, putting the brakes on at a time when they should have been going full bore for success. For who can afford to lose a full season of the best kind of publicity a motor cycle manufacturer can get—winning Grands Prix?

Certainly Suzuki took full advantage of their major business rival's withdrawal. Barry Sheene may have failed to make any impression whatever upon the 750 cc formula internationally, but his 500 cc Suzuki took him almost effortlessly to his first world title. Opposing him on the big 500 cc Yamaha was Johnny Cecotto, racing under the banner of the Caracas-based team Venemotos. In Cecotto's immature hands, the machine that had been such a victorious mount for Agostini throughout 1975 was unable to put up any real challenge. Although it was generally considered to be quite capable of earning at least second place to the ultra-fast Suzuki, Cecotto simply did not seem to have the ability to get it to respond to its full potential.

When Cecotto returned to Caracas as the world 350 cc champion at the end of 1975, he had been greeted by a crowd of 20,000 at the airport. Thousands more gave him a rapturous welcome as he drove through the streets of the city in an open car, in presidential style. He was given a contract from a jeans company, another from a firm that sold sun-glasses, yet another from a cigarette company. A clothing company paid him £25,000 ($50,000) to wear their gear. His annual earnings reached more than £250,000 ($500,000). The Venezuelan President, Carlos Andres Perez, feted him at a televized banquet—and Venezuelan motor cycle sales trebled.

MV Agusta tried to sign him. He bought himself a £10,000 Ferrari—and burnt the clutch out the first day he drove it. Soon he was asking £7000 ($14,000) appearance money and, at times, getting it. But by the middle of the 1976 season his winning streak had faded. It seemed that he just could not handle the 500 cc Yamaha. Too often he was left sprawling in the road while Barry Sheene, the man he was trying desperately to catch, disappeared into the distance.

He became pompous, a prima donna who seemed to bear no resemblance to the happy-go-lucky character he had been only 12 months before. His organization was chaotic. Often he would turn up for a Grand Prix without bothering to confirm entries; he would be allowed in only

Cecotto with Dunlop master technician Tony Mills at the Paul Ricard Circuit, France. His mechanics said that his engineering know-how was limited to demands for new tyres.

because of his status, without hotel bookings or arrangements for paddock parking space. Venemotos became known as Team Chaos.

Unlike Agostini, who had persuaded Yamaha to make four ratios for each of the six gears on the 500 cc machine, Cecotto had little or no engineering know-how. He was unable to give his team any feedback. Some of his mechanics said that he was limited to demands for them to change the tyres. They were frustrated because none of them seemed to be able to get across to him the fact that he should be able to help them solve other problems, where as much as 2 seconds a lap could be saved. Instead, he argued that the Yamaha simply was not competitive.

The failure in communication meant that he was often forced to ride an ill-prepared machine, and was pressed into unnecessary risks in a bid to make up for shortfalls in performance. Naturally enough, he made every effort to compensate for these defects by sheer riding brilliance. There was no doubt that he had plenty of that, but on its own it was not nearly enough to give him the advantage that could so well have been his even before he fired up the machine. His bravery was also unquestioned—as he demonstrated on the OW31 at Daytona. But while he still was capable of flashes of brilliance, his consistency had disappeared. Compared to the 350 cc races, the 500 cc division was tougher. It became an issue of hard acceleration and heavy braking, and he could not cope.

In mid-season, just before the Dutch Grand Prix, Cecotto's mentor Andres Ippolito, who had guided him on his way to his 350 cc world title, withdrew him from the 500 cc championship series. Ippolito, a Yamaha importer in Caracas and the power behind Venemotos, felt that the £250,000 a year youngster was putting himself too much at risk, and had crashed his machine too often. (It was also rumoured that Team Chaos were running out of spares)

Cecotto's withdrawal, and Phil Read's highly publicized domestic problems which caused him to retire from the series at Belgium, made Barry Sheene's task that much easier. And on July 25, 1976, at Anderstorp, Sweden, he clinched the championship for Suzuki and won his first world title.

Thus, at the close of the 1976 season, Yamaha seemed to have been pushed back into the shadows of the Grand Prix scene. But even as Suzuki put yet more gloss on their sales pitch, with the current 500 cc champion to promote, top executives at Yamaha were planning a return to full works support for Grand Prix racing. The two world stars chosen to carry the Yamaha banner through 1977 could hardly have been more different in character: Steve Baker, the Chaplinesque American, and Johnny Cecotto, the precocious Latin. Agostini, the man who had served Yamaha so well, was also pencilled in on the secret list, for factory support through a dealer in his homeland, Italy.

It was a strange pairing of talents: two men who had gone in opposite directions throughout the preceding season. It also seemed strange to many observers that, for the first time, Yamaha had not included any European riders in their team. Yamaha's budget for attending each race was in the region of £20,000 ($40,000). With a full season of Grands Prix, and vital international prestige events to contest, the investment was considerable, and maximum media exposure was naturally essential. For this purpose, Baker and Cecotto were ideal, covering the whole of the American market between them.

Sadly, this policy also meant the break up of the old familiar teams of mechanics who had become as well known as the riders on many of the world's circuits. They now went their separate ways—men like Nobby Clarke, who had been on the championship scene since 1961, Iain Mackay, and Vince French, at the time a very disappointed man after his frustrating experiences with Cecotto's Venemotos team.

Inevitably, Yamaha's choice of Cecotto was questioned by many, both inside and outside the company. But they reasoned that if he could be motivated to reach his full potential, there was not a rider in the world who could better him. It was a calculated gamble. If it paid off, the

Barry Sheene's world-beating 500 cc Suzuki, the RG500, which took him to his first world title in 1976.

resultant publicity for this second-generation Italian superstar would be boundless, and Yamaha would reap their rewards in two particularly promising markets—South America and Italy.

The question remained: after his disastrous season in 1976, how much interest did he still have? Could he recapture the greatness he had shown so spectacularly in 1975? In my view, Cecotto had become his own worst enemy. Self-control would have been the answer, but the good life, the girls and the fast cars had over-ruled that crying need. There had been no hard-line manager to force him to come to terms with the responsibilities that accompanied his remarkable break-through—only Ippolito to guide, rather than coerce. Under his new masters—the tough and highly experienced personnel from the racing factory in Japan, a high level of professionalism would be demanded of Cecotto for 1977, and a positive response to the discipline they were bound to exert upon him. His personal finances certainly benefited immeasurably from the trust Yamaha placed in him. After spending a good deal of the winter of 1976-77 searching out possible sponsors, he stood poised to collect what promised to be the richest payout ever taken by a professional road racer—something approaching £300,000 ($600,000).

Steve Baker, the other name to be emblazoned on Yamaha's Grand Prix machinery, was an entirely different proposition. Quiet, unfussy and totally dedicated: that was the mark of the 23-year-old American. His springy hair, which looked as if it had 25,000 volts shooting through it, topped a sparse frame that hardly seemed strong enough to hold up a 250, let alone a 750 cc machine. Looking distinctly owlish in his rounded glasses, with a high pitched voice, Baker seemed anything but a racer—until he climbed aboard the fearsome OW31. Then he was virtually unbeatable, as he had proved so often during the 1976 season. His determination on the track was quite terrifying. The big OW31, an absolute monster of blurring speed and blow-torch acceleration, held no fears for him, even though his lightness gave him a distinct problem when it came to trying to hold down its front wheel under heavy twists of the throttle.

Baker had started racing in 1971, as a raw novice of 18, in Vancouver, Canada. Becoming the top junior rider in America, his uncanny talent was first noticed by Bob Work, the race director of Yamaha Canada. This was the beginning of a long and close friendship between the two men. Work gave Baker a contract to race for the Yamaha team in Canada and he spent the next few years commuting from his home in Washington to Canadian race tracks. Baker is unusual in that he has never been on the breadline, like so many other professional racers: his tremendous talent made sure of that.

It was not until early summer 1976 that he really arrived on the European scene, when he won the difficult and arduous Imola 200. "That was just fantastic," he recalled. "Bob and I had so much trouble in just getting the bike down to Imola. I don't suppose too many people gave us a chance of even finishing there, let alone winning the race." Baker and Work had set themselves up in the Amsterdam workshops of Yamaha and were waiting for the OW31 to arrive. It was late, very late. At last it arrived, almost at the last minute, and Bob Work immediately got down to the job of getting it into race trim. He sweated over it all day and got the intricate jig-saw of the engine together—only to discover a fault which meant that it all had to be taken apart again. He snatched a sandwich and a coffee, and then began to reassemble the machine. It took him all night—and the rest of the following day. With time running out, he loaded the bike into a truck and drove it non-stop from Amsterdam to Imola, south of Milan. "It was the most incredible spate of work I've seen", said Jerry Wood, Yamaha's workshop manager. "He must have worked non-stop for 50 hours. And at the end he was still cheerful, still happy. And he wasn't a bit worried about setting off straightaway for Imola. How can you beat that sort of enthusiasm? Impossible. What a tremendous guy he is. No wonder he and Baker hit it off so well—they're two of a kind."

At Silverstone in summer 1976, the Japanese rider Takazumi Katayama let his enthusiasm get the better of him, checking the Australian Jack Findlay and then causing Baker to tumble. White-faced and angry, Baker managed to contain himself although he was clearly shaken by the experience. It took a great deal of effort from Work for him to prise out of Baker what had really happened. When he got his answer, the mechanic was ready to storm off in pursuit of the aggressor. A few minutes later, Katayama, smiling and apparently unconcerned, arrived at the pit box to apologize. "Ah, but that's racing . . ." he murmured (which, of course, it was not). Work had to be dissuaded from any action on the spot—while Baker, still prepared to show some grace, refused to lodge an official complaint. "That's just the way he is," said a friend. "He would have forgotten the incident the day after, on the premise that it's not worth worrying about what happened yesterday. He just wants to get on with the job and not have lunatics getting him to fall off. Usually, he's so quick they can't get near enough anyway!"

I remember talking to Baker about his prospects for the 1977 Grand Prix season, on one of his many transatlantic trips from his home in Washington."I haven't ridden a 500 cc too much," he admitted blithely, "but I guess it won't be too big a step to switch from the 750 to the 500." The fact that he would be drawn up against Barry Sheene did not seem to trouble him overmuch. "Barry's got more experience than me, sure. And he's raced and won on tracks I haven't even seen. But he doesn't worry me. I'm a quick learner—maybe it's because I put everything I've got into concentrating on the job. And once I've got some experience, then Europe will be just like everywhere else. I can only get better with experience on the Grand Prix scene—and there are plenty of people around who will be happy to help me out." Baker's greatest ambition had always been to ride in Europe and make a bid for the world titles. Back in 1976, before he knew that Yamaha were going to award him a works contract, he confided: "I'd love to have a go. I still think the finest riders in the world are here in Europe and it really has to be something to beat them all and become world champion. If I can get Yamaha thinking my way, who knows? It might just come off."

Baker had no illusions about the responsibilities that accompanied a works contract—in this, a striking contrast to Cecotto, his partner to be. "I feel you have to try hard all the time. You can't let up or someone else will have you. I've been a professional racer all my working life, aside from a short time as a mechanic, so I know what it's all about. I know the risks and understand the responsibilities when you work for a factory like Yamaha. Their investment is gigantic and they need people with a responsible attitude. Otherwise it's all for nothing."

Just before Christmas 1976, Baker and Cecotto were summoned from their homes in Washington and Bologna to join the rest of the team in Japan and to meet the press. While they were there, they were fitted for the newly improved 500 cc OW20 and 750 cc OW31. Everybody in the racing world assumed that the riders would be signing their contracts while they were at Hamamatsu. But with typical stealth, Yamaha had completed these formalities back in October, long before anybody knew for certain that the company was officially interested in bringing the two men together for 1977.

The success of the OW31 the previous season had been met by a resounding clamour from riders throughout the world, all itching to get their hands on one of these all-conquering four cylinder two strokes. For 1977, the company decided to market a limited number of OW31 replicas (the works machines were known within the company as OW310s, for obvious reasons!). 20 machines were allotted for the European market, and 50 for the rest of the world. For the first time, they were all fitted with

Yamaha's two main contenders for 1977—the YZR750 . . .

monocross suspension, which had previously been restricted to works models.

In Amsterdam, Rodney Gould pored for hours over a list of the names of those men who might do the machines justice. The company had decided to make them available only to a select band of men, those who had proved themselves capable of handling the OW's immense power. Even at £7000 ($14,000) a time, including a spares kit, Gould received plenty of enquiries—by phone, letter or even in person, from hopeful riders who felt they could sway his opinion in their favour.

Mitsui, the London-based Japanese marketing company who handled the sales of Yamahas in Britain, were allotted five OW31s. Two of these were made available to Barry Sheene. An earlier difference of opinion had left Yamaha's top executives in a state of some disenchantment with the young Londoner, and thus they were not prepared to *give* him two of the most sought-after machines in the world. However, if he had bought one at the going price of £6571.63, Yamaha would have been prepared to loan Sheene one other, with the proviso that he broke free from Suzuki and gave Yamaha exclusive advertising rights. Choosing carefully from a queue of sponsors, Sheene finally decided to stay with Suzuki and concentrate on a defence of his 500 cc title, rather than attempting a takeover of the 750 cc.

Such was the reputation of the OWs that Tom Herron, the double TT winner in 1976, offered Allan Robinson of Mitsui £10,000 ($20,000) for a machine. "I was so upset when I had to turn him down", said Robinson. "Herron is a truly superb competitor, and deserved one. But there was nothing I could do. I could have sold twice, three times, what I was allotted. Everybody wanted one. But I must say we felt that not everybody who wanted one would be able to handle it." Robinson insisted that the

. . . and the YZR500.

men who did manage to buy an OW signed a contract promising that they would not resell their machines until October 1977—the end of the season. Resale values would have exceeded the original price set by Yamaha by thousands of pounds.

As the 1977 Grand Prix season got underway, it seemed that Yamaha were about to make a triumphant comeback. To most observers of the racing scene, the combination of the OW20 and OW31, Steve Baker and Johnny Cecotto, backed up by full factory support, seemed to present an awesome challenge—one that even Suzuki would be hard pressed to meet. But Grand Prix racing is never that predictable.

Young Johnny Cecotto scarcely had a chance to prove, one way or the other, whether he could sustain the high level of performance required of a world champion throughout the season. At the Austrian Grand Prix he crashed heavily, breaking an arm, and that put him completely out of action for the second and vital half of the 1977 season.

1977 was also the year in which Agostini's star finally faded. By the end of the season he found himself on top of the unwanted pile. Even his mechanics had lost confidence in him: when he was bad, they said, he blamed the machine; when he was good, which was not too often in those two years from 1975, it was all down to him. Perhaps the fight of the hungry man had left him; perhaps the edge that would take him right to the brink in a tussle for victory had been dulled by the knowledge that he

Cecotto and Agostini in the 500cc race at Silverstone, 1977.

did not really have to do it—he had more than enough money in the bank and 15 world titles to show for his glorious past.

The final blow to his chances of being retained by any manufacturer for future seasons must have come at the British Grand Prix at Silverstone, in August. He was down the field on what was probably the fastest machine in the 500 cc race—and struggling to fight off Kevin Wrettom, a virtual novice, who was after his ninth place on a 350 cc machine. There was a lot of headshaking that day as the most famous rider in motor cycling plodded up the pit straight. He was, quite cruelly, devaluing his own fine reputation.

Even worse, he was openly critical of Yamaha, the factory that had given him so much. Earlier on they had offered him a job as managing director of Yamoto, the Italian importers of Yamaha, as a token of their appreciation for all his efforts since they had signed him in 1974. It was a generous gesture, but Agostini turned it down.

It is not generally known that Yamaha are infinitely kind and helpful to men who have brought them recognition and success. Loyalty is rewarded; but lack of it brings instant retribution—not dramatic, explosive scenes of dismissal, rather a gentle easing out of the picture. This was now the case with Agostini, and there is rarely any coming back, as men like Phil Read would readily admit.

Just before Christmas 1977, Agostini finally announced that he was

Baker on his way to victory in the 250cc class at Daytona, 1977 . . .

quitting motor cycle racing for car racing. It was perhaps a timely move. Although nobody could understate his immense contribution to the sport, and to Yamaha in particular, the enduring truth about racers—that no one can afford to live on his reputation alone—had suddenly begun to hit home.

Agostini confided the news to me before anybody else, but when I wrote about it in my newspaper, the *Daily Mirror*, few people could really believe it. They had no way of knowing the tremendous struggle he had had to get rides for the 1978 season. He had tried to get the former British champion Steve Parrish's 1977 Suzukis, even though they had been put through a gruelling year of racing, by asking the German importers to use their influence. But when that bid failed, just like all the others, Agostini was left with little alternative but to call it a day and switch to motor cars. Although he had been under pressure for some time to make such a move, he did not want to go the way he was eventually forced to take.

It was a sad departure, and the sport lost a charismatic character who had brought excitement and colour into the lives of millions of enthusiasts all over the world.

It could not be argued that either Cecotto's or Agostini's performance on the track was totally unpredictable, though naturally Yamaha were disappointed. But in the case of Steve Baker, the out and out professional, Yamaha could be forgiven for wondering if fate itself was against them. From the beginning of the season, Baker had problems on the track. He was very shaken by an accident at Imola, Italy, where he saw his friend Pat Hennen take a terrible tumble; for a time, he was convinced that Hennen had been killed. Then he ran into a spell during which he could hardly stay on his machine. It seemed that every time he went out, he would screw himself up to superlative effort and then fall off. He was of course having to compete on circuits he had never seen before, and was facing Barry Sheene at the top of his form.

Few of us realized that he was also enduring dreadful personal problems. For Steve's sister, the girlfriend of his best friend and adviser,

. . . and aboard the 500cc Yamaha at Belgium—the series that Yamaha really wanted to win.

Bob Work, could not see eye to eye with his own fiancée. The two girls spent a great deal of time in conflict and eventually caused a split between Baker and Work, who had previously been quite inseparable. It all came to a head in Holland, before the Dutch TT, when the two men gave full vent to their tempers and almost erupted into a fist fight. The Japanese were amazed—to have women in the pits, interfering when so much was at stake, was unthinkable to them. The girls were banned from the pits and from the team's hotel, while Work readied himself to fly home to Canada in order to escape the awful scenes.

Despite such a disastrous start, Baker won the 750 cc Superbike championships—if he had not, he would hardly have dared to show his face in Europe again. In the 500 cc series, the title that Yamaha really wanted, he finished as runner up to Barry Sheene. But by then the damage had been done. My view is that Yamaha would have accepted the lesser honour of the 750 cc title quite happily, realizing that Baker was feeling his way in the championships, and would have been delighted to back him for 1978 and another crack at Sheene's all-conquering Suzuki. But the embarrassing issue of the squabbles between the two girls, and the fact that Baker had not taken firm action to stamp it out and send them home, overshadowed the natural ability and bravery he undoubtedly possesses. The rest of the racing world was taken by surprise when Yamaha announced that Baker would not be racing for them in 1978. Baker himself, I think, had been prepared for this decision way back in the middle of the season, when he realized that his efforts to capture the blue riband 500 cc title were not going to meet with success.

Specials: Kel Carruthers and Kenny Roberts

One name synonymous with success at Yamaha is Kel Carruthers and he, more than any other man, was the force behind the Kenny Roberts climb to the very pinnacle of Grand Prix achievement: three successive 500cc world titles.

When it came down to it, of course, Kenny had to get on the machine and ride it to victory. But whenever he went to the line, and long before it, he had the backing of Carruthers, one of the shrewdest brains in the sport.

The partnership might have been hewn from rock; for they are both tough characters with a will to win that is fearsome in its intensity and awe inspiring to those outsiders like me who occasionally are allowed to see it in full flow at close range, as at the pre-race planning stage when riders, engineers and mechanics all get-together to plot the pathway to a win.

Ideas, encouragement, schemes, tricks and tips pour from Carruthers in his matter-of-fact manner; precisely the attitude and forthrightness appreciated by Roberts, a single-minded character with no patience for posers or fools, and with a great deal of respect for the opinion of a seasoned expert like Kel.

There are, naturally, differences of opinion between them but their mutual respect has left little room for interlopers; they stood shoulder-to-shoulder in everything, each man totally appreciative of the other's value to him and to the team. And Carruthers was most certainly the power behind the Roberts' glitter. Whether Roberts would have been quite the force he turned out to be on the international scene without the guidance and support of the race-wise little Australian is a point worth debate.

For it could be argued that such a massive natural talent as Roberts would anyway have forced its way to the surface. But whether it would have done so with the same impact, had Carruthers not been on the scene, is questionable.

As it turned out the influential Carruthers saw in Roberts the very copy of his own determination to succeed; it was as if Roberts was the Carruthers alter-ego. And the Grand Prix contests from 1978 onwards were certainly enriched by the experience injected by Carruthers into the formidable skill possessed by Roberts.

With Kel's knowledge and Robert's long hunger for competition at its highest and toughest levels with no fear to make its progress even stumble, it was, I suppose, completely natural for him to accept Kel's counsel. And that's the way it was . . . with, of course, those questioning differences that generally led to an absolutely mutual satisfactory arrangement.

Carruthers was world champion in his mid-thirties when he clinched the 1969 250cc world championship for Benelli. And then, a year later on a Yamaha, he was runner-up to Rodney Gould in the 250cc title and second to Agostini in the 350cc class. It was the brand of credential that made a man worth listening to. But more, he had done it with great style and bravery - for the middle-weight classes were hard-fought and no quarters were given or asked.

He battled tigerishly with Agostini, Gould, and Jarno Saarinen and was always in the thick of the action. He won Daytona's 250cc race twice - 1970 and '71. And was second to Saarinen in the prestigious 200-miler in 1973. He was also the first foreign rider ever to win an American national event when he thundered home first in the Atlanta 125-mile event in 1971. And throughout it all he was building a reputation as a man to have on your side.

It is amazing that, despite his great gifts of bravery and skill, he did not win more than one world title. After Benelli found they could no longer support him following a crippling strike Carruthers decided that Europe had lost its racing charm and discovered to his great joy that he could live just as well on seven races a year in the USA as he had been doing on 30 on the other side of the Atlantic. His whole outlook on life changed; his lifestyle surely did, and meanwhile Kenny Roberts' future was starting to take on a new rosiness as the young American wiped out all the junior opposition at home. The experienced Carruthers and precocious Roberts were about to meet.

In mid-summer 1983, with Roberts five points adrift of the American wonderboy Freddie Spencer in the 500cc world championship, Kel like Kenny was pondering on his future - and made a fascinating re-run of his career as a power behind the scenes at Yamaha from his San Diego, California base. We sat for three hours, discussing the entire spectrum of his colourful relationship with Yamaha, his moods, his first meeting with Roberts, his efforts on the engineering front and his views of the Grand Prix scene. This is his story . . .

"I raced for Benelli in 1969 and was happy to do it again the following year. But around Christmas time I got a letter from them that dropped the bottom out of my life right then - there had been a three months strike and they wouldn't be able to give me any bikes because four-cylinder 250s had been banned so they were going to have to move up into the 350/500cc class. They were very sorry, they said, because they had Renzo Pasolini, the great Italian rider, to look after and they wouldn't be able to get me any machinery. They had only enough bikes for him. Fair enough.

"I didn't know what to do. But Rodney Gould was in America and I wrote and asked him if he could get me fixed up with Yamahas to take to Europe. He got me a new 250, but there were no new 350's - but Don Vesco had a used 350 and he said I could ride his bikes at Daytona.

"I rode them in early 1970 and won the 250 race for him; I was in front of Dick Mann in the big race, the 200-mile, until the crankshaft broke. There was a fair old chance I might have won, but for that problem.

"Anyway, that's the way the luck goes in racing. I was upset, of course, but I was delighted that I'd managed to win the 250 and so was Don.

Roberts with Stars and Stripes, and flanked by an equally youthful Barry Sheene at the first Trans-Atlantic trophy series, USA V UK, clash

"Don told me that if I wanted to spend a year or so in the States he would help me out. In the meantime I went back to Europe with the Yamahas.

"Yamahas, then in America, were a write-off in a racing sense. They had a few guys doing dirt tracks on production bikes . . . road race machines. But they were nothing, and plainly, needed to be developed into a bigger force. With all their resources Yamaha obviously were ripe to make an impact and I would see it.

"I did my season in Europe in 1970 and decided to go back to America to see what the future there might hold for me. Vesco and I got together and I set up at his workshop in California; I had a couple of machines, but I looked after his bikes and operated the dyno and generally helped with the development. Don's idea of going racing was a little strange to me - he felt you just took the bikes out of the crate, screwed them together and off you go. I had, I felt, a bit more to offer than that.

"So I was able to help out there, I was a pretty good engineer and knew what I was doing on the insides of a bike. I was busy, because aside from looking after my own machines I was working with Vesco and taking care of Cal Rayborn's equipment, too. But Yamaha were paying me on a bonus scheme and things were looking up. In fact, I won every 250 race but one in America that year and I won Rhode, Atlanta, the first time Yamaha had ever won a national in America.

"But, as always, there's a big disappointment at the end of every rainbow. And when we went to Ontario, just about the last race of the year, I was in super - confident mood and thinking I could win anywhere - but I was dropped back into second place on the last corner of the last lap and lost by half a wheel . . . my 350 was just no match for the final blast of a 750. I had led all the way, but just got blown off in the critical sprint.

"So I thought: that's that. I'm not riding a Yamaha 350 anymore against the big 750's, it's crazy. So I decided to go back to Australia; I'd made more money that year than in five years racing in Europe. For instance, when I won the double Atlanta I came home with 20,000 dollars - and that was real good money. But there was plenty of big money around in America just then. I could not complain I had not had my share.

"Though I missed out on some 15,000 dollars at Ontario, I won the 250 race and had that second place in the big race and was paid about 15,000 dollars. If I'd won the both of them I'd have taken away more than 30,000 dollars and for those days . . . 1971 . . . that was some pay day! And I was half a wheel away from that little fortune. Imagine!

"With what I'd earned I thought I might go back home and open a motel and forget about racing. But Kawasaki came up with an offer, though I didn't fancy it too much, and it made me have second thoughts. So much so that I went to Yamaha again, talked about the prospects for another year, and they matched the Kawasaki offer. And it was a whole bunch of money. I'm not saying how much - but it was a lot. It would have been a lot for these days - but for 12 years ago it was tremendous. I thought I might as well stay.

"The contract was that I'd help Kenny Roberts with his bikes from the garage I had set up in the house I'd bought in San Diego.

"Kenny was Yamaha's Junior rider; he'd been racing for them since 1970 and in 1971 he was a first year expert. So he was riding in the same races as me. We drove to all the races together - and the condition of my contract and my job was to teach him as much about road racing as I could. Look after his bikes - and help him out.

"But we didn't have a good year. The bikes were brand new and pretty unreliable and they cost us a good few wins. But all the time I was getting in deeper with Yamaha, and getting to the point where I was just about Yamaha-America on my own. It was suddenly all revolving around me and my headquarters in San Diego.

"They decided to farm out their entire race programme in America and I was given the road race responsibility: somebody else got the dirt track programme.

"They gave me a budget, bikes and parts and they said: Go and do it! I already had the base, of course, but now I had a budget of 70,000 dollars to play with, too. Out of it I had to pay the mechanics, find a transporter and cover the expenses. It wasn't easy. And I really had to keep on racing to top up the budget and finance further the whole set up. I certainly didn't make any money out of that Yamaha contract!

"The team was Kenny, Don Castro and Gary Fisher - and me, riding to make money. I even lost cash on the deal and had to get into my own savings, but I wasn't too worried. I knew it was a way to get going on a new future. They would have preferred I didn't race - but, even at my age, I was still the number one rider in the team and did as well as anybody even though Kenny did win the National Number One plate.

"But the next year we really started getting our act together, all the experience we had gained was put to good use. And with Kenny in the team as number-one things looked really good . . . and were! We still had Castro with us, but then Gene Romero joined as well.

"By then I had a 2,000 foot workshop - we weren't working from behind my house any more - and we had lathes and all the stuff needed to give serious support to a race team. But Yamaha-America as such didn't exist then, it was Kel Carruthers Racing that was Yamaha race HQ in the USA so far as Yamaha were concerned.

"But things had gone on at one hell of a pace; I was now working hard on development for Japan, doing modifications and the like. All the modifications we did, all the work, was all set down on paper and sent back to Yamaha-Japan in a constant feedback.

"It all came to a head for me in 1973. I was still being pressed by Japan not to race anymore - they figured I was too valuable to them. After all I *was* Yamaha racing in America and the US market was more important to them then than Europe. Daytona, for instance, was the biggest race in the world so far as they were concerned - and the American nationals carried more weight in their minds than the Grand Prix in Europe.

"They agreed to let me do five events in the year - to keep *me* happy, I suppose, even if *they* weren't - and I was second to Saarinen Daytona; I won Talladega, second Atlanta, fourth or fifth Ontario, but I did even better than Kenny that year.

"I never used to practice. He was testing my bike for me - and I'd go out and race after maybe six or seven practice laps. But it was all getting to be too much for me. We were understaffed, despite taking on an extra mechanic, but I was working all night, trying to squeeze in a qualifying lap or two and then racing while I was still looking after the team. It was madness. And finally Japan told me to pack it all in . . .forget it! And I thought: Thank God. Because really I just didn't have time any more.

"I suppose when I look back that must have been the turning point for me, when I stopped being a rider and started in the engineering and development business for Yamaha full-time.

"Halfway through the year I went to Japan to test the 700. I was there for five days doing the final testing; I was the only one who had ridden it aside from Gary Fisher, who didn't do too much on it. They had been testing it and running for about a year and they asked me to do all the final assessments on it with Japanese test riders.

"At the end of '73 they sent me the second and third production 750's to continue testing at Ontario and Daytona; I took my whole crew on the trips and we linked with a Japanese engineer.

"The improvement from how it had been when we rode it in Japan was unbelievable. There it was impossibly bad, awful.

"They had told me it was good . . . but had one problem. Over 160 miles an hour it used to shake its head. It scared the life out of me. It was so bad you wouldn't believe it - it was out of control.

"When I took it out on the first day of the final testing there was a lot of wind about at the test track and the thing was all over the road . . . it was just diabolical.

"I said I thought the swing-arm needs lengthening. They did it overnight and when we went out the next day it was 100 per cent better. We played with the shocks and we got it pretty good, up to production stage. But it didn't stop there . . .

"We all went back to the factory and they opened up an engine for me and I gave them changes to make and they did everything I wanted. Nothing drastic - but, for instance, there was no lip on the oil seal behind the gearbox sprocket. I was afraid it might fall out like they used to on the old 350's.

"The bolt that held the gear on the primary shaft was something like a 10mm thickness and I had it replaced with, I think, a 16mm, a good hefty thing compared with the first one.

"This was only a small part, of course, of a much greater issue but it showed me that I was somebody they took notice of when I had an idea or a modification that I felt would improve the situation.

"I think I was probably the first non-Japanese who had earned this sort of respect. They were happy to do what I suggested; it was all based on the

1981 Championship Team (LtoR) Tilbury, Carruthers, Roberts, Mikawa, Clarke

feedback I'd been giving them from America. They obviously had seen that I was talking sense and it all served to put me in a position where I was made to feel I was an important part of the future for Yamaha.

"From that point on, until I moved into Europe with Kenny, we did virtually all the development work on the production race bikes at my workshop. They were the only sort of machines that could be raced in the States . . . the factory back in Japan could build all their fancy four-cylinder 500s, but we couldn't use any of that stuff. We had to use and race the production bikes, the 250's and 700's and later 750's, all homologated units.

"So far as I know the factory didn't do any development work from '74 until about 1978 when I came to Europe. They did some 750 frame work - but all the engines mods were stuff that I'd done in America.

"I reckoned I was about a year ahead of the factory in Japan. We had Daytona to go for and I was in charge of the whole business there. They lined up the Japanese one side, Agostini was there, and Kanaya, and I had my riders, Kenny, Romero and Castro, the boss Mizzo from the factory, introduced everybody and said; 'Kel's in charge . . . If there are any problems, sort them out with him'. And I knew then, I guess, that I had arrived on the scene in a big way.

"We did Daytona and Imola with production stock bikes. And then at Rhode, Atlanta, we came out with three-under-one-over-the-top exhaust pipes and other trick bits, and we ran for the rest of the season on them. The factory didn't get to them until the end of the year, we were just so far ahead.

"I wasn't making a fortune out of it, though I had a big enough budget by now from the factory to play about as I wanted, and all the experimental stuff I was doing was totally acceptable to them back at head office. The only way I made any money for myself - because the official budget was all used up - was in selling race bikes out of crates at my workshop. Yamahas in America didn't supply bikes with spares kits; riders just got a bare bike. None of the dealers carried spare parts and these guys would go off racing and, hopefully, pick up a few spares here and there wherever they were racing. But I had a 24 hour service on virtually any Yamaha road race part with express delivery all over the country - so I sold almost every part sold in America off the shelf. I used to carry bits that nobody else had. It didn't really cost me anything other than the money I'd laid out for the parts. I had all the shelf space I needed and with the help of a friend we got a good business going.

"I used to sell about ten or fifteen bikes a year and with the parts service going so well I did, at least, start to make some money over and above all the outlay that the development and race team budget demanded.

"Along the way I even allowed myself to get conned into doing the dirt-track bikes and that was a big, big mistake. I had enough on my plate as it was . . .

"I'd prepared a dirt track machine for Kenny, a 700 four-cylinder miler. Somebody else had built six frames and I got hold of one and we made it really special, it was an absolutely tremendous flyer. It was assembled like a road race bike . . . really nice and neat . . . and the other five were built like the regular dirt trackers. They had connecting links in the rear chains - they didn't understand about rivet links and wiring bolts and they were generally quite shoddy.

"Ours was in contrast a beauty. And it could go like the wind . . .

"The guy who was supposed to do the frame work didn't do it and we got lumbered with the whole lot - and we had too much to do. Kenny won all the *road* races, but we were working flat out in every direction. And the dirt track programme for me was a disaster. The road was the right way for us. The dirt certainly was not . . .

"Kenny was hardly any help at all. He is basically a motor cycle racer - and a great one - but on the dirt he had no clues what to do. I thought he would be really good at it, but he doesn't understand it. He had some ideas, but they weren't always on the right track. And I couldn't give him any advice because I knew nothing about the business.

"When the bike was good he could ride it right and make it do its job. But when it went off and it was bad he was stuck and he'd have you changing forks and wheels and suspension like you wouldn't believe.

"It was all simply because we didn't know what to do. Had it been road race problems then it would have been alright because I would have known what was going on and what the bikes were supposed to do . . . but on dirt . . . well neither one of us had a speck of an idea.

"I was as pleased as I have ever been when eventually we quit the dirt scene and got back onto our strongpoint . . . developing road machines. And here I had a lovely time building the greatest little 250 you've ever seen in 1977 . . . a bike so nice all the current 250 and 350's are based on the ideas I had.

"I was to-ing and fro-ing to Japan, doing all the development work on the 250 and 750's, and they used to send engineers over from the factory to see me in San Diego and it was an exciting period. But it reached a nice peak for me when I set about this little beauty and saw it come to fruition in just the way I'd hoped it would . . .

"We gave it its first outing at Daytona in 1977. I called it my baby 250. And Kenny just ran away with the race until it broke a suspension unit - by then Kenny had slashed about seven seconds off the lap record.

"He used to ride a 250 that was not all that good yet used to win virtually all the races he entered. But this bike was not so hot that he could do it without trying. I did a real big development programme on the engine . . .

"I put a lot of thought and effort into the bike knowing from my long experience on 250's just what was needed to make it a little bit out of the ordinary and to give Kenny a machine that could stand up to his determination. Not just for Daytona, for the season.

"It was a hell of a lot of work, and I mean it! For instance, there was a week's work just modifying a cylinder . . .

"When we talked about the possibilities Kenny said he thought the engine was a little bit too far forward - and that's where we started.

"Skip Aksland's brother Bud and Pete Davies worked for me and we put our heads together to get it right. We stuck a bike up on the bench and let our eyes roam over it and we decided it needed lowering down. We worked out all the ground clearances and dropped it all down. Two inches here, two inches there. We took fork springs out of it and the springs out of the suspension. We worked out where everything would be when the bike bottomed. Then we took a look at the frame set-up and a guy who was working at Vesco's came in to help us - he was an ace!

"I told him what I wanted and he operated from my workshop for a week and he made up a jig and he bent me up the first main frame and I said 'OK that's all we need'. He left and we got down to putting all the bracket and special little bits and pieces on it and we ended up with this trick little 250 that weighed nothing and ran like a 350, really good. Really low and racy. And it was giving 60 horse power at the rear wheel and turning only 11,000 revs; it was certainly something to be proud of.

"We knocked about 35 to 40lbs off the older model. It was a lot. We just scaled everything down, used light tubing, milled the crankcases away; and I went to Yamaha's moto-cross department and raided their titanium nuts and bolts box.

"When we took it to Daytona for testing, Kenny, who was plainly pleased with the results of all our efforts, just destroyed the 250 lap record time and made it look easy. Steve Baker and his engineer Bob Work were down there at the same time and quickly fastened onto the idea that we were running something a bit extra-special.

"Stevie spotted its potential and said he wanted one so we built him one, too, for Daytona. He used it in Europe that year and it suited him down to the ground.

"But it was so disappointing when Kenny raced the prototype in the 250 event at Daytona . . . he was streaking away from the rest when a little part in the monoshock broke and put him out of the race. But it had done enough by then to have the Japanese factory men in a high state of excitement: the engineers thought it was the greatest thing ever.

"I sent the prototype to Japan for them to test and it finished up as the basis for all the current 250/350 frames. All they did was to move the engine forward just a little bit, because with the 350 it was a little bit light in the front end and they wanted the same frame for both 250 and 350s.

"It was just a tiny bit too small for some people . . . I mean, it fitted me, Kenny and Steve Baker perfectly because we were about the same size . . . but for others it needed scaling up a bit. Otherwise it was just a straight copy of my prototype and it became the first of the low 250 production racers.

"Why the factory in Japan was not doing all this kind of development work, and leaving it to me to get 250's and 750's right, was a bit of a mystery. But they seemed to be working back to front . . .

"With the race set-up as it later became they would build a factory bike and then a year or two later would make a copy production racer version. But with the 250s and 350s it used to be the other way round - they would make a production bike and then they would modify it to become the factory, say, 350. Like the one Agostini rode. But there was nothing special about them and not really all that good; they would use chrome alloy instead of steel, but otherwise the bikes were not much better than the production stuff. The enginers were just about standard . . . barely better at all than the production Yamahas.

"They didn't have too much to work off, they were copying production bikes and making their factory machines from that set-up. It seemed to me to be the wrong way round. So what I did was to build in America a factory bike, an original. They saw the wisdom in my move and once my work had been done on it they would go ahead and produce it.

"As if all this was not enough to think about there was a good bit of pulling from Europe and pushing from America and Japan for Kenny to get into the world championships. The dirt track programme so far as Yamaha were concerned had by then collapsed and Kenny was left with only about five road races to do in the year in the States. It was pretty obvious he would be under-employed, but that there was a huge market to be served in Europe and a big public curious about this fantastic rider Roberts.

"He had made one or two forays . . . Imola, Italy, and the Trans-

Atlantic match race series . . . and had shown just what an exciting competitor he could be. I'm sure that a lot of the affection still felt for him in Holland, our European HQ, stems from the 1977 season in Holland when he was leading the 250 race - on our little baby, incidentally, - and fell off. But he got back on again and finished second and they loved him for it.

"The Yamaha bosses had recognised the need to widen their horizons and get Kenny into the front line of championship racing and in 1978 he and I came to Europe to do just that. I didn't want to, I'd done that scene and I felt that now I was settled with a good home in California I really could do without all the hassle of trailing across Europe. In the end I didn't have too much choice, there was a feeling that my contract in America might be under threat because of the reduction of the demands with the withdrawal of the dirt race programme and the shrinking, therefore, of the entire calendar with just five road events to prepare for. Yamaha were just not that enthusiastic about the situation in the States and they told me I should go along with Kenny to Europe. Being faced with that sort of pressure I decided to go along with the plan, and we set up a business deal . . .

"We pooled Kenny's contract money and mine. We went to Goodyear and got some money off them; then Lektron put in some cash and so did Champion Spark Plugs and we put it all into a Corporation, K. & K.

"I was President with 49 shares. Kenny was vice-president and he had 49 shares, and Ken Clarke, from Yamaha-America, had two shares because Yamaha wanted somebody to have a casting vote if things got out of hand, which they never did.

"It was my job to put it all together and get the team to Europe. We had two 250's, two 750's and one 500, with back-up parts promised from the factory, to tackle the Continent. Yamaha-America bought us a big Mercedes van. Goodyears sent a tyre technician to stay with us throughout the season - and away we went.

"We did Daytona and won there and set off for Europe and the Grand Prix scene with a lot of hope and confidence. I pulled in Nobby Clark and Trevor Tilbury, two superb mechanics who had been around for a long time, and they were paid by America. There was financial backing, of course, from the States but for all practical purposes we were just a little private team. We were so far away from those distant shores, America really had little or nothing to do with it; we used to phone them up on a Sunday night after a race to tell them what was going on, but that was just about it so far as contact with home-base was concerned. All the parts came to our Amsterdam headquarters direct from Japan; we had a bank account in Holland. And Kenny and I had agreed how much we'd take out for wages and how much we would put into the team - and we had an arrangement that at the end of the season I would sell my shares to Kenny and so would Ken Clarke. I did the job for a salary-plus expenses, so what was left at the end of the year was Kenny's.

"All my development work by then had stopped and I was making a

1979 World Championship Team
Left to right: Mikawa, Tilbury, Roberts, Carruthers, Clarke

full-time effort to get the Grand Prix effort into good shape; it was real hard work. But it was worthwhile because Kenny, fully justifying all the faith Yamaha had in him did really well.

"He should have won the 750cc championship, but he had some bad luck. A couple of really unfortunate things broke, a chain adjuster on the line in Belgium when he would have won, then a steering damper bracket at Assen and he would have won there, too.

"And I'm sure he would have taken the 250 title with a bit more going for him; but the Goodyear tyres were a big let-down. He won the first race in the Argentine and he was leading in Spain when the tyre went away and it did it again in France when he was in front. Then he had to miss the final two rounds because he had already signed to do two 750 races in Canada and in Laguna Seca. To win the 250 title he needed to have a good lead if he was to miss those final rounds. I believe he would have been able to build enough of a lead to be champion had we not had those, mainly, tyre problems.

"Goodyear, unfortunately, were simply not up to it. It was all new to them and we struggled to get it right, but it was a line of technology where they were not sufficiently experienced.

"In Austria we had almost 150 tyres for the 250 and 500. We didn't even have enough room to carry them ourselves so Dunlop carted the Goodyears down to Spain for us . . . that's how difficult things were.

"It was hard graft. We used to change the tyres and do everything ourselves, not like nowadays. But it was worth it because Kenny won the 500 title first time, first try. By the middle of the season he had given up on everything but the 500 championship - he concentrated all his effort in that class.

"It was heartbreaking in many ways because he was first fastest in practice at the Nurburgring and didn't ride in the race and again at Silverstone and never started. He was just using the 250 as practice and then, after qualifying - often quickest - he would park it.

"But he couldn't manage to do both Grand Prix classes, it was too much of an effort and far too wearing to do both of them on the top level. One or the other, if not both, would have suffered eventually and we would have finished up with nothing for all our effort.

"One of the big problems was that organisers always put the 250cc race on directly before the 500 and he was getting off one bike straight onto another and having to chase round different lines and with a machine of totally different characteristics.

"But he was in an awkward position. Here was this hot-shot rider from America, this highly-publicised star, and he just had to win at least one title in his first year or he would have lost some of his credibility. In truth he might have won the three he set after - the 250, 750 and the 500. But as it turned out he won the 500, the one we never expected him to win.

"When we look back now it really was a magnificent achievement - but, with a little more luck, we could have been looking down the years on three titles in Kenny's first full season in Europe.

"If people had not much regard for him before he left America, and thought he was just a home racer, then they certainly sat up and took notice that year.

"And when you remember just how badly organised we were it makes it an even more remarkable breakthrough; we were finding our way in more ways than one. Sometimes it was chaos - the van we had was hardly ready for a full Grand Prix and international race season.

"I remember we left Venezuela for Amsterdam and at our compound behind the workshop there was the van. It had a nice paint job, and it looked okay. But it had no shelves in it, no places for the bits and pieces, no ways to hold the bikes or anything. And we were about a week away from our first European Grand Prix - we barely had time for any work on setting up the team. We just had to rush along as best we could.

"We had all the spares and stuff coming from America, from Japan and catching up with us from Venezuela, and that was our set up. I was up working until the early hours of the mornings fitting shelves and drawers. And that's how it seemed to be for the entire year . . .

"I was the Jack of all trades; I was the team . . . The engineer, the chief mechanic, the cashier, the secretary, I made the entries . . . I did just about everything with Nobby Clark and Trevor Tilbury to help out.

"The one comfort I had was that I had managed to arrange to have my family travel with me. Kenny and I both had big motorhomes, probably the first time they had every been seen on the motor bike Grand Prix scene, and they gave us a good deal of comfort which we would otherwise have not enjoyed. I had said to the factory that unless I could travel Europe under these conditions then I wasn't interested in going - and that's the way it was for the next 12 years or so.

"Kenny and I had almost lived in each other's shadow for a long time before that first blast at full time Grand Prix racing; I was his mentor, his dad, his companion . . . just about everything to him . . . when he was signed up by Yamaha. They spoiled him rotten, he had everything he wanted from them just by asking. And even though I had little or nothing to do with his dirt tracking I was responsible for him when he went road racing. That's the way the factory wanted it to be.

"He used to come and stay at my house in San Diego and I'd help him with his bikes and with advice about racing. He was just a freckle-faced kid, a teenager, and he's changed a whole world since those days. You'd hardly recognise the unsophisticated character of the early days in the great champion he is now.

"Whenever he went outside America, principally to Europe, Yamaha used to send me along with him. Ages before we had set up the Grand Prix team I'd go along with him to the Match Races or to Imola or anywhere else as an insurance against him wandering off or losing his way.

"He was hopeless. All he wanted to do was to race bikes and he couldn't be bothered about all the other stuff . . . organising plane tickets or hotel rooms. So I used to do it - or Yamaha would simply send the tickets, and he had nothing to think about.

"But he was infamous for getting himself lost; it used to be a standing joke between us that he did so many U-turns to my place when he had lost his way yet again it cost him a fortune in tyres.

You can imagine with all this close proximity between us Kenny and I had grown into a partnership that was deep in its friendship and held mutual appreciation for each other's respective skills . . . him as a rider . . . me as a developer and engineer.

"In the second year I think we brought racing up to the standard it had required for years, to the same sort of organised level that Formula One cars had, with all the proper backing and support.

"We had learned a lot from our first year and I was determined to put it to good use for 1979; so even as the factory Japanese looked after Johnny Cecotto, with all the parts in boxes, out of the back of a truck, and with a cook doing his stuff on a two-burner stove in the middle of the paddock, we got ourselves into a pretty tight-knit and well-organised situation.

"We set up camp properly. We were still financed from America, but I suspect, it was with money routed from Japan and we were able to get

1st 500 cc Championship Winner for Roberts 1978

down to it in the way I knew was necessary. So I had an extension built onto my motor home, we had a big Mercedes full of shelving and places for everything. We worked under cover, in a full sized annexe and in far greater comfort than anybody else.

"In the third year, 1980, we were elected to be *the* Yamaha factory race team. We weren't the little team on our own any more, we were stamped with the full, official recognition from Japan as the Grand Prix team.

"They sent us a Japanese engineer, permanently on our team, and we just changed the colours we'd been racing under and set about winning the third world title in a row. The engineer and me worked in harmony to get it all running good - but now we were contracted to Japan. But nothing else really had changed, we went racing just as we had done before. We were still sorting out our own problems.

"What had changed was Kenny. The first year was easy...if I thought it

Left to right – Roberts, Carruthers, Lawson at the Dutch T.T. Assen 1983

was going to rain I'd put wet tyres on the bike, if I thought it needed intermediates I'd do it and Kenny would accept it, take my view and advice without questioning. But inside three years it had all changed and he would say 'I want this on it . . . or that' and had become rather more assertive in his ideas for the bike.

"Now Kenny has got to the stage where a lot of the time he is right, but people assume that a rider is always correct. Well, that's just not so. They make a lot of mistakes; but why should they know? It's not like the old days when the rider used to go out, find something was wrong with the bike and come back and fix it.

"And there's so much staff to play about with these days, so many variations to work on and so many spares to get it all right when it's not running smoothly.

"Team riders nowadays will practice, feel there's something not dead right with the bike, explain if they can what it is and a mechanic or engineer goes and fixes it and the rider often has no idea what's been done. He knows something has been done in the general area of his complaint or his suggestion, but usually he doesn't really know.

"I would never not do something to a bike that Kenny had asked for. I would certainly argue with him and tell him I wasn't going to change what I'd done if I felt strongly enough about it, but I'd never send him out thinking we'd done something he had asked for and we hadn't done it.

Carruthers shows Kenny Roberts his lead at the German Grand Prix at Hockenheim 1981

"Sometimes is is almost impossible, when you are setting a bike up on a rider's instructions, to identify what the problem or trouble is - and sometimes it's so minimal an issue that you can't correct it or change it, but the rider still feels you can. In the end there are some things a rider just has to live with. When you cannot possibly make one further improvement to the machine that is what the man is left with and he has to face up to making do.

"Eventually, when you're trying to work out something to do to improve a bike or cure an ailment in it, you run out of time or things to do with it and the rider just has to live with it and get down to riding it. Good or bad, he just has to get down to . . . that's the bottom line. That's his job.

"It's got to a stage now where you can work for a whole week on the bike, sweating your guts out and wracking your brains what to do next to make sure you've got the best prepared machine in the race, and then forget that you have the best rider in the world in Kenny and when he goes to the line he can probably win anyhow. And you worry that you haven't got the bike good and prepared well enough for him to win.

"You get to the stage as a mechanic of thinking you haven't got the machine dead right and Kenny can't win and you've let him down - and you forget that he could win on a lesser bike over men who have better, quicker machines, simply because he is the greatest. He gets you thinking like that, he gets you to that stage, and I don't know why.

"He's been a rogue at times. He's taken a bike out and practised and decimated the lap record and come back and said 'It's a load of garbage, I can't ride it, it's rubbish. Get it right. And you can't believe what he's saying. You look at the times, look at the bike, and you can't believe your ears. And you wonder where you can go from there.

"I worry a lot about my responsibilities and I certainly get sleepless nights before a Grand Prix. I just want to make sure that when Kenny goes to the line we have given him the best possible chance of winning, that we have done our part and what's left is his responsibility. It's all down to his skill - because the machine is perfect. At least that's what we strive to do. Sometimes it can go wrong . . . just as it did at Assen. Disastrously.

"We were all set for the Dutch TT, 1981, and it was going to be a great Yamaha show. All the big bosses were over from the factory, all eager to see us wipe out the opposition, and it turned into a nightmare, an absolute disaster. It was such a chaotic collapse you would not have wished it on your worst enemy. And it was all my fault; I've never felt so badly about anything in my life.

"To make matters even worse Barry Sheene, who had joined the team, was left pushing a spluttering machine when the flag dropped and he couldn't get going. And when the pack roared away, not only was Sheene still there - though he manfully shoved the bike for about 100 yards trying to get it going - so was Kenny. Stuck on the line, going nowhere at all, cursing like you've never heard and struggling vainly to get underway.

"The trouble was the brake pad was in the wrong way round, and that was my responsibility, and a whole series of incidents that followed made us lose sight of the problem. I asked another mechanic to check the front end for me because I had to go away and do something else, I was always running here there and everywhere doing all sorts of jobs, but the ultimate blame must lie with me.

"There had been an almighty mix-up. And it wasn't even the race prepared bike that Kenny had the trouble with; it was the spare. But it was the one he decided he wanted to ride at the last minute. And it was back in the tent! My son Paul went for it and pushed it to the startline, five minutes before the off. Kenny said he wanted to ride it because it had rain tyres - but when he came back from the warm-up I'd prepared to put intermediates on it because I just *knew* that's what he'd ask for. And I was right.

He was on the line, the grid was jammed of course because there was only a short time before the start, and one of the mechanics came running over to say that Kenny had complained there was something wrong with the front end . . . when I looked I saw the brake pad had welded itself to the disc. And that was our race run.

"It was an awful time for us all, me most of all. But, mercifully those sort of errors are few and far between, they don't happen too often because normally anything like that is spotted long before the race. And, generally, whatever problems are likely to arise have already been recognised in practice - the freaks, of course, cannot be budgeted for.

"After the three halcyon years of three championships, 1978, '79 and '80, things went a little awry for us. And I suppose it was due a lot to the fact that we were involved in a development programme whilst we were trying to win world titles. It's enough to concentrate on one without the added complication of the other.

"When you remember Kenny, in his first year had to take on the world's great road racers on circuits they mostly knew, but he didn't, he won 10 championship rounds, won the 500cc title and was second in the 750. Quite a remarkable achievement.

"Then a year later he retained the 500cc crown despite the horrendous crash he had testing in Japan. He was knocked about a great deal - he had very serious internal injuries and a severely damaged back, in fact he was fortunate he didn't break it. The doctors told him he would be lucky if he could even sit on a motor bike in three months, let alone race one. But inside two months he had won the second Grand Prix of the season.

"He was in a great deal of discomfort and his back played up for ages afterwards, but he is the sort of character who tends to put that out of his mind and will ride the pain barrier. That's why, when we talk about preparing machinery for him, I feel it my responsibility to ensure he has the best I can do for him - he deserves it. He gives *his* all and so should his back-up team give theirs. Whatever hours they have to work, whatever difficulties and problems they may face.

"There are times, of course, when things are difficult for everybody . . . like the development years. And, naturally, when Kenny is trying to win on bikes that really are not up to the fine standard he requires, and the one needed to beat off the other factories, he does get frustrated. And 1981 and 1982 were two such years. He was angry a lot during those two years - mainly, I guess, because he was having to try and compensate with guts and skill for machines that were not up to the job.

"The V-four, for instance, that bike was just wrong. A lot of little things . . . sideways suspension . . . power characteristics were wrong . . . wouldn't handle . . . the power came on with too much of a rush and it magnified the problems we had with the frames. Power curve was all wrong. It was out a year too early, I suppose, but we were stuck with it. There was not alot we could do with it.

"The one before it, the square-four, was simply too heavy. Kenny fell off one in Austria and it broke in halves, but he never liked it too much. And I spent all my time doing modifications - I was up to my knees in shavings in the tent working on Barry Sheene's bike, and Kenny's too. It was hard work, I used to machine the cylinders, the heads and re-grind the ports. I was nearly dizzy with all the effort.

"Those two bikes, the OW54 in '82 and the V-four, a year earlier, both left us with a lot to do. And, to a great extent, Kenny felt the factory had let him down, he went through the entire 1982 season, for instance, feeling that the bike wasn't good enough, blaming the people around him and terribly disappointed at the factory's failure to fix him up with a winner.

"I don't know how he felt towards us, the engineers and the mechanics travelling and working with him, but our feeling was that we could only do our best on what we had to work on. We couldn't get a better job done for him - we felt a bit bad towards him, deep down, because I think we blamed him for not helping the factory as much as maybe he should have done. And that was the cause of a lot of the trouble.

"I viewed it like that at the very start of the project, even before the season got underway, he should have spent more time in Japan at the factory helping with the development. And they needed his guidance.

"It all rebounded later on in the season - but he was between contracts at the time, maybe trying to work something out for his future with the factory, and he didn't get into the project. By the time he had sorted out his contract the programme was well under way without him - and, it's my own view, he should have been involved from the beginning. But that's what happens with riders tied up with teams - they get to arguing about their contracts from, say, October or thereabouts and they don't get into the development programmes for the next year's bikes until it's almost too late. Sometimes not at all. And that's no good to anybody.

"When it came to the halfway mark in the season, around June, there was a four week break. But instead of going to the factory for two weeks to put some ideas and help out with the engineers, Kenny went back to America.

So we were left to make-do every week. It's a position you are in the most of the time, but sometimes, like that year, you are deeper in the hole than you want to be and you can't get out of it too easily. That's when everybody . . . riders . . . engineers . . . mechanics . . . should all pull hard together.

OW 54 Prototype Broken in Two by Roberts in the Austrian Grand Prix crash

Kenny Roberts in grim mood.

"Then, on top of it all, we had the added problem of difficulties with the tyres. That suddenly jumped into being a whole new technology on its own - with so much power being pumped out so savagely the tyres were taking a hell of a battering. And by the time you had fiddled about with them, changing them, trying to figure out what compound to use, there was less time to spend working on the engine or the suspension. The sessions between practices just started to become so frantic, with so much to do, so much to change and with so many variations, that those final 30 minutes or so before the practice ended became monstrous and really taxing on all our resources.

"It's a tremendous testimony to Kenny's total professionalism that he did as well as he did considering the overwhelming difficulties he was facing - but then nobody could ever question his dedication.

"I put it on a par with that shown by Mike Hailwood and Agostini. In terms of comparison - and it's always dangerous to try and skip generations when you are comparing racers - I would say there was nothing between them. They were the three really outstanding riders of my time in racing . . . Mike for his sheer genius and his ability to ride any bike you put under him and still win . . . Kenny for his will-to-win, his awesome determination and his skill . . . and Agostini for his brilliance, particularly at a time when he won all those titles on the run with few others around to challenge. He still had to ride, still had to be good, to do it and there were times when it was hard for him, particularly when he changed from four-strokes to two and he knew very little about them. But he was such a quick learner and such a natural competitor, always with something in reserve, that it looked easy . . . he made it look easy, of course. The greats always do.

"They can't analyse what it is they have - they can just *do* it. Ask any of them how or why and they have never been able to answer. You can either race like them . . . or you can't. But there are fewer men who could race to their standard than you could count on one hand.

"Kenny doesn't fall off too often, neither did Hailwood or Ago. They all had the ability to piece everything together and it all added up, balance . . . courage . . . bravery . . . skill . . . to an unbeatable combination.

"I was listening to Eddie Lawson and Kenny talking about braking markers at the Dutch TT, they were placed all wrong at Assen, and Eddie was asking Kenny where he anchored, what marker? And Kenny said . . . 'Well, nowhere in particular, I just put the brakes on when I feel it's right'. He just knew, his instinct told him, where to slow down but he couldn't describe why . . . it was a feeling.

"He's probably the most brilliant rider in the world on fast corners, he loves them, and he can pick up race winning milli-seconds by beating the other guys through those sort of swoops. The slower stuff, those low gear bends, is all about bravery these days. Especially in 500's. It used to be that the flat-out, high speed dash called for every ounce of courage you had . . . and it still does . . . but now you have the added need to be brave in the dive into those slow corners, the late, late braking, and the ability to hang on in there when the power comes blistering on at the exit from the corner. The bike wants to go over backwards, step sideways, spit you off as quickly as it can, and you have all those guys at your elbows, early in the race, all trying to control the same problem. Hanging on the traction is the biggest job they have when they squirt that power on.

"Look at the horrific Franco Uncini crash in Holland (1983) when he was pitched off over the high-side when he put the gas on coming out of the corner. That said everything about the dangers I'm talking about; when a rider as brilliant as Franco gets caught out then you know it's a big problem that takes a lot of care and handling.

"It broke away and started sliding. He had to turn it off a bit and it got traction again and high-sided him. In the old days he would have just fallen down, but now the tyres are so good it just grips again right away and unless you're careful you're off.

"But to my mind the 250 is still the easiest bike to fall off, that's the hardest class to race in. You can't afford to make any mistakes, you've got to be right on the limit all the time, right up in the power band. If you go into the corner in the wrong gear you're in all sorts of trouble and you need to be on the ball throughout the race - whereas with the 500 you could make a similar mistake, but you just pull it a bit tighter, knock it back a gear and give it the gas a little earlier and you pick up everything you lost. You can't do that with a 125 or a 250, once you've made the error, you've lost the advantage . . .

"This, of course, covers the whole range of problems that Kenny faced when he was attempting to do the three classes in one season. It's no wonder he was getting himself in a tangle mentally, having to cope with such a wide variation of aspects in racing at the highest level and against the specialists in their own class - men who only raced one class - he was faced with enormous difficulties which outsiders find hard to understand.

"The benefits of rationing yourself to a single class could be seen to be working right away when he stuck to the 500cc events in Grand Prix's - and he became a far more formidable rider. It paid off with three championships and you could see him getting happier and more relaxed as he had less and less to worry about; Kenny's problem, you see, is that he has to give 100 per cent in everything he does and it was hurting him that he could not do it and race full out for the three classes he originally aimed for.

"I suppose that if there was ever a time when Kenny's scary determination could be seen to be working at its most efficient rate it must have been in the 1983 season. He gave Freddie Spencer a 26 point start in the championship and with sheer gutsy riding, some of the best I have ever known from him, he whittled away the lead.

"He was almost frightening in his intensity, and I certainly would not have liked to have been out there trying to stop him when he set after Spencer for the title. Everytime, it seemed, Freddie got off to a great start and Kenny was left to catch-up. There were a few minor problems throughout the season with the bike, but it was most times pretty good and certainly fast.

"But the way Kenny was set to go made up for any tiny deficiencies the bike may have suffered; he was in tremendous form: he caught and past Spencer in Belgium to pull to within five points of him. Spencer must have felt terribly demoralised having to surrender such a huge lead - normally, I would say, a titlewinning margin - to a born winner like Kenny. He just did not know how to give up. And while some may argue that Freddie had trouble with the tyres or his bike a couple of times there was the Spa Grand Prix that showed he was just blown away by Kenny's all-out, do-or-die spirit.

"Kenny went underneath him at the hairpin at the top of the start-and-finish straight and it was a way of demonstrating to Spencer that if he left the smallest gap Kenny was going through . . . no matter what.

"After that Kenny piled on the power and Freddie was left without a hope of catching him.

"Something you do tend to overlook about Kenny, and it's what made him so special and such good value for money to Yamaha, was his ability to wring the most out of the bike when it was maybe not at its best - he'd

Roberts nips under Spencer at the Belgian Grand Prix and nearly spills as he accelerates too hard. 1983

gripe that it wasn't right, and moan if we couldn't possibly do anything more to it to make it faster or handle better, but then he'd go out and do it. He wasn't phased thinking that he didn't, after all, have the quickest machine in the race. If he thought he didn't have the best he'd damn well try his utmost to make sure it went the fastest.

"Spain in 1982, again, was proof of his willingness to go for it when the chips might be down. He rode like a genius that weekend - and, in fact, he always considers that it was his hardest ride ever. He said he was over the edge all the way round, right throughout the race, but he didn't back off. He couldn't. He doesn't know how. And when you are faced with that sort of rival you know you have your work cut out to beat him off . . . and that was Freddie's big, big problem in '83. Any other guy on the same Yamaha as Kenny's may not have been quite the stumbling block - but the Roberts brand was stamped on an ambition to finish with his fourth champion- ship in the year he said he would quit and it turned him on!"

A Hat-trick of Championships

At the end of the 1978 racing season, two world champions met up for the first time at a celebration party. Kenny Roberts and Heikki Mikkola had come to the Yamaha house on the edge of the lake at Vinkeveen, a few miles south of Amsterdam, to celebrate a spectacular double first for Yamaha: the 1978 500-cc world championships for both road racing and motocross. It was a happy gathering for riders, mechanics and staff from the company's European headquarters, the welcome end to two tough yet almost faultless campaigns.

For Heikki, the Finnish expert, it was familiar ground: he had been world 500-cc motocross champion twice before. For Kenny, the ice-cool Californian, it was an entirely new experience, for this was his first world title, taken from Barry Sheene, the Suzuki lead rider who had held it for the past two years.

Kenny, the sandy-haired keep-fit fanatic, had come a long way since his days as a 16-year-old when he won his first title, the Oregon 100-cc Short Track State Championship. Two years later he had become a full-time professional with not too much money but a whole lot of natural talent which virtually ensured that his pockets would soon be bulging with dollars. His all-round experience—of one mile, half-mile, short track, long track and road racing—placed a world championship easily within his reach—if he could be bothered to cross the Atlantic to Europe to take up the challenge. "After I'd won the AMA Number One plate, the top title in the States, in 1973, there was a lot of pressure on me to come to Europe for a world title," he told me, "but I resisted until now, 1978. I'm sure glad I did."

If Barry Sheene saw any threat looming over his racing kingdom, he identified it with Roberts. He received an early warning in 1977, when Roberts took four wins from six starts in the Trans-Atlantic Match Race series and left the world champion wondering what had hit him. He did not stop there. He went on to Italy for the Imola 200 and won both the 750 cc and the 250 cc races, collected another first place in the 250-cc class at Paul Ricard, France, and slipped in behind the winner Steve Baker in the superbike event. "I guess I'm getting the hang of this European road racing," he said in that laconic manner that has become his hallmark, "so I figure it might be a good plan to get over there among them and bring something home."

He paused on the way to snap up the victory laurels at the Daytona 200, the race everyone wants to win and one that had so far eluded him despite several dramatic attempts. Returning to California with his manager and friend, Kel Carruthers, he picked up the brand new 500 cc Yamaha and set about the long haul through the summer of '78 to the highest pinnacle in road racing.

Kenny Roberts flat out on home ground—at Daytona, 1978.

The 500-cc title is the finest in the world, the ultimate accolade of a rider's skill. Riding in his first Grand Prix season and on unfamiliar ground, over circuits he had never even seen before, Roberts proceeded to wrest this crown from the ambitious Englishman, Barry Sheene. Luck had little to do with it, despite Sheene's illness early in the season, caused by a virus he picked up at the Venezuelan Grand Prix. He said that this made him feel weak and unable to concentrate, but once he had recovered Kenny's performance must have seemed like a weekly relapse to him. Indeed, Sheene, poised to weld a motor car racing career onto his bike racing interests, had no real answer to the power, pace and determined style of the knee-scraping American.

1978 became a frustrating year for the Suzuki captain. Not only did he suffer the pressure put on him by the Roberts Yamaha, but he felt the stress of an internal threat: for men drafted into the Suzuki team to help him, in fact ended up beating him. That issue reached almost ludicrous proportions at the West German Grand Prix—the final round of the championships, held at the Nurburgring. While Roberts needed only a fourth place, Sheene had to get his Suzuki home first, or all his title hopes would be gone. The Dutchman Wil Hartog was recruited to help Sheene, as was the Frenchman Michel Rougerie and, almost at the last minute, the young Italian Virginio Ferrari, a rider with virtually no experience of works machinery. There were bets that Ferrari, famous for his rather exciting style, would fall off. In fact it was the ultra safe but superbly fast Hartog who crashed, for the first time in two years, while he was ahead of

Author Ted Macauley, who organized Mike Hailwood's TT comeback and his farewell appearance a year later, in 1979, shares a moment of despair with the great man in the paddock alongside the famous course. The Senior TT machine, the year-old 500 cc Yamaha, had suffered steering damper problems and Mike was forced out of the race he was sure he could win. Only two days before, despite a lay-off of eleven years, he had returned to the Isle of Man to clinch his tenth world title with victory in the Formula 1 race, indeed a fairy tale.

Sheene. Meanwhile, Ferrari had cleared off, leaving Sheene trailing behind, well back in fourth place. Sheene said later that he was waiting for Roberts, a place ahead of him, to break down. But that was not to be and within seconds of crossing the line, Kenny and his team were all wearing black and yellow tee-shirts, made secretly a few days before, that proclaimed: "Kenny Roberts World 500-cc Champion".

Kenny's hi-fi voice, well lubricated, switched onto full volume for the prize presentation and the high jinks went on well into the night. He was in greater danger of falling and hurting himself as a result of his drinking ambitions than he had been during the afternoon's race. He rode then with perfect control, suppressing all the time his natural instinct to ride to win. Later, we talked in Amsterdam as he helped his wife Patti to pack for home. "I could not have dreamed of a better end to the season," he told me. "The 500-cc championship! That's really something. It's the one I wanted, some sort of official recognition on this side of the Atlantic to go with all that I won at home in America."

In parallel to Kenny's 500-cc campaign, Heikki Mikkola, another fitness enthusiast, set about his task of retaining the 500-cc motocross title. Throughout the season he was to display an uncompromising confidence that left little room for hope among those who wanted to dislodge him. His prediction before the season started was simple and direct: "The title? I'll win it." His claim was backed up by his performance. With three races to go, he had amassed a record 299 points and won 14 of the 24 Grand Prix events. He headed the championship table from the start of the season until its end.

The story of 1978: Kenny Roberts gets the champagne while a rueful Barry Sheene looks on.

Mikkola had seen Hondaman Brad Lackey as his main rival and his forecast turned out to be accurate—but he refused to allow Lackey to close on him. The Honda finished 18 of the 21 races in which Lackey started. Mikkola's Yamaha failed only once—in the Swedish—when the chain slid off and jammed the drive sprocket. To the strength of his seemingly unbreakable machine, Mikkola brought two special qualities—fearless riding, and superb fitness of a degree that can stand as a lesson to competitors in every branch of motor sport. That, as much as anything else, allowed him to shake off the crippling effects of a mystery bug that threatened to sabotage his chances early in the season. At Sittendorf, for the Austrian round, Mikkola was still fighting off this illness and allowed Lackey to get within two points of him. But by the time the next round in France fell due, he was back to perfect health and Lackey had to say farewell to any chance of the title.

With Mikkola and Roberts scooping up the major titles in motocross and road racing, it was left to one other Yamaha rider to recoup some of his lost glory and complete a hat trick of Yamaha championships— Johnny Cecotto. His target was the world 750-cc title. Ironically, the

Heikki Mikkola powers his 500 cc Yamaha through the mud: the Number One combination in motocross.

major threat to the young Venezuelan's second world title was Kenny Roberts. But the rigours of the 500-cc season had left Kenny disenchanted with the idea of clinching the superbike title as well, and while he made a manful effort in the last two rounds — Laguna Seca and Mosport — it was to be Cecotto who won the crown and rejoiced in revitalized status.

By then, Roberts had already done enough to satisfy both spectators and his bosses. And, taking nothing away from Mikkola, who had done it all before, I do not suppose that anybody who saw Roberts take his title will ever forget the spectacular way in which he did it.

Kenny's fourth title hopes evaporated in a blast of indignation — not in San Marino, the last Grand Prix of the '83 season, but in Sweden in early August. That was when Spencer, the gentle Louisiana churchboy bared his teeth and showed Roberts just what a hard man he could be when it came to the showdown.

Kenny was leading with two corners to go of the Anderstorp airfield circuit when Spencer in a desperate do-or-die bid drove underneath him and forced him onto the grass.

"I think Freddie went berserk," said Kenny later, "he had no idea what the outcome might be and he might have had us both in hospital. It was a dangerous, inconsiderate manoeuvre, but if he wants the title that badly he's welcome to it."

Spencer, having forced Kenny off his line, rode on to win – but the bad taste left in Roberts' mouth after the incident gave added spice to the final clash in Italy, the San Marino Grand Prix in September.

A massive crowd turned up at Imola – but, really, Kenny's task was impossible. He needed to win and Spencer had to be forced down among the also-rans, as low as third. Kenny was up to his job – he won alright. But his support rider, Eddie Lawson, failed him. He could not get his Yamaha in between the King and the young pretender...

But for me the title was won and lost in Sweden – and I would have lost money on a race-hardened veteran like Kenny being ridden off the track by a kid like Spencer, for all his genius. Kenny was furious, of course, and refused to speak to Spencer after Sweden. When it came to Italy and the San Marino Grand Prix the Roberts' ire had been channelled into fierce determination...but could not do it alone.

His greatest race friend, Randy Mamola of Suzuki, said he would surrender the lead if he could let Kenny in for a championship – but, as it turned out, he was never in with a chance. Roberts rode as slowly as he could; Lawson as fast as he dared – but the back-up Yamaha man could not get onto the pace, and so Roberts must go down in history as probably the only man to win a Grand Prix on his brakes.

Above
Barry Sheene in Yamaha livery.

Below : Holland – Roberts
aviates at the Dutch T.T. 1983.

*Above: Kenny Roberts at the
Austrian Grand Prix 1983.*

*Below : The victory spray
for Roberts. Mamola looks on.*

Above: Kyalami, South Africa, March 19 1983; 500cc Grand Prix opening round. The American Freddie Spencer and his Honda NS 500 – 3 cylinder, 2-stroke won the first Grand Prix of the 1983 Season.

Right: New Zealander Graeme Crosby, who quit the team at the end of the 1982 season.

Above: Eddie Lawson on the outside line.

Right: Salzburgring, Austria 1983: 500cc motorcycle Grand Prix, Mamola (Suzuki no. 6;), Katayama (Honda no. 8), Haslam (Honda no. 35), Roberts (Yamaha no. 4) and Spencer (Honda no. 3) in the battle for the lead.

Moto-Cross

Yamaha's moto-cross ambitions, for so long left dormant in the shadow of road racing achievement, were fuelled by three Scandinavians - Torsten Hallman, Mikkola and Hakan Carlqvist.

There were others, of course, but these three in my view were the vanguard of Yamaha's bid to become a force in the highly competitive world of off-road racing. The huge commercial benefits that lie in prospect for the fun-bike, trail market, meant that Yamaha simply had to join in the effort to secure sales and guarantee identification with the potential customer through the publicity generated by success at the sport.

Hallman by his technical wizadry and far-sightedness and Mikkola and Carlqvist by their eye-catching skill, strength and bravery in the 500cc class, underlined the depth of determination these wondrous men had. All three enjoyed a perception for the sport, and its finer points of development, that gave Yamaha a boost to send it alongside road-racing as an interest to grip a huge following.

Yamaha could be criticised as late-comers, and maybe there was some shortsightedness among the hierarchy that failed to recognise earlier the vast possibilities, but when they did finally wake up and move into the off-road market battle they went in with considerable force. And the main standard bearers were those three Scandinavians . . .

Hallman's part in the framework of Yamaha's arrival on the world scene was, basically, his faith in the revolutionary suspension system, the mono-cross, invented by a Belgian engineer, Lucien Tilkin.

Suzuki had taken up the first option on Tilkin's idea - but for some reason best known to themselves they idled on it and the impatient inventor, disappointed at seeing his brainchild scrapped, happily listened to Hallman when he posted his intentions on the system.

Hallman, the world champion turned development expert who had offered his services to Yamaha towards the end of his riding career, could see the potential. But the Yamaha engineers were not so sure . . .

"I could see it had a future, said Hallman at his home in Sweden, I trusted it. But there were lots of doubts at the factory. However, on my say so, they bought the patent for a lot of money."

It was *the* most radical change in moto-cross and, as Hallman said, the biggest decision he had ever had to make in his relatively short time with the company, one year. In truth it was the most important of his career with Yamaha - and he began with the company early in 1971. Within a year he was faced with the Tilkin system . . .

"It was so difficult to explain why it was so good, so much better than

First Yamaha Moto-Cross bike 250cc, 1971.

Engine 250cc Yamaha YZ 1971.

Bengt Aberg, Luxemburg Grand [...] winner – the last 4 stroke to win [...] Grand Prix.

Spain 250 MX 1973.
Hakan Andersson on his way to world title.

the old system", he said, "and it was a terribly hard message to get across to the traditionalists . . ."

There was no harder, more unswerving traditionalist than Andersson. He hated change. He reckoned he had been hired to win races, not develop machinery and he refused even to test the moto-cross.

"Hakan's refusal shocked me", said Hallman, but he was an out-and-out traditionalist. He ate the same food all the time, drove the same make of car, went on holidays to the same place every year and he liked to race the same sort of bike - he didn't want to be involved in anything radical.

"I worked hard on him, but he would not budge from his stance. Having been given the go-ahead from the factory, having developed the system perfectly into a Yamaha frame it was all a bit annoying.

"But I suppose it *looked* different. It was certainly heavier. Originally we had built the mono-shock into a Yamaha . . . then we built a machine around it.

"We continued to develop it until we had reached a stage where the revolutionary new machine was pretty close to the one Hakan was already riding, the one he was used to.

"He was still resisting any overtures to ride it; his view was that he didn't want to be fooling about with anything new and he was forceful in his view that he would not break his training to ride it and test it at a time when he felt he was doing okay anyway. Then the factory stepped in and he was left with no choice.

"He was still reluctant, but he could feel the benefits and the difference between the new system and the traditional methods of suspension. Like I'd told him he wouldn't get so tired, it made life easier. And the whole dream I'd had came true when he won the first Grand Prix of 1973 on it.

"He was so happy. And after that he never went back to the old bike again."

All those arduous days and gruelling sessions around a Belgian test track spent by Hallman and Tilkin had paid off - soon the rest of the off-road race world was copying Yamaha's lead. Previously all the emphasis had been on horse-power, brute force, and the need to improve a rider's lot through suspension help was not a priority with any Japanese factory. If you had the power, it seemed they thought, then there was no reason why you should not win . . .

Suddenly, by Hallman's belief and Tilkins' theory, the moto-cross scene was revolutionised. It was the single, most vital change in off-road racing since the sport started.

When Andersson got underway he won the world 250cc title and Yamaha picked up the manufacturers championship; it was full justification for Hallman's relentless effort and persuasion. Soon, 20 or 30 factory representatives were watching the suspension war that was starting. Rival factory spies hustled to get a glimpse of Andersson's race winning suspension - but by then they had been taken by surprise and Yamaha's Belgian 250cc moto-cross Grand Prix devastated the opposition.

First M/X Grand Prix win at the Belgium 250cc in 1973. Rider: Hakan Andersson.

Unknown even to Hallman Yamaha engineers, taken totally by the success of the system had ideas to install it in their road racing programme.

Hallman, it seemed, could do no wrong. He was the brains behind the DT line. He turned 1971-72-73 into superbly successful development years and lifted Yamaha right to the top after they had spent 10 to 12 years barely interested in off-road and certainly not prepared to give it the support they had put behind road racing.

He had more than fulfilled his promise on the three-year development contract he had organised and after he became interested in marketing, too, Yamaha offered him the Swedish importer set-up.

The graduate technical engineer who had made a name through racing - and four world titles - and who had put Yamaha's name ablaze across the moto-cross front received the reward that the company always seems to strive to do when they have been well-served.

"It was all very exciting", said Hallman, "I had seen the boom coming years before I joined Yamaha. I had been to America and seen it start to happen there. And when I joined forces with Yamaha, and they believed in what I was trying to do and supported it so well, I knew the rewards for us all could be great. They came right up to my expectations".

Heikki Mikkola as "promotion man" for Yamaha at the French 500cc Grand Prix, 1982

He added: "The factory engineers were very wise; they knew nothing at all about moto-cross. But they were prepared to listen to somebody who did. They allowed me to get on with what I could do best . . . develop a good bike. I rode a few times, but I was way past it, my back had gone and the old legs, too - and they realised my greater value was at my workshop".

His butchery on Yamaha off-road ideas when he first joined the company was a bit startling; he chopped and hacksawed a 250 until its whole profile had changed. He altered frame dimensions, riding positions and front angles and moved pegs about - cut frames and welded them back together. He was commuting from Japan and to and from his workshops in Upsala, near Stockholm.

Hallman and Eneqvist of Sweden produced this HL 500

Yamaha may not have always been absolutely certain that all his ideas would work - but they stayed with him. His budget was not immense, but it was enough to help him to do what he wanted. Suzuki were streaking away with all the off-road honours and the publicity that went with it; Yamaha needed to catch up fast. And Hallman could not have been bettered as a man to do just that - he put the pain of years of racing behind him and in 1971, shortly after he had started his programme, he gave Yamaha their first world championship points with a seventh place in Holland. Then the 125 with Tommy Johnsson won the Swedish Grand Prix . . .

He had ambitions for a 500, too; a two-stroke and tested it in Holland. But it was far too fast for the frame, it vibrated so badly it could hardly be ridden. It was too mighty an engine, too small a cradle and the project was abandoned without the bike ever winning a race . . .

The feeling for 500's never really left Hallman and in 1977 he was enthusiastic about an XT500 that had been built for the USA for desert racing. "Everybody in Europe wanted one", said Hallman, "but Yamaha didn't have a mind to sell it there.

"Anyway, I bought one from an American rider and put the engine in a home-made frame. I had the idea to race it and Bengt Aberg, the 500 champion in 1969 and '70, was keen to ride a good four-stroke and said he'd give mine a go. The bosses at Amsterdam shook their heads, they were not nearly as enthusiastic as I was and didn't believe in my idea that the four-stroke could be a top ten runner.

"My idea was that for a small budget - 150,000 Swedish K's (about £13,000) we could enter the Grand Prix's and generate a lot of publicity and even if we didn't win that the coverage would be worthwhile . . .

"I was disappointed that I had been turned down so I went to the very top - to see Kuratomo San. It took him just five minutes to agree to my suggestion - he understood my way of thinking and he could see what a great return we could have for a small outlay. Straight away Bengt won the Luxembourg Grand Prix . . . it was a win that was its own answer to those who doubted the scheme".

If Yamaha had strength in reserve, way beyond the shores of Japan, it lay in moto-cross thinkers like Hallman. But then he was unique, a rare blend of expertise and determination. The tracery of technical development was interwoven throughout Yamaha with his own belief that what he was striving to do was worthwhile and would work. That he had to be both patient and persuasive is further legend to his character.

He had to try and transmit his boundless energies for his various projects - principally the moto-shock - into the minds of men who were not so sure as he was that new ideas were in Yamaha's best interests.

But Hallman had shown he was a competitor in all things and winning the confidence of the men who mattered, those with the money and budgets to support him, were merely another obstacle to be cleared.

Make no mistake the battlefronts then were not so much the hills and dips and corrugations of the circuits but the boardrooms and office desks where traditional ideas were acceptable and where innovative men like Hallman, for all his good reputation, were regarded with suspicion and doubt. Change, until good sense prevailed, was not viewed favourably. That's why men like Hallman, who can battle through, are worth their weight in bullion to company's like Yamaha. And, let's not forget, he asked the factory if he could join them . . .

It happened with another man, too. His name: Mikkola. Look what he did for Yamaha's name in moto-cross . . .

He was another caller to Amsterdam and the longer servers among the staff recall how Mikkola revitalised the factory moto-cross effort at a time when it was tending to fall away; he, said Paul Butler, re-awakened Yamaha's interest when it was faltering.

But then, explained Butler, Yamaha had enjoyed a long affinity with Finnish firebrands - the likes of Tepi Lansivouri and Jarno Saarinen in road racing had sparked their original interest in such characters - and Mikkola fitted ideally into the bracket. The Japanese liked the total commitment and 100 per cent honest-to-goodness purpose of the Finns - and even a little temper now and again was acceptable provided it was a motivating force. And that was exactly what it was with Mikkola.

His telephone call was Yamaha's connection with another world title; this time the one they really wanted, the 500 moto-cross championship.

Husqvarna's loss was most certainly Yamaha's gain - the former (1974) world 500cc and 250cc (1976) champion was a prize catch at a time when morale among the moto-cross connection was pretty low and few people felt motivated alongside the preponderance of consideration on being given to the road race department.

His two world titles in 500 - '78 and '79 - excited the imagination and almost gave a certificate to Yamaha's future role in off-road competition.

The rather dormant moto-cross interest turned into one of intense effort and concentration and Mikkola, the solidly professional, fiercely ambitious, if often muddy, superstar found himself on level footing with those road race aces. The spotlight had tended to bathe the road racers and leave the off-roaders in the shadows. Mikkola, really, altered all that...

Just as surely as Hallman's influence had been seen to take Yamaha into new areas of achievement technically Mikkola's advanced them great strides as a dominant force in the 400/420cc branch of the sport and as it was a fight from the back it was made more notable. In quick succession, after the wilderness years, Neil Hudson clinched the 1981 250cc class - and Danny La Porte did it again a year later, and the manufacturer's championship went with it.

The years of unstinting, gruelling competition played their part on Mikkola's battered body and he had to make 1979 his final year because of too many injuries, too many accidents and a toll too great to bear. But his mark on the factory had been great; his worthiness immeasurable.

It was his further guidance on Hudson, through his demanding keep-fit schedule, that helped the youngster make it to the top. It was an area of the sport he felt absolutely essential and he set up a winter training camp that has dropped many a fit man to his knees - and yet sent him back into the fray a much better competitor . . .

Roger de Coster may have been considered a prize catch - but it would have been extremely difficult to lure him from Suzuki; he was Mister Moto-Cross and Suzuki valued him so, he was strongly identified with them. Then there was Joel Robert, but his rough-and-ready outlook, his occasionally outrageous behaviour (like stopping to relieve himself in front of the organisers when he was in the lead in one race) hardly endeared him to the men who had the money to spend on buying winners. So when Mikkola cropped up it was like a gift that was a pleasant surprise - Yamaha had the right man, the right machine, and the title of 500cc world beaters was theirs for the asking. The commercial men, too, were delighted. For moto-cross sales relate directly to track success and bike exposure . . .

It's no matter of luck that in 1983, for instance, Yamaha was selling around 25,000 moto-cross bikes in Europe alone. And the feeling at the company was that you just did not sell them if you were not racing and the potential customer could not see them up front.

All that vital linkwork from the early seventies and into the eighties . . . the ties between Hallman and development . . . Mikkola and the major

"Carla" Carlqvist in action

Henk Van Mierlo   *Marc Velkeneers*

success of 500cc titles . . . was all a foundation to build underneath the continuing challenge in a highly competitive area. And, who knows, without that basis from which to work, without all that spade work, would the era of the magnificent Carlqvist have ever happened?

And here the wheel turns full circle - for it was that man Hallman, exercising his influence and wisdom once more, who recognised the vast potential and winning ability of the former ice hockey teenage star.

His loyalty to Yamaha had him draw up a dossier on the big, rough and tough Carlqvist and to get in touch with his Amsterdam base to recommend . . . strongly . . . that Hakan be snapped up as quickly as possible to further 500cc ambitions.

Carlqvist was another one of those fiery characters so much admired by the Japanese; this sort of explosive attitude seemed to go hand-in-hand with a desirable tenacity, so necessary among the off-road riders taking their chances for the big prizes.

But the six-foot blond Hakan curbed his rashness and harnessed it all into fearsome determination and brave, spectacular dash over the roughest terrain, against the toughest, most experienced opposition.

His 1983 performance in particular more than adequately demonstrated all those qualities recognised so early by Hallman; he trapped a nerve in his back and had rib injuries but he still rode through the pain barrier with a panache and style that was unmatched in its sheer determination. His confrontation with the excellent Malherbe was a season-long serial of a moto-cross man re-born.

And, as before him in the 500cc class, he set an inspirational standard in the Mikkola manner that most certainly excited not only all those paying customers but the men he had to work with - and the workshop in Amstelveen was a happy place to be whenever Carlqvist was in town.

The big and robust personality cloaked the stutter that hampered him slightly - a gentle impediment that added to rather than took anything away from the rough riding superstar's popularity.

Mikkola, married with two children, made his home in Hyvinkaa, Finland, when he was forced out of the sport he had done so much to promote - but he and the famous mechanic who had served him so well, Heikki Pentila, and the pair of them viewed Carlqvist with a respect that said volumes for their support of the continuation of the pedigree.

In 1980 Yamaha's moto-cross line-up was Carlqvist, supported by Hallman and Eneqvist of Sweden; Andrew Vromans, backed by D'Ieteren Sport, Belgium - each to contest the 500cc class with Jeff Nilsson and Marc Valkeneers in the 125cc class.

Nilsson, another ice-hockey player turned racer, had a fine record in the Swedish championships at both junior and senior levels.

Velkeneers, a Belgian, had been his country's national 125cc champion - and had the remarkable record of winning ten races in his first year as a junior. He joined the senior ranks at 16 - and clinched the national title. The FIM banned him from the 1979 moto-cross Grand Prix challenge because, they said, he was too young - so he spent the season in national events . . . often beating the more experienced riders who had enjoyed big time success.

Vromans, another Belgian, took up moto-cross after getting so badly hurt playing football that he had to quit what was his first love. He and his wife Marianne set up home in Arendank, Belgium, and he made 7th place in the 500cc MX Grand Prix season of 1979.

The bikes they had were . . .

Bike specifications in Moto-Cross Racing.

YZ80

Engine

Type	2 Stroke, single
Displacement	79 cc
Bore/stroke	49,0 x 42,0 mm
Compression ratio	8,1 : 1
Max. horsepower	12.5 Kw (17 HP)/11.500
Max. torque	10.3 Nm (1.05 Kg-m)/11.500
Lubrication system	Mixture oil/fuel (20 : 1)
Starting system	Kick
Gearbox	6 gear

Dimensions

Overall length	1745 mm
Overall width	785 mm
Overall height	990 mm
Wheelbase	1185 mm
Min. ground clearance	225 mm
Seat height	740 mm
Fuel tank capacity	4.7 lit
Weight (Net)	62 kg
Tires front	2,75-17-4PR
Back	3,60-14-4PR
Brakes front	Drum
Back	Drum

YZ125

Engine

Type . . . . 2 stroke, single
Displacement . . . . 123 cc
Bore/stroke . . . . 56,0 x 50,0 mm
Compression ratio . . . . 8,5 : 1
Max.horsepower . . . . 19.5 Kw (26.5 HP)/1.100
Lubrication system . . . . Mixture oil/fuel (32 : 1)
Starting system . . . . Kick
Gearbox . . . . 6 gear

Dimensions

Overall length . . . . 2115 mm
Overall width . . . . 950 mm
Overall height . . . . 1215 mm
Wheelbase . . . . 1430 mm
Min.ground clearance . . . . 340 mm
Seat height . . . . 940 mm
Weight (net) . . . . 85 kg
Fuel tank capacity . . . . 6,5 lit
Tires front 3,00-21-4Pr
Back 4,00-18-4PR
Brakes front . . . . Drum
Back . . . . Drum

YZ250

Engine

Type . . . . 2 stroke, single
Displacement . . . . 246 cc
Bore/stroke . . . . 70,0 x 64,0 mm
Compression ratio . . . . 8,1 : 1
Max. horsepower . . . . 29.5 Kw (40 HP)/8.000
Max. torque . . . . 37.0 Nm (3.77 Kg-m)/6.500
Lubrication system . . . . Mixture oil/fuel
Starting system . . . . Kick
Gearbox . . . . 6 gear

Dimensions

Overall length . . . . 2155 mm
Overall width . . . . 935 mm
Overall height . . . . 1195 mm
Wheelbase . . . . 1455 mm
Min. ground clearance . . . . 310 mm
Seat height . . . . 935 mm
Weight (Net) . . . . 97 kg
Fuel tank capacity . . . . 7,6 lit
Tires front 3,00-21-4PR
Back 5,10-21-4PR
Brakes front . . . . Drum
Back . . . . Drum

YZ465

Engine

Type	2 stroke, single
Displacement	465 cc
Bore/stroke	85,0 x 82,0 mm
Compression ratio	7,0 : 1
Max. horsepower	38.2 Kw (52 HP)/7.000
Max. torque	55.5 Nm (5.65 Kg-m)/6.000
Lubrication system	Mixture oil/fuel (32: 1)
Starting system	Kick
Gearbox	5 gear

Dimensions

Overall length	2175 mm
Overall width	935 mm
Overall height	1195 mm
Wheelbase	1480 mm
Min.ground clearance	310 mm
Seat height	935 mm
Weight (Net)	102 kg
Fuel tank capacity	9,0 lit
Tires front	3,00-21-4PR
Back	5,10-18-4PR
Brakes front	Drum
Back	Drum

In 1981 the team was: Carlqvist, Vromans, Vimond and Velkeneers - with Neil Hudson, the boy from Bristol, who had been second in the 1979 250cc title to Carlqvist; and back-up rider Dave Watson, from Gloucestershire, another former schoolboy racer who had taken the top prize in the British under-18 Championship.

Their machines were . . .

YAMAHA FACTORY MOTO-CROSSERS SPECIFICATIONS

	YZM125	YZM250	YZM500
ENGINE	2-stoke, watercooled single	2-stroke, watercooled single	2-stroke, watercooled single
DISPLACEMENT	123 cc	245 cc	487 cc
MAX. HORSEPOWER	Over 30PS/11,000 rpm	Over 43PS/8,000 rpm	Over 53PS/7,000 rpm
IGNITION SYSTEM	C.D.I.	C.D.I.	C.D.I
LUBRICATION SYSTEM	Pre-mixing (20:1)	Pre-mixing 20:1)	Pre-mixing (20:1)
TRANSMISSION	6-speed gearbox	5-speed gearbox	4-speed gearbox
TYRE SIZE (F)	3.00-21	3.00 - 21	3.00-21
TYRE SIZE (R)	4.00 - 18	4.00 - 18	5.00 - 18
BRAKE (F)	Drum	Drum	Drum
BRAKE (R)	Drum	Drum	Drum
SUSPENSION (F)	Telescopic fork (air damper plus coil spring)	Telescopic fork (air damper plus coil spring)	Telescopic fork (air damper plus coil spring)
SUSPENSION (R)	Swing arm (with Mono-cross unit)	Swing arm (with Mono-cross unit)	Swing arm (with Mono-cross unit)
FUEL TANK CAPACITY	7.0 lit	9.0 lit	11.0 lit
CLUTCH	Wet Multiplate	Wet Multiplate	Wet Multiplate

In 1982 the team details were:

Name: Hakan Carlqvist
Nationality: Sweden
Date of Birth: Jan. 15, 1954
Race career:
   1976: Rode a Swedish importer's Ossa machine in 250cc World Championship
   1977: Took part in 250cc World Championship as a works Husqvarna rider.
   1978: Chalked up his first GP win in Spain. Placed 7th in 250cc World Championship.
   1979: Won 250cc World Championship.
   1980: Placed 3rd in 500cc World Championship. Won Swedish National Championship.
   1981: Placed 3rd in 500cc World Championship.

Name: Neil Hudson
Nationality: Great Britian
Date of Birth: Jan. 14, 1957
Race career:
   1978: Placed 5th in 250cc World Championship.
   1979: Place 2nd in 250cc World Championship.
   1981: Won 250cc World Championship.

Name: Danny Laporte
Nationality: USA
Date of Birth: Dec. 3, 1956
Race Career:
   1976: Placed 3rd in AMA 125cc Championship.
   1977: Placed 2nd in AMA 125cc Championship.
   1979: Won AMA 500cc Championship.
   1980 to 1981: Placed high in Super Cross & AMA Championships.

Name: Dave Watson
Nationality: Great Britian
Date of birth: Jan. 31,1961
Height: 183 cm
Weight: 65 kg
Race career:
   1976: Rode a YZ125 in schoolboy moto-cross in Northern Ireland.
   1980: Took part in under-21-years-old European championship. Won 500cc Motocross des Nations. Placed 5th in British National Championship.
   1981: Placed 8th in 250cc World Championship.
*The family moved to Gloucester, England from Northern Ireland when Watson was 16 years old.

Name: Jacky Vimond
Nationality: France
Date of birth: Jul. 18, 1961
Race career:
   1977: Made a debut in National Championship. Won 10 races.
   1978: Won French junior class (125cc) Championship.
   1979: Won French 125cc Championship.
   1980: Won French 125cc Championship.
   1981: Placed 9th in 125cc World Championship.

Jacky Vimond working hard.

Yamaha 125cc 1983

Name: Marc Velkeneers
Nationality: Belgium
Date of birth: Aug. 5, 1961
Race career:
  1975: Made a debut in National Championship. Won 10 junior class races.
  1976: Took part in 250cc National Championship.
  1978: Won 125cc National Championship.
  1979: Placed 2nd in 125cc World Championship Belgian GP, and 3rd in West German GP.
  1980: Took part in all the rounds of 125cc World Championship and placed 4th in final ranking.
  1981: Placed 4th in 125cc World Championship.

Name: Bob Hannah
Nationality: USA
Date of birth: Sep. 26, 1956
Height: 178cm
Weight: 63 kg
Race career:
  1974: Won junior 250cc race in California.
  1975: Took part in 10 club events, California, winning 18 races.
  1976: Won AMA 125cc Championship. Placed 6th in AMA 250cc Championship.
  1977: Won Super Cross Championship. Placed 3rd in AMA 125cc Championship, 7th in 250cc Championship and 2nd in 500cc Championship. Placed 2nd in Trans AMA Championship.
  1978: Won Super Cross AMA 250cc and Trans AMA Championships.
  1979: Won Super Cross and AMA 250cc Championships.
  1980: Placed 3rd in Trans USA Championship.
  1981: Placed 4th in Super Cross Series. Placed 5th in AMA 250cc Championship. Placed 4th in Trans USA Championship.

Yamaha 250cc 1983

Name: Broc Glover
Nationality: USA
Date of birth: May 16, 1960
Height: 176 cm
Weight:75kg
Race Career:
  1974: Made a debut in a local amateur race.
  1975: Finished 3rd in Los Angeles high school moto-cross.
  1976: Placed 2nd in AMA 125cc Championship.
  1977: Won AMA 125cc Championship.
  1978: Won AMA 125cc Championship.
  1979: Won AMA 125cc Championship.
  1980: Placed 2nd AMA 125cc Championship. Placed 5th in Super Cross
        Championship and 2nd in Trans USA Championship
  1981: Won AMA 500cc Championship. Won Trans USA Championship. Placed 8th
        in Super Cross Series.

Name: Scott Burnworth
Nationality: USA
Date of birth: Jan. 24, 1963
Height: 175 cm
Weight: 66 kg
Race career:
  1980: Placed 6th AMA 125cc Championship.
  1981: Joined the YMUS team. Placed 6th AMA 125cc Championship.

Name: Mike Bell
Nationality: Canada
Date of birth: Aug. 8, 1957
Height: 189 cm
Weight: 78 kg
Race Career:
  1972: Made a debut in a local junior race.
  1974: Won Canadian National Championship. Won 13 night races in a row.
  1976: Won CMC night National Open Class Championship.
  1978: Placed 6th in Super Cross Championship.
  1979: Placed 3rd in Super Cross Championship. Placed 2nd in AMA 500cc
        Championship and 2nd in Trans USA Championship.
  1980: Won Super Cross Championship. Placed 2nd in AMA 250cc Championship.
  1981: Placed 2nd in Super Cross Series. Placed 2nd in AMA 500cc Championship.
        Placed 4th in Trans USA Championship.

There were two new faces drafted into the line-up for season '83. They were "Diamond Jim" Gibson, the 125cc title chase leader, and the second American to join Yamaha; the first, of course, was Danny La Porte. The second man was Dutchman Henk van Mierlo.

It was a formidable array of talent that attacked the titles in 1983 and here is the list of the men and their mounts - with their back-up support.

125cc GP		Team
Jim Gibson	Factory bike 0W67	Yamaha Motor Denmark
Pekka Vehkonen	Factory bike 0W67/YZ 125 k	Ov Arwidson Yamaha
Jacky Vimond	YZ 125 Factory bike 0W67	Sonauto Yamaha
John Hensen	YZ 125 k	Yamaha Motor (Nederland)
Jan Postema	YZ 125 k	Yamaha Motor (Nederland)
250cc GP		
Danny La Porte	Factory bike 0W68	Yamaha Motor Denmark
Jo Martens	Factory bike 0W68	D'Ieteren Sport Yamaha
Dave Watson	YZ 250 k	Mitsui U.K. Yamaha
Soren Mortensen	YZ 250 k	Yamaha Motor Denmark
Matti Tarkkonen	YZ 250 k	Arwidson Yamaha
Henk van Mierlo	YZ 250 k	Yamaha Motor (Nederland)
Jean-Paul Mingels	YZ 250 k	Sonnauto Yamaha
500cc GP		
Hakan Carlqvist	Factory bike 0W64	Hallman & Eneqvist Yamaha
Jukka Sintonen	Factory bike 0W64	Ov Arwidson Yamaha
Neil Hudson	YZ 490 k	Mitsui U.K. Yamaha
Franco Picco	YZ 490 k	Belgarda Yamaha
Michael Heutz	YZ 490 k	Mitsui GmbH Yamaha
Side-car GP		
Ton van Heugten-Jaap van Vliet	TR1 V-twin engine	Yamaha Motor (Nederland)
Josef Brockhausen Hubert Rebele	XS Twin Engine	Mitsui GmbH Yamaha
Emil Bollhalder-Charly Büsser	XS Twin engine	Hostettler Yamaha

m Gibson   *Dave Watson*   *Neil Hudson*

And this is how their machines measured up . . .

Model Specifications	YZM 125	YZM 250	YZM 500
Engine type	2-stroke, watercooled, single, YPVS, Rotary Disc Valve Induction System	2-stroke, water-cooled, single YPVS	2-stroke, air-cooled, single, YPVS
Displacement	123cc	246cc	487cc
Maximum Power output	more than 33 PS at 11.250 rpm	more than 44 PS at 8.250 rpm	more than 56 PS at 7.000 rpm
Ignition system	C.D.I	C.D.I	C.D.I
Lubrication method	Pre-mix	Pre-mix	Pre-mix
Transmission	5-speed gearbox	5-speed gearbox	4-speed gearbox
Tyre (front)	3.00 - 21	3.00-21	3.00-21
Tyre (rear)	4.00 - 18	5.00-18	5.00-18
Brake (front)	Drum	Drum	Drum
Brake (rear)	Drum	Drum	Drum
Suspension (front)	Telescopic (air/oil spring)	Telescopic(air/oil spring)	Telescopic (air/oil spring)
Suspension (rear)	Swing arm with mono cross	Swing arm with mono cross	Swing arm with mono cross
Fuel tank cap.	7.0 litres	9.0 litres	11.0 litres
Clutch type	Wet multi-plate	Wet multi-plate	Wet multi-plate

The factory reports for the 1983 season make fascinating reading; they add up to the drama of titles won and lost and give a rivetting insight to the battles, at all levels, for off-road honours . . .

Grand Prix 250cc of Spain

Circuit: Very hard
Weather: Sunny
Spectators: 16.000
Bikes' equipments:

Bike of	Rear shock/spring	Tyres	Airfilter	Plug
La Porte (YZM)	Öhlins	Dunlop/Bridgestone	Phase 1	Champion
Martens (YZM)	Öhlins	Dunlop/Bridgestone	Phase 1	Champion
Watson (YZ)	Öhlins	Dunlop/Bridgestone	Phase 1	Champion

Though his results were not bad, Danny deserved a better score. Leading the second heat from the start, reigning world Champion Danny La Porte was on his way to a brilliant win when his front wheel partly broke a few laps before the end! That left Danny with the fourth place, the victory going to Belgian rider Jean-Claude Laquaye; Jobé, second, and Jo Martens, third, also profited from Danny's problems.

Jobé had won the first motto, ahead of La Porte and Van der Ven. Jobé had the best start, Danny started in fifth spot to conquer the second place later which was earlier the property of an impressive Mortensen (1st Grand Prix on his YZ Yamaha - he later crashed after hitting a big stone and retired) and also Jo Martens (crashed, dropped down to seventh). Martens signed a good second heat, Mortensen had a disastrous start, missing all his chances.

The Spanish round, again run on the very hard and difficult circuit of Sabadell, was not profitable to three other Yamaha riders; Dave Watson managed only a tenth place (crash in 2nd heat). Tarkkonen ended with an eight place in heat two. In heat one, his chain came off while he was riding an excellent fifth place. Dutch sand rider Henk van Mierlo did not really appreciate the Spanish conditions. He finished both heats but only in 16th and 19th position.

Grand Prix 250 cc of France

Circuit: Very muddy
Weather: Rainy
Spectators: 10,000
Particularities: Best production bike: YZ (Dave Watson)
Bikes' equipments:

Bike of	Rear shock/spring	Tyres	Airfilter	Plug
La Porte (YZM)	Öhlins	Dunlop	Phase 1	Champion
Martens (YZM)	Öhlins	Dunlop	Phase 1	Champion
Watson (YZ)	Öhlins	Trelleborg/Pirelli	Phase 1	Champion

The French Grand Prix 250cc turned into a disaster for reigning world champion Danny La Porte, who could not score any points on the race track of Château-du-Loir, near Le Mans. The race day was spoiled by constant rain, and the circuit was transformed into a muddy arena!

While Jobé was winning both heats, Danny and his mechanic were desperately trying to find the reasons of two engine seizures.

Jo Martens rode brilliant races. Second behind Jobé in heat one Jo was on his way to the same place in heat two, but he lost two places at the end as he got stuck in a very muddy section.

Dave Watson had also a profitable day, scoring a fourth and a fifth. Other Yamaha riders came in the points: Tarkkonen, Mortensen, van Mierlo, and the young French Gervaise, actually the only Frenchman to score a point in his "home Grand Prix".

In the championship Jobé is leading his countrymen Laquaye and Jo Martens. Danny is fourth, but already 37 points behind Jobé. But people say: "Nothing is impossible in racing". . .

Grand Prix 250cc of Holland

Circuit: Sand
Weather: Sun and rain
Spectators: 14.000
Particularities: Moto-cross is a tough job! S.B. Mortensen, Yamaha Denmark rider, has undergone a difficult operation before the start of the GP season. Difficult is the word, really! Suffering often in the winter from heavy neck pain, Mortensen was later told by doctors that his life was in danger, with only one muscle holding his neck! Operated in emergency, Mortensen has since recovered well, but despite some good performances, the Danish rider is still far in the current championship classifications. But he should have better days later this season. He deserves it, after a long period of health troubles.

Bikes' equipments:

Bike of	Rear shock/spring	Tyres	Air filter	Plugs
La Porte (YZM)	Öhlins	Dunlop/Pirelli	Phase 1	Champion
Martens (YZM)	Öhlins	Dunlop	Phase 1	Champion
Watson (YZ)	Öhlins	Dunlop/Trelleborg	Phase 1	Champion
Tarkkonen (YZ)	Öhlins	Trelleborg	Phase 1	Champion

"The rider in front of me slipped off" Danny said, "to avoid him I had to go out of the track. My engine stopped, I lost some time to restart it. I was mad. I had to do all the job again!"

Danny did a good job coming back to fourth place. Van Mierlo secured an excellent fifth place, a deserved reward knowing Henk's problems.

At the top of the race Jobé brilliantly managed to keep Jo Martens a few seconds behind him. During forty minutes, both riders offered a great show to the 14,000 spectators of Markelo. In the last laps, Jo released his pressure and the gap immediately increased to almost ten seconds.

"As I passed a lapped rider, I almost crashed", Jo said. "I then lost all chances and I secured my twelve points."

Dave Watson this time got two points but was not happy: "I did not ride well", he said. "I should have done much better. It is a bad day for me."

A crash in heat two, cost points to Matti Tarkkonen, who left the top ten. Only Mortensen was missing by the finish. The Danish rider had a bad start, made his way through the field but soon crashed and retired (handlebars bent).

At the championship, Jobé has increased his points capital with the maximum. He now leads Martens, Laquaye and La Porte and has a comfortable margin on all of his rivals.

Once again, rain welcomed the 250cc riders on Saturday, May 7th in Markelo. But luckily, the sun won from the rain on Sunday, and the Grand Prix of Holland could be run in reasonable conditions.

On this sandy course, Yamaha riders La Porte and Martens were determined to go for their first 1983 Grand Prix win. But the current championship leader, Georges Jobé was as much determined to win as his main rivals, and his two excellent starts gave him a good advantage.

In heat one, while Jobé was easily leading the race, Martens and La Porte were struggling to emerge from about twentieth place.. So did other Yamaha riders, Tarkkonen, Watson and Mortensen.

The reason was simple: behind the first five at the start, a big crash occurred, blocking a lot of top riders into a complicated "pile up".

Martens and La Porte furiously rode impressive races, coming back to second and third places half way through the race. But Jobé was leading by 40 seconds and unbeatable.

In the late part of the race, Danny managed to pass his teammate, saving two more points in the championship.

Tarkkonen and Mortensen also managed to get back in the points. Watson and van Mierlo, eleventh and twelfth, failed. For the Dutchman, this was a dramatic race; he badly twisted his right ankle during Saturday's practice. Starting 5th, Henk just escaped from the big crash, but he could not hold his place and dropped out of the points.

"Here in Markelo, most of the corners are right ones, and I really cannot use my right foot. Therefore, I lose a lot of time in the corners. I am having bad luck, this season", Henk said. "Like in France, where I lost a fourth place as my chain went off (stone). And now, I twist my ankle at my home Grand Prix!"

Despite continuous pain, Henk van Mierlo started in the second moto. His start was brilliant, he was fourth behind Jobé, Martens and Van der Ven. La Porte was seventh . . . but lost more than ten places during the second lap . . .

Grand Prix 250cc of Bulgaria

Circuit: Hard
Weather: Dry
Spectators: More than 50,000
Bikes'equipments:

Machine of	Rear spring/shock	Tyres	Airfilter	Plugs
La Porte (YZM)	Öhlins	Dunlop/Bridgestone	Phase 1	Champion
Martens (YZM)	Öhlins	Dunlop	Phase 1	Champion
Watson (YZ)	Öhlins	Dunlop/Trelleborg	Phase 1	Champion
Mortensen (YZ)	Öhlins	Dunlop	Phase 1	Champion

Dave Watson flying

GP 250cc of Bulgaria

More than 50,000 spectators attended the surprising overall win of their hero, Dimitar Rangelov. Rangelov and championship leader Jobé shaped the best results; each one a first and a second place.

The weather was sunny and dry. Dry also were Yamaha riders' results! Danny La Porte crashed in heat one as he was following the leaders; in heat two, he could not stay with them and had to secure a third place.

The day was dramatic for Jo Martens: in the first lap of heat one, Jo hit Watson's back wheel and crashed. Danny could not avoid his teammate, hitting his right arm. This incident ruined Jo's day. He desperately tried to race but the pain in his arm was so heavy that Jo was denied the chance of getting any points in the championship.

Other Yamaha riders were not too lucky: Watson, Mortensen and van Mierlo only scored points in heat one. Tarkkonen crashed twice because of local riders. So did Henk van Mierlo in heat one, when he was riding an excellent fourth place!

All those incidents combined with Jobé's performances have put the Belgian rider in an incredibly strong position in the championship, after only four races: Jobé leads Jo Martens, still second, by 58 points!

Grand Prix 250cc of Germany

Circuit: Very hard, dry
Weather: Warm sunny
Spectators: 15,000
Bikes' equipments:

Bikes of	Rear shock/spring	Tyres	Air filter	Plug
La Porte (YZM)	Öhlins	Dunlop/Pirelli	Phase 1	Champion
Martens (YZM)	Öhlins	Dunlop/Bridgestone	Phase 1	Champion
Watson (YZ)	Öhlins	Dunlop/Bridgestone	Phase 1	Champion

Particularities:
Henk van Mierlo crashed during the official time training on Sunday morning. Although seriously injured, the Dutchman managed to get on his bike again and ride it to the finish line, where he fell off. Carried in emergency to the nearest hospital, Henk van Mierlo was urgently operated and the doctors were forced to remove a kidney. Back in Holland already, Henk hopes to race again in the future.

Soren B. Mortensen had an excellent start in heat one, but the Danish rider did not keep his third place for more that a lap: he crashed and retired (handlebars bent). In heat two, he had a bad start, was coming back but again crashed and retired (same reason).

On a track which he has known for years, Jean-Paul Mingels held a good sixth place in the heat one but soon before the finish he hit his left foot badly and was forced to retire. The same foot would hurt him too much in heat two and Mingels again retired after a bad start. Mingels, presently in excellent position to become the new 250cc French champion, does not compete all the grand prix.

Danny La Porte on a high.

"I'm not any more in a good position to run a full season", he said. "I have to be my own mechanic, and I basically concentrate on the national 250cc title. Sometimes, I still suffer from my heavy crashes of the last two Paris-Dakar rallies. Especially my left foot becomes painful as soon as I hit somewhere in a race, or during a practice session. This foot is my worst souvenir from the 1982 rally . . ."

This Grand Prix season had started reasonably for Danny La Porte. But after the opening round in Spain, it all went wrong for the reigning world champion. France, Holland, Bulgaria . . . three Grand Prix which brought a lot of points to George Jobé, putting Danny a long way behind.

This situation had to change, and it did change, during the recent German Grand Prix, run at Beuern, a famous old but still interesting racing track. La Porte already warned everybody during the official training, as he signed the best time, immediately followed (two hundreds of a second . . .) by an excellent Dave Watson. Both Yamaha riders were determined to gain as many points as possible in Beuern.

Starting in third place, Danny La Porte quickly moved to first and easily controlled the race. While the American was "flying" to his first

Neil Hudson with his foot down.

win of the year, Dave Watson, ninth after one lap, made an impressive come back to second place, his last victim being his compatriot Whatley. Jobé had a bad start and also quickly moved to the front rows; he finished fourth.

The Belgian rider and his eternal rival, Danny, started the second heat together. For a couple of laps, Jobé chased Danny and both riders were already far ahead of everybody else. In a corner, La Porte braked too hard and fell, Jobé passed him and went away, taking the victory to his account. Danny's crash cost him about 15 seconds, but the American preserved easily his second place, winning the German Grand Prix overall.

Dave Watson had a disastrous start (about 25th) and rode brilliantly back to sixth place... just behind Jo Martens. Dave passed Jo just in the last lap, but the Belgian rider could not afford to be beaten and repassed Dave before the finish.

Two-times fifth, Jo was not too satisfied: "Beuern is a very hard circuit; it is very fast, and I couldn't get used to it. Any way, very hard, fast circuits still remain my weak point in racing . . ."

Other Yamaha riders failed to get points in Beuern: Matti

Heavy going for Honda: two muddy bikes, Andre Malherbe (left) and Graham Noyce (right)

Tarkkonen, twelfth and eleventh, had two bad starts and was still suffering from a recent ankle injury.

Grand Prix 250cc of England

Circuit: Deep sand, dusty
Weather: dry sunny
Spectators : 15,000
Bikes' equipments:

Bike of	Rear shock/spring	Tyres	Air filter	Plug
La Porte (YZM)	Öhlins	Dunlop/Pirelli	Phase 1	Champion
Martens (YZM)	Öhlins	Dunlop/Pirelli	Phase 1	Champion

The British Grand Prix traditionally run in Hawkstone Park on a very sandy course has been totally dominated by a two-man show. Danny La Porte and Georges Jobé have scored equal points, each rider winning one heat and finishing the other heat in second place. This status quo has of course not changed the current championship situation, as Jobé still leads Danny by 60 points.

In heat one, Jobé quickly took the lead while Danny was fighting his own way in the middle of the field, around the eighteenth place in lap one. If Jobé could not be threatened by anybody, Danny furiously passed all his rivals, including strong men Martens and Van der Ven, to finish second.

In heat two, Danny and Jobé offered a real "fighting" festival to the spectators for twenty-five minutes. Then Jobé made a mistake and Danny ran away to win the heat, but not the Grand Prix.

Jo Martens scored two fourth places. As a great sand specialist, people were eventually expecting better results from Jo. Would Jo still suffer from his injured arm in Bulgaria? Soren B. Mortensen, fifth in the first motto, held the fourth position in heat two until two laps before the end; he unfortunately had to retire (engine seized), losing precious points in his struggle to enter the "ten" of the championship.

Matti Tarkkonen, still riding with a painful ankle, managed to finish twice in the points. In front of his home crowd, Dave Watson had a disastrous day. Soon in the first heat, Dave had to ride without goggles (some places of the circuit had been watered, and Dave had got so much water and mud on his goggles that he had been forced to throw them away) and finally he had to stop, giving an excellent third place up because he just couldn't see anything . . . In heat two, Dave was riding in fourth place when a heavy crash brutally stopped him. Dave had lost a lot of precious points . . .

GP 500cc of Switzerland

Circuit: Relatively dry (much rain on Saturday)
Weather: Dry
Spectators: 30,000
Bikes' equipments:

Bike of	Rear shock/spring	Tyres	Airfilter	Plug
Carlqvist (YZM)	Öhlins	Trelleborg/Michelin	Phase 1	NGK
Sintonen (YZM)	Öhlins	Dunlop/Pirelli	Phase 1	Champion
Hudson (YZ)	Öhlins	Dunlop	Phase 1	Champion

500cc Payerne

The opening round of the 500cc world championship series was at Payerne, Switzerland, a beautiful and spectacular circuit which again attracted about 30,000 moto-cross enthusiasts.

Favourite of this year Grand Prix season, Yamaha's top rider Hakan Carlqvist was determined to ride an impressive first Grand Prix. With the best training time, Carla clearly started ahead of all his rivals in the first heat. During nine laps, he remained the master of the race, despite a continuous pain in his back: "I suddenly got heavy cramps during the second lap", Hakan said. "The pain was really big and I just could not keep riding as well as I wanted to." Despite the heavy pain , Hakan managed a fourth place in the opening heat.

Iffendic, France, July 3, 1983: 500cc Moto-Cross World Championship high flyers.

The dusty road to the title: Malherbe and Carlqvist (No. 8)

Brad Lackey

It was Carla again leading the field from the second start, but his pain quickly became so heavy that he lost all his speed and tempo, dropping from first to eleventh quickly: "It was impossible to go on. Anyway, I was out of points. Therefore I stopped." Carlqvist's troubles profited his major rivals in the championship: Malherbe, Noyce and Vromans.

The other Yamaha factory riders were not too lucky: Sintonen could not avoid a bike soon after the first start and crashed. When laying on the ground, two riders rode over his left arm.

Taking the start of the second heat with a sore arm, Sintonen could only manage a ninth place.

Neil Hudson, riding a standard YZ490, rode a brilliant fifth place in the second motto. Victim of an early massive crash in heat one, Neil lost much time and bravely tried to come back in the points. But his rear brake had been damaged in the crash, and despite his efforts (twelfth after 20' race), Neil had to stop.

Grand Prix 500cc of Austria

Circuits: Hard, dry
Weather: Dry
Spectators: 14,000
Bikes's equipments:

Bike of	Rear shock/spring	Tyres	Air filter	Plug
Carlqvist (YZM)	Öhlins	Dunlop/Pirelli	Phase 1	NGK
Sintonen (YZM)	Öhlins	Pirelli/Dunlop	Phase 1	Champion
Hudson (YZ)	Öhlins	Metzeler/Dunlop	Phase 1	Champion

Beaten by his back pain in the Swiss Grand Prix, Hakan Carlqvist has proven during the Austrian Grand Prix, held in Sittendorf (area of Vienna), that he is one of the most motivated riders to clinch this year's world champion title.

"Carla" rode a brilliant first race, leading from start to finish. In heat two, Carlqvist was also in a position to win. In the late stages of the race, he had a very close duel with Graham Noyce who finally beat him by a whisker. But Yamaha's number one rider won the Grand Prix overall, and, more important, could catch some precious points back from his main rivals, Noyce and Malherbe. Carlqvist has currently surrendered 17 points to Noyce, and 14 to Malherbe.

Jukka Sintonen had two brilliant races in Sittendorf. With a fourth and a sixth, Jukka has much improved his position in the championship.

With Neil Hudson also scoring a sixth and an eighth place, Sittendorf turned out to be a much better day than Payerne for Yamaha.

Grand Prix 500cc of Germany

Circuit: Extremely muddy
Weather: Rain
Spectators: 10,000
Bikes' equipments:

Bike of	Rear shock/spring	Tyres	Airfilter	Plug
Carlqvist (YZM)	Öhlins	Dunlop/Trelleborg/ Michelin	Phase 1	NGK
Sintonen (YZM)	Öhlins	Dunlop	Phase 1	Champion
Hudson (YZ)	Öhlins	Dunlop	Phase 1	Champion

Carlqvist's factory motocrosser

Rain likes moto-cross, obviously! The 500cc German Grand Prix in Northeim was held in incredibly muddy conditions. After many changes on the track, the first heat could be started . . . almost when the second heat was scheduled: Actually heat two started around seven o'clock!

In heat one, Carlqvist quickly took the lead, Malherbe being his closest rival, 15 seconds behind. Unfortunately, Carla later got a flat tyre that forced him to slow down. Luckily, only Malherbe could profit from this problem, the Yamaha rider securing the twelve points of the second place.

In heat two, the victory went to Malherbe again. Carla had a poor start (fifteenth) and moved up to sixth place. "I made some mistakes" Carla said. "In the beginning, I was following Noyce, who finished second. I had a bad ride in this race . . ."

A mistake cost Neil Hudson the fourth place in heat one: he finished sixth. In the second motto, he was eliminated as the chain of his bike went off.

Jukka Sintonen had a crash soon after the first start and retired. In the second race he managed a seventh place.

German Yamaha rider Michael Heutz was in the points for a long time in the first heat but a crash cost him his points. In heat two, a rider crashed into Michael's bike, damaging the exhaust pipe. Heutz who is still recovering from a serious winter injury was forced to retire.

Grand Prix 500cc of Sweden

Circuit: Sand, muddy
Weather: Rain
Spectators: 20.000
Bikes' equipments:

Bike of	Rear spring/shock	Tyres	Airfilter	Plug
Carlqvist (YZM)	Öhlins	Dunlop	Phase 1	NGK
Sintonen (YZM)	Öhlins	Dunlop	Phase 1	Champion

In front of his home crowd, Hakan Carlqvist had two excellent races, and scored 27 points for the championship. As his main rivals, Malherbe and Noyce, only scored respectively 10 and 18 points, "Carla" is now much closer in the current championship standings. And there are still eight grand prix to go!

Rain was again present during the races, but it could not spoil the sandy track conditions. In heat one, the race was first led by Vromans, followed by an excellent Sintonen (he loves sand riding!) and Carlqvist. Later Vromans crashed and Sintonen replaced the Belgian rider at the best position: the first one! But "Carla" would not allow his teammate to have his first ever heat win, and a few laps before the finish, the Swede passed Jukka, taking the victory.

Hakan Carlqvist at St. Antonis. The final round of the 500cc World Championship,
21.8.1983.

Grinning bunch. Left to right: Torsten Hallman, Bengt Aberg, Paul Butler.

In heat two, Carla quickly moved to third place, behind Everts and Noyce. Later he passed the British rider, and rushed to the leader. But Everts brilliantly resisted Carlqvist during the last two laps, scoring his first ever heat win in grand prix. "Carla" had missed the "double win", however, the overall win was for him. He was closer to the leader in the championship.

Disaster struck for Sintonen just after the start as he was one of the victims of a massive pile up (slight hand injury).

It was also a bad day for Neil Hudson who left the circuit without a point. Unfortunate involvement in crashes had been his lot, too.

Grand Prix 500cc of Finland

Circuit: Sand, some hard places.
Weather: Dry
Spectators: 10,000
Bikes' equipment:

Bike of	Rear shock/spring	Tyres	Air Filter	Plug
Carlqvist (YZM)	Öhlins	Michelin	Phase 1	NGK
Sintonen (YZM)	Öhlins	Dunlop	Phase 1	Champion

The battle went on, during the Finnish Grand Prix, between Andre Malherbe, Hakan Carlqvist and Graham Noyce. However, the Grand Prix was won by the still-fast Tapiani Pikkarainen, who delighted his home crowd twice in the day.

The Finnish public was rather pleased in heat one as Pikkarainen and Jukka Sintonen offered a fantastic battle, with the main stars, Noyce, "Carla" and Malherbe left behind. As the race was going to its end, the tension went up as Sintonen closed on Pikkarainen. In the last laps, the Yamaha factory rider tried all what he could to pass his compatriot and win his first ever Grand Prix heat. But Pikkarainen controlled the race till the chequered flag. Sintonen, suffering from a slight hand injury (Sweden), finished only seventh in heat two. "Sandwiched" between Noyce and Malherbe, Carlqvist was not too happy as his fourth place could have been much improved if his rear brake would have worked.

Neil Hudson, second fastest time in practice (. . . between Carla and Sintonen), lost his chances soon after the start in a crash caused by another rider, but came back to ninth place. Neil had the same problem in heat two, was fighting again to come in the points. . . until a lapped rider made him crash. Hudson seems to have a subscription to lady bad luck, this year, and he certainly deserved a better Finnish Grand Prix on a track which he particularly likes (Neil won there in 1982).

In heat two, the two strongest riders of the moment, Malherbe and Carlqvist, had a splendid battle for the first place. Both riders gave what they had and it was Malherbe who beat the Yamaha rider by a whisker. Noyce finished sixth.

In the championship, Noyce left his leadership to Malherbe, conceding also precious points to Carlqvist.

Grand Prix 500cc of Italy

Circuit: Very hard
Weather: Dry
Spectators: 20,000
Bikes' equipments:

Bike of	Rear shock/spring	Tyres	Air filter	Plug
Carqvist (YZM)	Öhlins	Pirelli	Phase 1	NGK
Sintonen (YZM)	Öhlins	Pirelli/Bridgestone	Phase 1	Champion
Picco (YZ)	Öhlins	Pirelli		
Hudson (YZ)	Öhlins	Dunlop	Phase 1	Champion

Once again, the 500cc category turns out to be the most interesting and fascinating one of the season, Hakan Carlqvist is chasing the leader André Malherbe by just four points. And Graham Noyce has still a chance, thirteen points behind the Yamaha rider.

The Italian Grand Prix was a complete success for Carlqvist, who won the first heat brilliantly and finished second in the next moto, after a very impressive come back.

In heat one, Carla succeeded to his teammate Sintonen after a few laps and built a solid leadership which nobody managed to threaten. Behind the Swedish rider, a lot of changes happened! Sintonen regularly losing places, or Malherbe desperately trying to take the second place from the local hero, Franco Picco.

Beside Carlqvist, Picco and his YZ Yamaha were stars of the race. Picco, number 12 in last year's championship, had passed through difficult times early in the season. The first Grand Prix were for him nightmares . . . and Picco decided to miss the Scandinavian campaign, staying in Italy to prepare "his" Grand Prix. Obviously a good idea, judging from the results in Italy. Picco is now eleventh in the championship, but will not participate in the US Grand Prix.

Picco and Malherbe were finally separated as Picco stalled his engine, lost time to restart it, and as Malherbe fell, hit by a lapped rider. Those problems profited Thorpe and Everts who finished behind the winner. Picco ended fourth, Malherbe sixth, behind Noyce.

Picco had the holeshot in heat two . . . followed by Malherbe. The Belgian needed six laps to pass the Italian and run away to catch the victory and fifteen precious points. Early in the first lap, Carlqvist was hit by Semics. Carla restarted in the 35th position and furiously gained place after place: twentieth, fourteenth, eleventh, . . . after ten laps, the Swede was fifth already. Eight laps later, he passed Picco, second. In Lovolo, Hakan was really the strongest. He was the fastest . . . with Malherbe and Picco.

Sintonen retired in heat two; he was involved in a massive crash during the early stages of the race. Neil Hudson once again didn't have a good day; starting from 15th place in the first race he finished ninth. In the second race, Neil was twenty-seventh after the first lap; he finished thirteenth.

Yamaha success was completed by the young Italian rider Claudio Di Carli, who scored his first championship points by finishing sixth in the second heat.

Grand Prix 500cc of USA

Circuit: Quite hard, but much water during the first heat (a lot of water had been spread before the race, to avoid dust).
Weather: Dry sunny
Spectators: 7,000
Bikes' equipments:

Bike of	rear shock/spring	Tyres	Air filter	Plug
Carlqvist (YZM)	Öhlins	Dunlop/Pirelli	Phase 1	NGK
Sintonen(YZM)	Öhlins	Dunlop	Phase 1	Champion

Hakan Carlqvist on the podium at St. Antonis, 21.8.1983.

Hakan Carlqvist's victory "wheelie" at St. Antonis, 21.8.1983

Hakan Carlqvist and Yamaha are leading the 500cc world championship after the US Grand Prix, run in Carlsbad, at the end of June. Carlqvist, now achieving his fourth 500cc Grand Prix season, has taken the lead for the very first time in his career. Hakan, "number 3" after a "running in" year in 1980, took again the number three in 1981, but much closer to the number one and two . . . Last year, the Swedish rider was denied his chances to become world champion before the Grand Prix season even started. An arm injury kept "Carla" away from the Grand Prix circuits for some time, and later on, his come back was hindered by a finger injury. "Number 8", Calqvist had a troublesome "opening round" this season as he suffered some back injury during the Swiss Grand Prix. But it all went well for Carlqvist from the second Grand Prix on, except in Germany, perhaps.

Finishing the Italian Grand Prix just four points behind the championship leader, Malherbe, Carlqvist dominated his rival completely in the US Grand Prix. Carlsbad was a Yamaha festival with Carlqvist scoring a "one-two" and Broc Glover, Yamaha US official rider, scoring a "two-one". In heat one, Carlqvist beat Glover by thirty seconds. In heat two, Glover won by ten seconds, while Carlqvist had to battle with another American ace King. Carla kept his second place and secured his victory in the Grand Prix. Conclusion of the specialists in California: "only Carlqvist was able to beat the best Americans . . ."

It was a difficult day for Carlqvist's rivals in the championship: Noyce got two seventh places, Malherbe a sixth and a fifth. This gave Carlqvist a twelve point advantage in the championship.

Reigning champion Brad Lackey was making a temporary come-back and he signed reasonable results: fifth and sixth.

Jukka Sintonen managed a ninth and an eighth in his first US Grand Prix, while Hudson, eleventh in heat one, suffered again some bad luck later: he was involved in a crash at the first corner in heat two and left the race with an injured thumb.

Carlqvist, demonstrating his absolute calm and responsibility, clinched the 500cc title at St. Antonis, close to Eindhoven in the south-east corner of Holland – but there was hardly a Dutchman to be seen.

The circuit was a mass of Swedes – and after their hero Carla had ridden to restrained sixth and fourth places to amass enough points to take the crown they carried him shoulder high from the circuit.

But there were shocks, too, lying in store. For though Carlqvist was retained in defence of his superbly won title Yamaha dropped Hudson, his 500cc team-mate, La Porte, Gibson and Sintonen. The cold blast of commercial blunders made, the need to conserve money and an over-capacity line-up among the moto-cross men, dictated drastic changes . . . just as they had done in the road race set-up. But at least Yamaha were not alone in their shake-up – Suzuki were hit even harder on their racing front.

Pro-Am

The daunting, gladiatorial commitment of the eager young rivals in the Pro-Am RD 350 Cup series, Yamaha's most vividly moving advertising placard, gave Britain's Saturday afternoon television viewers some of their most thrilling watching. For there is nothing so exciting as turning the full glare of the spotlight on enthusiastic hopefuls, all out to do their level best to get recognition, when the adrenalin is pumping through their veins.

It was as if Yamaha had cast a magic spell over racing when, following on the success of the XS 400 series in Germany in 1978, it was planned by Paul Butler to urge importers to adopt the same format to give wide exposure to the potential of the RD 350s. The RD350 was the perfect machine for the job. And the concept was quickly appreciated and the bandwagon set in motion.

Germany, France, Britain, Switzerland, Denmark, Holland, Sweden and Belgium all became hosts to this most spectacular of events. Television, quick to note the breathtaking pictures it was providing, fastened on and soon the screens of Europe were filled with the heart-stopping sight of ten and more riders, elbow-to-elbow, jostling fearlessly for the lead with a chasing pack trying to get on the pace.

I do not think I fully appreciated the phrase fast-and-furious until I saw my first Pro-Am and then I was hooked. But from 1981, the first RD350 Cup season, a new dimension was added to racing, an innovation as excitingly staged as any of the seasoned Grand Prix clashes.

There is no quicker way to expose raw talent than to mount budding championship contenders on equal machinery and turn them loose with only their natural skill to provide the dividing line. And with no financial outlay young riders were allowed to give full vent to their ambitions without the penalty of a crash that could empty their bank accounts. But, more importantly, they were suddenly placed in a position where they could gauge their ability against others on equal terms and if they found they could not go through with it they could simply stop racing with no great financial loss.

The proof of the RD Cup's value as a training ground for potential Grand Prix contestants is shown by the riders who have made the breakthrough: Alan Carter, at 18 the youngest man ever to win a Grand Prix when he picked up the French 250cc title at Le Mans in 1983; Martin Wimmer, another GP winner, from Germany and Rob McElnea, the sensation of 1983 with victories for Suzuki at the Isle of Man TT and in the F1 championships in Holland, at Assen, and at Donington Park.

Andy Watts, a bank clerk from East Anglia, is another product of the Pro-Am series and an extremely useful Grand Prix rider; from France

Above: Martin Wimmer

*Right: Martin Wimmer,
Hockenheim – September 26,
1982*

came Patrick Igoa, Thierry Rapicault, both in world title racing, and Philippe Robles, a European championship entry. Germany saw Wimmer through his apprenticeship - and then funnelled the rather more lurid Harald Eckl into Grand Prix racing. Then Anders Skov, a Dane, moved up through the RD ranks and into the classics.

There is Stephen Maertens from Belgium and Michael Melander, from Sweden, both European title graduates; Christian Etienne, from France, in the Endurance and F1 championships; Steve Chambers, England, Joel Roche, France, Rob Bakker Holland and Frenchman Phillipe Pagano who all have the potential to make the breakthrough that sent tiny Yorkshireman Alan Carter into the world reckonings.

If there is hope for the future it rests on these basic foundations; from them can be built a whole new generation of Grand Prix men to follow in the footsteps of Kenny Roberts and Giacomo Agostini, two champions at the heart of Yamaha's anxiety to under line the need to nurture and develop young talent. Both Roberts and Agostini, the Marlboro-Yamaha Grand Prix team leader, feel that they should give the full benefit of their long experience in racing to the up-and-coming kids. So much so that Roberts, worried about Alan Carter's over-eagerness and subsequent crashes throughout 1983, organised to take the boy hero back to California with him for six months to strengthen him and advise him on racetrack style. Nobody prompted Roberts; he had seen for himself the huge promise in Carter, the biggest success story of all the Pro-Am series, and wanted to insure it for Yamaha.

The harvest reaped by Yamaha for an annual outlay of around £250,000 was phenomenal; the goodwill it generated among riders who would otherwise have little chance of showing their skills was enormous, too. The company name blazed through Europe's TV systems, spectators in countries where the RD Cup rounds were staged packed the circuits to see the young chargers doing their best on £1,700 machines and, through it all, there was only one serious accident - to a Swiss rider who was killed. Aside from that unfortunate incident, and despite the closest racing you could see anywhere in the world, injuries were comparatively minor.

Paul Butler, the prime mover who took over the Press and Public relations duties for Yamaha in Amstelveen in 1982, said: "I think the racing excited everybody's interest. It was by far and away the most thrilling of all the speed events on television, for instance, and I'm sure it helped to create a whole new following for the sport. Importers and dealers were deeply involved and could see dimly the value in terms of publicity for the make. Everywhere the series were staged the general appeal was the same; riders, too, benefited hugely. Not only were they able to race on machinery they didn't have to pay for, they were being paid . . . and well paid . . . to do it. All those shoe-string racers suddenly found they were in the money - and, more importantly, being thrust into the gaze of both the public and the sponsors who could further their careers even more. No wonder we were always over subscribed with riders wanting to get in on the act."

Once the idea had been mooted it was quickly taken up. The French, for example, who hardly ever need any encouragement when racing is involved speedily organised a competition. Gauloises agreed to sponsor a series and Dunlop backed them.

In no time at all the "Coupé Gauloises", probably the keenest of all the events, was under way. And in 1983 it attracted 170 riders, the survivors of pre-season qualifying; it's all fierce, competitive racing and there are heats and semi-finals to get into the grand finale. Like Germany prize money is paid at each event and on final standings; the winner received two brand new TZ250's and full sponsorship from the Patrick Pons shops for one full season in the European championships. After that, if he proves good enough, he is drafted into the Word Championship team.

In France, where the series is superbly supported by the dealers, there are ten events run in just about every corner of the country. Patrick Igoa was the 1980 winner: Rapicault won it in 1982 - and showed his Grand Prix worth by taking third place at Le Mans in the 1983 French 250cc championship round, only his second GP. Britain followed suit - Robert Jackson, then with Mitsui, realised its potential after Butler's urgings and swiftly organised a series that gripped everybody's imagination. Across the North Sea Denmark holds RD Cups at senior and junior levels - they are races totally controlled by the Federation; but Yamaha-Denmark award a new RD 350 to the winner of each competition.

Compared, say, with France and its mobile administration centre, its huge press service and regular team of technical inspectors, the Danish set-up is quite small. The competition is relatively tiny because there are so few circuits in the country, so most of the events are run in neighbouring Sweden. There are usually about twenty riders with only five events; but in the great tradition of the series the racing is every bit as fierce, even with fewer numbers, as it is in France or the UK. Denmark's first series winner was Michael Nielson - and his runner-up was Anders Skov, a fine prospect, who could probably make it to the top.

Switzerland used 250's in their RD Cup because there was no 350 market - but that, however, was scheduled to change in 1984 when they were due to race the new 350's.

The competition is almost totally financed by Yamaha's Swiss importer Hostettler, an enthusiastic supporter of racing over a long number of years. It is held over ten rounds - but as there is a ban on road racing in Switzerland seven rounds are farmed out to France, Italy and Germany. The remaining three, all hill climbs, are cleared for home venues by the Swiss authorities; it's ironic that the only fatal accident in the Cup series was in a hill climb . . .

Holland was the sixth country to adopt the kids who wanted to go racing RD Cup style. And the KNMV organise the series that involves eight circuits and 70 riders. In Sweden and Belgium the RD 350 has always dominated the production class - in Belgium, for example, 95 per cent of 500 entries are RD 350's. For as a production/promotion racer there has never been a finer machine, nor has there ever been one more extensively raced; there are some 1,000 of them in competition in Britain in 1983.

The ultimate aim is to win the overall European Pro-Am title - and Yamaha stage a big final at the end of the season. In 1982 it was run at Brands Hatch - and engineering student Steve Chambers, just 19, from Lincolnshire, England, won by two-tenths of a second from Alan Carter. And the first five riders home were covered by the tiny margin of only 1.2 seconds. It was probably the most unique motorcycle event covered by television - and the response was tremendous. Shell and Dunlop were so encouraged by it all that they confirmed their ongoing interest for 1983 even before the riders had dispersed.

The 1983 final was set for the Hockenheim-Ring, the tough Grand Prix circuit, with 24 riders in the line-up....five each from Britain, France and Germany; four from Holland, two Swiss; and one each from Denmark, Sweden and Belgium.

What about the machine? A British motor cycle writer tested one in 1983 and his opinion: "Yamaha had set themselves a very difficult task when they came to design the new RD350LC. The old model, first introduced to Britain in 1980, was so good it's damn near impossible to improve upon. The 350LC has become the ultimate production racing machine, and there are few other bikes on the road that povide such a brew of race bred performance for so small an outlay.

"But Yamaha obviously saw the 350LC falling behind the opposition in sales brochure one-upmanship. The LC has only had 'ordinary' mono-shock suspension at the rear, and there were no high-tech features to sell it to a public bombarded by super-trick, high performance middleweights".

The writer, Mat Oxley, of Motor Cycle Weekly went on: "Yamaha obviously reckoned that the addition of a rocker arm rear suspension, their Power Valve system and a racey styling job would be enough to once again convince the punters that the 350LC is the ultimate sports middleweight.

"Yamaha have always been at pains to remind the public just what RD stands for. They're proud that they've managed to put a bike on the road that is so directly descended from their all-conquering TZ racers, and it's only on the track that you can really push an LC to its limits".

The new Yamaha RD350LC employ more racing technology than any street machine yet produced. Though the heart of the new machine is still the totally-proven, 350cc twin cylinder, two-stroke, everything is changed from the crankcase up. The new engine uses the Yamaha Power Valve System straight from the factory road racers. It also features an electronic governor in the transistor ignition system, improved carburation and liquid cooling system. The chassis and styling of the 1983 RD350LC is completely new. Nothing was retained from the 1982 version.

The chassis itself is directly copied from the factory Grand Prix racers with wide-spaced frame tubes and rigidly-triangulated. Rear suspension is also taken from the Grand Prix machines: a rising rate monoshock with

R.D. 350 Cup Action

the single suspension unit mounted behind the engine unit to achieve the lowest possible centre of gravity. Short front forks have increased stanchion widths for greater resistance to flex and the cast alloy Italic wheels are of a new, triple-spoke design.

The most significant engine modification is the adoption, again from the racing department, of the Yamaha Power Valve System for the first time on any street machine. Operated electronically via a microcomputer, the Power Valve is exclusive to Yamaha and changes the timing of the exhaust port according to the engine's speed.

The result of all these modifications to engine and chassis is that the 1983 Yamaha RD350LC is faster, has more acceleration, better handling, better braking and even more striking styling than its predecessors. An amazing achievement considering that the *original* RD350LC was a machine usually discussed in superlatives!

The 1983 Yamaha RD350LC uses all the technology of the racetrack to produce a machine that can attack the twists and turns of back-country roads faster and in more safety than most motor-cycles today . . . regardless of size.

It is the most powerful 350cc machine ever produced for use on the road, putting out close to 60bhp at 9,000 rpm! Even more amazing is the fact that it is still basically the same parallel twin that kept Yamaha firmly ahead in the two-stroke performance race for almost two decades!

Just like the TZ-series road racing twins, Yamaha have continually upgraded the unit so that now, 1983, it bears little resemblance to the original. But its ancestry is undeniable. No high-performance two-stroke has a longer or better pedigree. This 1983 version has a six-speed transmission and liquid-cooling, plus a host of power-boosting items which takes its performance into the superbike class.

The Yamaha Power Valve System (YPVS) is the most obvious of these. The RD350LC is the first street machine to be equipped with the system and, in fact, it's only a couple of seasons since it was first introduced on the Grand Prix road race tracks. Without the YPVS it is impossible to achieve both the maximum power potential and the maximum torque possibilities from the same engine. Basically, advancing the exhaust port timing gives more power to a two-stroke at high rpm and retarding it will spread the power across the low speed and mid-ranges to obtain good torque. Exhaust port timing is controlled by the height of the port and YPVS is the only system that can vary this height to suit the power demands. Normal two-strokes are bound by the actual port height as cast into the cylinder barrel.

Yamaha's Power Valve is a cylindrical block placed horizontally across the exhaust port, with a cutaway to match port dimensions. At high rpm, the cutaway and port blend together to form the largest possible exhaust opening. At lower rpm, the Power Valve revolves so that it blocks off part of the exhaust port. Effectively the top edge of the exhaust opening is lowered so that the timing of the exhaust operation is delayed.

A microcomputer is linked to electronic sensors which monitor engine speed. The computer then electronically operates the valve, rotating it to achieve the best possible exhaust port size and timing for any given rpm.

A novel feature of the RD350LC YPVS operation has been incorporated because this is the first time that it has been used on a street machine. As soon as the ignition is switched on - and before the engine is started - the valve rotates to clean itself of any carbon deposits that might have built up during previous running. Thus, no regular maintenance of the valve is necessary.

Electronic controls also play a part in the ignition timing. The capacitor discharge system (CDI) fitted to the RD350LC also includes an electronic governor. Sensors monitor engine loads and adjust ignition timing to perfectly suit any situation. Coupled with the YPVS, this adds greatly to the mid-range pulling power and assists in improving fuel economy. Another measure which gives the RD350LC first class fuel efficiency in addition to added power is the balance pipe which links the two intake ducts. This also allows the machine to idle evenly on closed throttles, with smooth power pick-up at low rpm. The efficient liquid-cooling system has been further advanced for 1983, bearing in mind the increased power output of the new machine.

A new alloy radiator is utilized and the better heat-dissipation of aluminium means that the unit can be reduced to a lightweight, single core design without affecting cooling efficiency. A plastic louvred guard protects the radiator against damage and a newly-incorporated thermostat controls the water flow. This shuts the flow off for quick warm-up or when the engine is running too cool in winter temperatures but opens up to the maximum to prevent the engine overheating. The RD350LC coolant temperature is always in the safety zone.

The cooling system is now "sealed" in automotive style with a recovery tank to handle the expanded, heated water when the engine is running, instead of it disappearing down an overflow pipe. This eliminates the need for constant water level checks and topping up . . . though obviously this must still be done at service intervals.

Other smaller, but still important, modifications to the 1983 RD350LC include the left side crankcase cover constructed in fibre-glass-reinforced plastic. Engine width is reduced by 6mm and overall weight is lessened.

The screw-type clutch operation has now been replaced by the TZ racing type in which a straight axle is controlled by a cam rotated against its end by a cable-operated lever. This gives a straight push to part the clutch plates, rather than the rotary motion of the screw drive. The result is much more positive clutch engagement.

The link between the RD350LC and the Yamaha factory racing machines is unmistakable. The first glance confirms that with the triangulated chassis, rising rate suspension and 20 litre fuel tank supported by the widely-splayed top frame tubes.

Any machine that has the performance potential of the RD350LC must also have the handling to match. Which is why Yamaha have gone to the full racing chassis for this 1983 street machine. Frame tubes are set wide apart to give the most rigid support for the engine and extra structural rigidity is gained by the fully-triangulated construction. The engine uses the unique Yamaha 'orthogonal' mounting to reduce vibration. The engine pivots in the chassis on the rear mounting and is anchored by a rubber-bushed mounting at the front. The tension on this bush can be adjusted to harmonize with the vibration of the engine and damp it out before it gets through to the rider.

Suspension is by rising rate monoshock, with the gas/oil shock absorber mounted low down ahead of the swinging arm and linked to it via a bell crank. This centralizes the weight mass and also carries it very low down in the machine to get the lowest possible centre of gravity. This rising rate suspension offers progressively more resistance and stronger damping, the more it is compressed. At the other end of the scale, spring reaction and damping are at their lightest when there is the least loading on the suspension. The high tensile steel swinging arm pivots on needle roller bearings. Short telescopic forks look after the front suspension and fork leg diameter has been increased to better cope with the stresses of high speed cornering.

The twin disc brakes at the front and single rear unit are slotted to allow for the heat expansion of prolonged hard use and high-efficiency, semi-

Alan Carter, youngest ever winner of a Grand Prix, French 250cc, aged 17, in 1983

metallic pads cut out brake judder and noise. They are also more effective in wet weather than the normal asbestos components. Yamaha's latest cast alloy wheels are of unique configuration with a small, six-spoke central hub carrying the three, staggered main spokes. These are of wide diameter with circular holes cut at their centres. The result is a supremely attractive, light and rigid wheel. Wide rims allow a flatter profile for the H-rated, high speed tyres, and also permit larger tyres than standard to be fitted if the rider wishes. Standard tyre size is 90/90 x 18 front and 110/80 x 18 rear.

The instrument panel is laid out in high-visibility, aircraft-style, with a central tachometer flanked by speedometer and coolant temperature gauge. Fuel is switched on by a rotary tap blended into the side panels, as is the helmet holder and chrome grab bar. Footrests are mounted on drilled alloy plates, swept up at the rear to protect the passenger's foot from inadvertant contact with the rear wheel. Ahead of the passenger footrest is an angled plate protecting the sole of the passenger's foot from the hot muffler. The narrow seat is sculpted to give positive positioning for both rider and passenger and its lines flow smoothly into those of the race-styled petrol tank.

The whole of this package is set off by the bright red paintwork of chassis and front forks plus the streamlined flow of gas tank, side panels and tail cowling. Standard for 1983 is the final touch: the racy steering head fairing and engine cowling. These accentuate the forward thrust of the bike's aggressive styling and have the practical advantages of improving air penetration and adding aerodynamic downforce for high speed stability.

The RD350LC specification:

Engine

Type . . . . Liquid cooled, 2-stroke, Torque Induction Twin
Displacement 347cc
Bore x Stroke . . . . 64.0 x 54.0mm
Compression ratio 6.0:1
Lubrication . . . . Autolube
Starting system . . . . Kick
Ignition . . . . CDI with electric advance
Transmission 6-speed

Dimensions

Overall length . . . . 2,120 mm
Width 740mm
Height 1,165mm
Wheelbase 1,385mm
Min ground clearance 165mm
Seat height 790mm
Weight (dry) 145kg
Fuel tank capacity . . . . 20 litres
Tyre (front) . . . . 90/90-18 51 H
Tyre (rear) 110/80-18 58H
Brake (front) . . . . Double disc
Brake (rear) . . . . Disc

For the RD Cup series the machine is kept as close to standard as possible – and the only changes allowed are to the main jet in the carburettor and the final drive sprocket. Stands and stand lugs are removed before the race. Indicators, mirrors, headlamps, too, are taken off and the front footrests are set higher than is standard. The pillion pegs are removed – and in place of the headlamp there is a small head-fairing.

When riders arrive at the circuit they draw a key from a helmet to establish which of the machines they will ride – then a team of mechanics, provided by the sponsors, set about adjusting the bikes and riding position to each rider's specification and requirement. Cheating is unheard of; scrutineering of the machine after a race is so strict it is almost impossible to achieve anything illegal and such is the spirit of the challenge it's a thought that enters very few heads, I'm sure.

An interesting breakdown of the numbers of RD's being raced throughout Europe shows that in Britain there are approximately 700; 100 in Germany; 405 in France; Switzerland has 70; Holland 150; Denmark 60 and Sweden and Belgium 50 each.

It is worth recording the profiles of each of the rising stars who contested the first European RD Cup Final at Brands Hatch in 1982, the event won by Steve Chambers, and to trace their progress from this high-speed, highly-spectacular apprenticeship into the top grade . . .

The phrase "Grand Finale" was never more justified than in the last flourish to the Pro-Am season – the European climax at the Hockenheimring in September 1983. It was frenzied action all the way, with the greatest of young Grand Prix hopefuls locked in a tingling chase for the title.

The lead changed seven times, despite the long hauls down the backstraight of the famous Grand Prix circuit, and at the flag Graham Cannell, a 23 year old from the Isle of Man, the mecca of motor cycle racing, was half-a-wheel ahead of Briton Steve Chambers, a 20 year old engineering student from Lincoln. Frenchman Philippe Pagano, aged 26, was third followed by Scotsman Niall McKenzie, German policeman Roland Busch, aged 22, and Swede Vesa Kultalahti, at 28 the oldest rider in the entire series.

Organiser Bruce Cox, the energy behind the British series, said: "It was the best race of the year – non-stop action and drama all the way and typical of the standard of racing we have come to expect from these young men".

Johnny Cecotto, (left) with Alan Carter at Hockenheim in 1983

Appendix
The Development of Two Stroke
Motor Cycle Engines

The following appendix consists of extracts from a paper presented to an engineering congress in Detroit, Michigan, in 1971. Drawn up by director Hiroshi Naito, the man in charge of Yamaha's motor cycle technology, and his colleague Nomura, the paper examined the root causes of the difficulties that invaded the development of two-stroke motor cycles. It has since become a standard work for anybody interested in such engines, providing an interesting insight into the matters of cooling, intake and exhaust systems.

During the eight years between 1961, when Yamaha first took part in Grand Prix racing, and the Italian Grand Prix of 1968, various improvements were made in the 125 and 250 cc classes. The increased performance results obtained during this period were even more than anticipated.

With the 250 cc engine, the 200 hp figure (3.28 bhp/cu in) was first surpassed in 1963, and a scant five years later the 125 cc engine attained 350 bhp/1 (5.74 bhp/cu in). The Table below shows the relative bore and stroke of the engines involved.

Engine, cc	Year	Bore, mm	Stroke, mm	Cylinders
250	1961-5	56	50.70	2
250	1965-8	44	41	4
125	1964-6	44	41	2
125	1966-8	35	32.40	4

This paper presents material covering various data on the development of our two-stroke cycle, high-output Grand Prix racing engine. It then goes on to discuss our production racing engine which is on the open market.

Because many unknown factors related to the small displacement two-stroke cycle engine cannot be taken into account, the "make and try" method plays an important part of theoretical research. However, the analysis of our data will indicate preferred directions for continued investigation of specific problems.

Design Philosophy

So that we can design and develop an engine that will out-perform the field on a racing circuit, our design philosophy must consider the basics of where to put performance emphasis. Accordingly, it is an absolute necessity that our racing engines possess good torque characteristics in the middle and low speed ranges and that our usable power band be 3000 rpm wide, at the very least. At the same time the machine must have a higher output than any other machine in its class.

Furthermore, performance within its class must not suffer in any way. For example, the engine output of the 125 cc engine class must provide a rider with a sufficiently wide power band. Most importantly, the effective power range past the power peak must be as wide as possible. In other words, there must not be a sharply decreasing slope to the power curve once it has passed its peak. The application of these principles allows us to emphasize power range rather than number of gear changes, with subsequent decreased lap times of the circuit as a result of fewer shift requirements. Without such a wide power range, there is a complete stoppage of power application to the wheels while the rider is shifting gears.

In passing, we can state that in the 125 cc class our four-cylinder engines had the same number of transmission gear stages as did the larger displacement two-cylinder engines.

On the other hand, with our super-power engines in the over-250 cc class, we could emphasize performance within the range of acceleration up to maximum horsepower. The reason for this is that there is seldom a need for the rider to use the maximum revolution range of these engines.

Initial Research

In engine design it has been established that in order to obtain higher output, we can raise the mean effective pressure in the combustion chamber. Another method of obtaining super-power is to raise the rpm of the engine, but this can result in the following disadvantages:

1. Mechanical component failure resulting from the increase in inertia of the reciprocating parts.
2. Problems imposed by the additional heat load.
3. Problems caused by increased mechanical friction loss.

Due to these three factors, the inevitable trend is to diminish the volume per cylinder; therefore, the multi-cylinder engine becomes a necessity.

In 1964 we felt that we had reached the upper limits of the twin and were obliged to switch to four cylinders. The primary obstacle in this transition was the layout of the two-cycle four-cylinder engine.

Because it was impossible to use the rotary disc valve system in a parallel four configuration, we were obliged to lay out a pair of parallel twins in either an over-under or a front-back configuration.

The second limiting criterion was that the wheelbase of the machine could not be lengthened beyond that of a twin, which meant that the total length of the engine was limited.

The third consideration was that, due to the likelihood of weight increase, a change from the water-cooled system of the twin to an all-air-cooling system was imminent.

In order to satisfy these requirements, intensive discussion and consultation between the designers and engineers finally indicated a forward, open V-type four engine. With this lay-out the bottom pair of cylinders was positioned 5° above the horizontal and the top pair was positioned another 60° higher. The power take-off was from the independent crankshafts (top and bottom), through an interconnecting and common idler gear, to an idler shaft that in turn powered the transmission through the clutch. Even in its water-cooled transformation (the engine was later modified to a watercooled system) the total configuration was extremely compact.

The measured output of the 250 cc four was 66 hp, which was a tremendous jump from the 56 hp of the twin. The general results, over and above horsepower increases, of the transition from twin to four were good, including such factors as heat load and durability. Because the power output was raised there were some subsequent problems with big end bearings, an issue which will be dealt with later.

In this manner, in its final form the V-four water-cooled engine was able to achieve 44 bhp with 125 cc displacement, and 73 bhp with 250 cc. In fact, this engine captured the World Grand Prix championships in both classes in 1967 and 1968.

Factors of High Performance Tuning

Intake System: Rotary disc valves as an intake system have been adopted for all our Grand Prix racing engines. We would now like to describe the performance of these valves in detail.

Intake timing: the best open-close timing of a rotary disc valve, as decided by testing, is not greatly influenced thereafter by specification changes of cylinder port timings and/or carburettor settings. In general, slight changes of opening timing do not cause appreciable changes in engine performance.

Valve closing timing is the factor that has considerable influence on engine performance. There is maximum rpm rise when the valve close is retarded. Accordingly, maximum horsepower of the engine is also increased, but torque at low engine speed is decreased. That is, the characteristic curve of engine torque is moved toward high engine speeds by this retardation.

On the other hand, the characteristic curve of engine torque moves toward the low-speed range of the engine when valve close timing is advanced. The effects are easily understood if one considers both the action of a rotary disc valve and the increasing pulsation effect due to inertia of gas flow in the intake passage at high speed.

Yamaha's production racing engines of the TD and TR series are piston valve engines (due to the limitation of the original design), and they have a more conventional intake system controlled by the piston skirt. However, the development of the highly efficient exhaust and scavenging systems made possible an improvement in piston timings.

So now these engines are capable of developing maximum horsepower equal to that of our original Grand Prix racing engine, which had been developed five or six years before, using a rotary disc valve, and whose design at that time was somewhat limited to the system then available.

A piston valve engine with approximately 90 per cent of the intake time-area (as compared with that of a rotary disc valve engine) can obtain almost equal maximum horsepower if the inertia and pulsation effects of mixture gas flow inside the intake passage are utilized effectively. However, performance of the piston valve engine is less than that of the rotary disc valve engine at the low and middle ranges of engine speed.

With respect to time/area of the inlet ports per stroke volume at maximum engine horsepower, rpm comparisons between rotary disc valve and piston valve systems show that the former has $180\text{-}190 \times 10^{-4} \sec m^2/m^3$ and the latter has $140\text{-}160 \times 10^{-4} \sec m^2/m^3$. The latter has 20 per cent less inlet-port time area. Through the analysis of various test data we found in general that the intake timings of racing engines tend to be constant, regardless of maximum horsepower rpm of the engine. In the case of the rotary disc valve system, intake opening timing is about 145° btdc, and about 65° atdc for the closing timing. The most suitable opening and closing timing for piston valve system engines is between 80° and 95° before and after tdc.

As is generally known, higher engine speeds require that the total open angle of the intake ports must be somewhat greater than the figures given above. However, if a larger opening angle of the intake ports is given to the engine, based only on a consideration of peak horsepower, starting characteristics become extremely bad. This happens because at very low engine speeds a large amount of mixture gas is blown back from the crankcase and there is not sufficient charge to cause the engine to start. Accordingly specification of intake port timing must also take this factor into account.

Carburettor: Until 1964 the AMAL type of carburettor, which has a separate float chamber was used. As this separate float chamber can be remotely mounted in a damping material, an important merit of this carburettor was that it was not influenced by engine vibration. However, its disadvantage was poor response under conditions such as rapid acceleration and deceleration of the machine. That is, the AMAL type carburettor had a disadvantage in that the gasoline flow rate to the venturi, as affected by rapid acceleration, varied from the normal carburettor flow rate. This happened because the mixing body and the float chamber were separate.

It is known that a mono block type of carburettor, which has the float chamber just beneath the mixing body, works much better than a carburettor with a separate float. However, on our earlier machine there were problems with the carburettor mounting system because engine vibration was transmitted to the carb. This caused extreme foaming, which made it impossible to obtain accurate jetting responses. This early mono block was therefore rejected; in 1964 a better mounting system was developed and use of this carburettor became practical. With it, engine response, including that under severe cornering conditions, was immensely improved.

Main bore: With Yamaha's 125 cc V-four engine, increasing the carburettor bore from 19 to 22 mm gave a maximum horsepower increase of three per cent, while medium and low ranges were increased 5.6 per cent. These increases were in accordance with our design philosophy and were therefore a successful modification.

Air Funnel: The air funnel is also an important factor that affects performance characteristics. In order to raise the performance of the total machine, we had to make the machine narrower each year. Therefore, the protruding lengths of the side-mounted carburettors had to be made shorter. This had an adverse effect upon the airflow within the venturi. Horsepower in all ranges dropped. The problem was rectified by varying the shape of the funnel to compensate for the loss. The factors that control the engine performance of the monoblock carburettor are the length L and the radius R of the funnel.

An increase in length L of the air passage will increase maximum revolutions, but midrange horsepower will drop. Optimum length L is L01.5 to 1.6D (carburettor main bore).

An increase in the funnel curve R raises maximum revolutions, but does not appreciably affect maximum horsepower. Consequently this has the effect of broadening the power band. From the point of view of fuel consumption, such increases in L and R can also result in great improvement.

Primary compression ratio of the crankcase: During development the usual crankcase compression ratio is assigned. Deviations within small limits do not seem to raise the performance appreciably. The normal primary ratio for our racing engines is about 1.5:1.

Timing and Shape of Scavenging and Exhaust Ports
The factors that have paramount effect upon two-cycle engine performance include:

    1. Exhaust system.
    2. Timing and shape of scavenging and exhaust ports.
    3. Shape of the scavenging passage.

The main factors governing performance improvement are the increase of the relative charge, based upon items 1 and 2, and the increase in scavenging efficiency, based upon item 3. In fact, the biggest contributions to our power increase efforts were the cylinder barrel changes encompassing items 2 and 3.

Suitable time/area values must be given to the scavenging and exhaust ports of a high output engine, and it is generally recognized that angle/area must be increased as the rpm limit is raised. Based upon that philosophy the factors discussed below should be considered.

Port Timing: This has the biggest effect upon engine performance, and it is established by the particular application of the engine. Speaking in general, the faster the scavenging timing (the higher the port), the more the torque curve is moved toward the low rpm range. Conversely, the faster the exhaust timing, the more the torque curve is moved toward the high rpm range.

However, the foregoing is applicable only to engine conditions that are near the normal configurations. The exhaust timing effect is considerably more pronounced than that of the scavenging timing. With the high speed engine of the racing variety, a suitable timing figure is generally assigned without regard for power peak rpm, in the same way that intake timing was treated previously. The figures are given in the table below for port locations A and B of the five-port system.

Port	*Timing, deg*	*System/Area*
Scavenging	About 115	A, B: tdc
Exhaust	About 85	A, B: tdc

Port Width: Although we have said before that general figures for port timing were assigned without regard for rpm, we must concede that suitable port width is roughly proportional to desired engine maximum horsepower rpm. While it is true than an increase in exhaust time/area raises the horsepower, it also increases the likelihood of heat problems in the piston crown. Therefore, since the port timing and time/area remain constant regardless of rpm, the figures assigned reflect the overall design philosophy. Again, increase of port width brings about ring protrusion into the exhaust port, with resultant failure of the ring. Determination of port width must take these elements into account.

At present [1971], depending upon the particular improvements of port shape and piston rings, the port widths in degrees (using the centre of the cylinder as the apex) of our engines are as high as 90° for Grand Prix racing engines and 80° for production racing engines.

The higher the engine speed the bigger must be the angle/area ratio, as previously mentioned. However, with regard to time/area a suitable value can be established without regard for engine speed. Suitable values for the time/area of the scavenging port are $80\text{-}100 \times 10^{-4}$ sec m²m³; those for the exhaust port are $140\text{-}150 \times 10^{-4}$ sec m²m³.

Now that suitable time/area values have been determined, our next essential element is the increase of scavenging efficiency. The first step is the determination of the flow of scavenging gases with regard to direction. This is determined by the balance of the entry angle of the scavenging gas, the shape of the transfer passage and the gas volume of the scavenging flow.

Port Shape: We employ two basic types of scavenging systems in our racing engines. With our Grand Prix racing engines there are main scavenging ports assisted by auxiliary ports. This is referred to as the three-port system. The system in use on our production racers consists of the main scavenging ports assisted by auxiliary ports very closely spaced to the mains. These two scavenging methods are based upon the differences in the intake processes.

The three-port system takes advantage of the rotary disc valve intake and subsequent vacant area to the rear of the cylinders. The five-port system is utilized on piston valve engines where the carburettor and intake port occupy the rear of the cylinder. Early production racing engines of the piston valve type did not use auxiliary ports.

Three-port system (rotary disc valve): The merit of the three-port system is its ability to increase scavenging efficiency by improving the shape and direction of the gas flow delivered by the main port. In effect, it creates a "looping" action that delivers the charge throughout the cylinder. A vertical angle of 45-50° is generally suitable for this purpose, and a port size ratio on the order of 0.4 of that of the main port will give good balance to the scavenging flow.

The five-port system: This is based upon the auxiliary ports having a horizontal angle different from that of the main scavenging ports and is directed toward a great increase of relative charge and scavenging efficiency. Depending upon on our use of this system the performance of the piston valve engine has been increased to a horsepower level close to that of our early Grand Prix engines.

Because this method is still under development we have not yet arrived at final conclusions; however, as an example of the data assembled and assimilated to date, we introduce the more outstanding statistics.

The five-port system has two sub-classifications A and B, designated according to port location. There are three types of scavenging passages. Classification is determined by conditions such as general design and production of the engines. The effects of each different type of scavenging passage on engine performance have not yet been fully discovered, but we would like to describe the two classifications A and B.

'A' Classification: Sub-ports of this type have a horizontal angle of approximately 90°. Accordingly, this system provides an engine performance similar to the combined effects of the main scavenging port and that of the auxiliary port in the three-port design. Depending upon that particular engine, some auxiliary ports have a vertical angular specification close to that of the scaavenging ports, whereas others have a vertical angle more like that of the three-port auxiliary. Fox example, the vertical angles can be illustrated as follows:

1. The 250 cc two-cylinder production racer (TD2) has a main scavenging port at 15° and up, with the auxiliary port at 0°.
2. The 350 cc two-cylinder production racer (TR2) has the main scavenging port at 0°, with the auxiliary port at 45° and up.

'B' Classification: In this sytstem the location of the auxiliary port closely resembles that of the three-port rotary disc valve engine. The effect is similar to the three-port system, and the vertical angle specification is close to the 45-50° of the auxiliary port. The ratio of the size of the main to the auxiliary is about 1:0.4.

The shape of the main scavenging passages is a factor that controls the smooth and efficient flow of the scavenging gas into the cylinder. More specifically, a gradual loop should be established between the crankcase and the cylinder opening so that loss from an abrupt change of gas flow will be minimized. Charging efficiency will be raised by utilizing the gas flow inertia to its maximum. The use of this transfer loop did not greatly improve maximum horsepower, but advantages were realized in mid and low ranges.

Exhaust System

With two-stroke engines performance is greatly influenced by the exhaust system. This is a very influential factor with respect to relative charge and delivery ratio.

Generally speaking, an expansion chamber is used on the exhaust system of the two-stroke racing engine. This system is divided into the following parts:

1. Small (usually tapered) exhaust pipe
2. Divergent cone
3. Exhaust chamber
4. Convergent cone
5. Tail pipe
6. Exhaust system

The theoretical analysis of the Yamaha exhaust system has not yet been completed, but based on current data available the following test procedure is recommended.

First, considering total volume and length of the exhaust system, and in order to obtain maximum at aimed engine rpm (with performance matched to the characteristics of the machine), the test should be conducted so as to achieve the widest possible power band, taking into consideration the inter-effects caused by the shape of each part.

Exhaust pipe (part 1): The exhaust pipe has a great effect on performance characteristics, and usually a straight pipe or a slightly tapered pipe is used. A long pipelength causes the torque curve to move toward a lower rpm range and a short pipe moves the torque curve higher. By selecting the proper combination of length and taper (a large taper, if used, will have an effect similar to that of a short pipe), it is possible to move the torque curve toward high rpm without decreasing maximum torque.

It is recommended that the length of part one be five to six times the dimension of the inlet diameter used. Suitable taper figures have not yet been established and are, for the most part, also dependent on the shape of the divergent cone.

Divergent Cone (part two): As for part one, by choosing a suitable combination of taper and length, the same effect can be achieved. That is, the torque curve can be moved toward the higher rpm range without substantial decreases of torque.

A greater improvement of performance can be produced by changing the taper of part two than can be achieved by changing it in part one. In addition, the taper of the divergent cone is normally of two or three stages in order to increase the suction effect of exhaust gas withdrawal. The length of the divergent cone should be about 0.3—0.4 times the total length of the exhaust system .

Exhaust chamber (part three): The exhaust chamber is the main factor in determining the total volume of the exhaust system. When this has a constant diameter, the effect on engine performance due to variations of its length is similar to the effect of part one. A suitable value for the length of part three, which is tested in conjunction with the total volume of the exhaust system, can give a large increase in the amount of torque. Generally, a torque peak point more toward the low-speed range of the engine will occur if a chamber with a bigger diameter is used.

Convergent cone (part four): The effect on performance by this part is also of considerable importance. If the taper is slight, the horsepower curve beyond maximum hp/rpm will decrease slowly. If the taper is large, the curve will fall rapidly.

This is, as described in the earlier section on design philosophy, a very important factor. It is also a key point in determining engine performance that fits the machine. There is an inter-relationship between length and taper, and therefore the shape of this part is strictly based upon a taper factor.

Tail pipe (part five): The shape of the tail pipe also has its effects. If the pipe is long or the ID small, higher engine rpm can be obtained. This will move the torque curve more toward high engine rpm. But if the ID is too small, heat problems will be caused, particularly piston crown overheating. Changes in pipe shape do not contribute to considerable performance changes, but they do effect minor increases in order to develop a better horsepower curve according to the specifications that determined parts 1-4.

Cooling and Lubricating:

Since 1965, all our Grand Prix racing engines have been equipped with water-cooled systems. The merit of this system is that it keeps engine performance stable under continuous, high speed operation. Moreover, it has been proved that the system has considerable effect on engine power increases.

Some specifications, such as expansion of exhaust port width, decreased width of piston top band, and decreased piston clearance, which could not be used in the conventional air-cooled racing engine due to over-heating, were applicable to water-cooled systems.

The performance curve moves toward high engine rpm when the temperature of cooling water is high. But performance deteriorates at all rpm ranges if the temperature exceeds 80° C.

Based upon several tests, the specifications of the cooling system were determined so that the engine would operate efficiently at a water temperature of 80° C.

One drawback of the water-cooled system is its weight, which is obviously greater than that of an air-cooled system. In order to minimize engine weight, various tests were conducted to determine the minimum weight of components, such as volume of cooling water, radiator, water pump and water jacket of the cylinder.

A forced lubricating system using an oil pump is used on our racing engines and lubricating oil is delivered to each part as necessary. In the engine section oil is delivered to the big end bearing of the connecting rod and crankshaft main bearing by a plunger type of oil pump

The most important factor in this system is the location of the nozzle that supplies oil through a crank pin to the big end bearing. The location of this nozzle was determined by theoretical analysis of crank motion and various tests.

Purity and other characteristics of the lubricating oil are also important; for this reason Castrol R-30 and Shell Super-M oils were chosen from several products.

In some Grand Prix races during 1967 we experienced a somewhat mysterious big end bearing problem. After an analysis of the oil it was found that this trouble was caused by a minute contaminant in the oil. Installation of a special oil filter between the oil tank and oil pump solved the problem.

Yamaha's Grand Prix mechanics were genuinely worried about the disastrous effects of seizures on their machines. Riders were usually going flat out in quest of world title points when the terrifying locking-up occurred. Every rider rode with a finger crooked cautiously over the clutch lever, ready to grab it at the first feeling of a seizure.

The oil contaminant was one of the reasons for the seizures. Materials that were simply not good enough for the job were another. Light materials caused the bearing cage to break up. When they were made more robust breakages, at least, stopped. A combination of better materials and improved oil feed directly onto the bearings was the answer; a channel was cut into the casing so that oil could be aimed directly onto the bearings. Cranks used to be tested for five hours at a time at 11,000 rpm—and, indeed, two benches were broken in the exhaustive efforts to find a cure.

Ironically Bill Ivy survived all manner of frightening seizures on Yamahas under great racing stresses—and then was killed when a piston seized on a Jawa he was riding during practice for the East German Grand Prix in 1969. His hand was not on the clutch, despite the lessons he had learned on the Yamaha.

Naito and Nomura concluded their report with a discussion of the problems that invaded engines during high-speed operation, also touching on some aspects of high-output design.

Ignition: Considerable increases in engine rpm made it impossible to maintain accurate and regular ignition when using a conventional mechanical magneto system. Specifically in the V-four engine, an irregularity of ignition timing for each cylinder caused engine performance to decrease. In order to solve this problem the magneto was improved and a new transistorized ignition was developed.

The transistorized ignition system is well known, but we tried using two different methods of electrical pick-up to work as the spark trigger. One utilized magnetic force and the other an electric wave. Development of these two methods was completed, but there were no observed performance differences between them. Therefore, the electric wave trigger was adopted simply by reason of its shorter development period.

The mechanism of the pick-up is as follows: between two pick-up plates, which face each other over a gap of 2 mm, a specific electric wave is constantly emitted. A change in the wave is caused by passing a blade with a special shape between these two plates, and this change is utilized as the igniting signal.

Several development tests verified the merits and demerits of the transistor ignition. The electric wave offered two advantages:

1. Easy engine starts due to quick response and the high absolute value of secondary voltage. Accordingly, spark plug failure could be reduced, and as a result the fitting of the correct heat range spark plug became easier.
2. Engine performance was stabilized as a result of accurate ignition timing.

Advantages outweighed the disadvantages of poor reliability and durability and variation of ignition timing due to characteristic transistor changes under different thermal conditions. In order to solve the foregoing problems careful selection of a high-quality transistor was necessary.

There is a close relationship between ignition timing and the secondary compression ratio. Both have some effect on engine performance increases. When the ignition timing is advanced the torque curve moves toward the low engine rpm range and horsepower at middle and low rpm falls rapidly after peak horsepower rpm. When ignition timing is delayed the reverse effect takes place.

When the compression ratio is raised performance is increased at middle and low engine rpm. In the case of a super-tuned engine a slightly lower secondary compression ratio gives the engine more flexible performance and permits easier operation on the race track. It is from consideration of these factors that ignition timing and secondary compression ratios are determined. Tests show that the following specifications are suitable for the racing engine: ignition timing, 20-

25° btdc; secondary effective compression ratio, approximately 8.0:1.

Connecting rod big end bearing: In the development of an engine with high rpm, the durability of some engine parts became a problem. The most important problem was durability of the connecting rod big end. To maintain a long life of parts at high rpm, it is apparent that sufficient lubrication is essential—and strength to withstand stress is vital.

Shortly after the racing season began we experienced rod big end bearing failures. We decided that the bearing in the retainer cage was too heavy and caused subsequent high inertia loads. The bearing cage was lightened by reducing the crank-pin diameter and by using a lesser number of needle rollers. In this way cage strength was not reduced.

But a new trouble occurred—flaking on the surface and breakage of the crankpin. It was found that this failure could be corrected by changing the location of the oil nozzle and using a crank pin of special material. Also, the thrust washers installed on both sides of the big end were removed so that frictional heat caused by thrust force from side play at the big end was eliminated. The movement of the big end was controlled at the small end through wider wrist-pin bosses so the rod could not touch the crank web. After these modifications were made we did not encounter any trouble with the big end throughout the Grand Prix series of 1968.

Piston effects on performance: These are influenced first by external profile. Design specification of profile must carefully consider thermal expansion and the movement of the piston head in the cylinder. It was observed in our investigations that if clearance between the piston skirt and the cylinder wall was insufficient a 2-3% decrease in horsepower would result.

The second factor influencing performance is the height from the upper edge of the piston ring groove to the crown. By decreasing the height horsepower can be raised, but overheating of the piston crown increases.

When the gap between the crown edge and the upper ring edge of the piston is narrow, thereby reducing random charge leakage past this area, the port timing can be more accurately calculated, thus increasing horsepower. Overheating occurs when the thermal transfer area between the upper band and the cylinder wall is decreased.

During initial development severe cracking around the piston pin bosses occurred; the trouble was completely eliminated by using semi-forged rather than cast aluminium alloy pistons.

Thinner piston ring width will extend performance increase to all rpm ranges. A 0.6 mm ring width has been installed on Grand Prix racing engines. To prevent piston ring fluttering at high rpm and to minimize blowby of burned gas, high pressure piston rings are desirable. A piston ring with pressure of 2.5 kg/cm² (35.56 lb/ins²) was used in our Grand Prix racing engines.

Thermal loads on the spark plug increased seriously at high engine rpm and high output. A few troubles arose, such as electrode melting and thermal cracks in the insulator. These troubles, which were closely connected with spark plug misfire, were very difficult to solve completely, but by using improved materials in the insulator and electrode, and by design changes for better cooling, the problems became negligible.

In order to maintain a better sealing effect on the crankshaft, to minimize friction loss and improve durability, a special seal with a Teflon lip coated upon the rubber base was used.

And to keep better sealing between the left and right sides of the crankcase on the two-cylinder engine, a labyrinth seal was installed on both racing engines and production engines. The seal eliminated friction loss between the crankshaft and the centre oil seal, and ensured near permanent reliability.

Picture Credits

Cecil Bailey, page 36; Tom Beesley, page 200; Champion Photo Service, page 97 (bottom left); Dunlop Central Photographic Unit, pages 144, 158; Features International, page 120/121; Dave Friedman Photography, pages 152, 162/3 (top); Foto Jan Heese, pages 89 (bottom), 103, 104, 105, 106/7, 108, 109, 114, 207, 213; H. P. Kumpa, page 120; Manfred Loscher, page 54; *Motorcycle News*, pages 64/5, 66; Nascar International Speedway, Photographic Services Dept, pages 41, 177 (top), 187, 189, 191, 192, 193, 194/5; Foto 'Olimpia', pages 125, 142, 154; Volker Rauch, page 42; Spalding Public Relations, pages 185 (top and bottom), 205; Universal Pictorial Press and Agency, page 51 (top); J. Wilson Clarke, page 97 (bottom left); Mick Woollett, pages 68, 113, 231, 232, 233.

Acknowledgements

I would like to acknowledge with great gratitude the help given to me by Rod Gould in the preparation of this book. Rodney was with Yamaha in Amsterdam until midsummer 1979 when he formed a business partnership with Mike Hailwood. I would also like to thank Volker Rauch and the Yamaha organization for permission to reproduce the majority of the photographs which have been included in this book.